D0218745

RACIAL SUBJECTS

RACIAL SUBJECTS:

WRITING ON RACE IN AMERICA

DAVID THEO GOLDBERG

ROUTLEDGE   NEW YORK   LONDON

"Hate, or Power?" first appeared in *American Philosophical Association Newsletter on Blacks in Philosophy* (Spring 1995): 12–14.

"Made in the USA: Racial Mixing 'n Matching" first appeared in *American Mixed Race*, ed. Naomi Zack (Rowman and Littlefield, 1995), pp. 237–56.

Lyrics from "Fear of a Black Planet" by Public Enemy. Copyright © 1988. Def American Songs, Inc. All rights reserved. Used by permission.

"In/Visibility and Super/Vision" first appeared in *Fanon: A Reader*, eds. Lewis Gordon and Tracy Denean Whiting (Basil Blackwell, 1995), pp. 179–202.

"Whither West? The Making of a Public Intellectual" first appeared in the *Review of Education/Pedagogy/Cultural Studies* (1994): 1–13.

"Wedded to Dixie: Dinesh D'Souza and the New Segregationism" first appeared in the *Review of Education/Pedagogy/Cultural Studies* (1996): 231–65.

Published in 1997 by
Routledge
29 West 35th Street
New York, NY 10001

Published in Great Britain by
Routledge
11 New Fetter Lane
London EC4P 4EE

Copyright © 1997 by Routledge

Printed in the United States of America on acid-free paper.

All rights reserved. No part of this book may be reprinted or reproduced or utilized in any form or by any electronic, mechanical, or other means, now known or hereafter invented, including photocopying and recording or in any information storage or retrieval system, without permission in writing from the publishers.

Library of Congress Catologing-in-Publication Data

Goldberg, David Theo.
  Racial subjects: writing on race in America / David Theo Goldberg.
    p. cm.
  Includes bibliographical references and index.
  ISBN 0-415-91830-8 (hardback : alk. paper) — ISBN 0-415-91831-6 (pbk. : alk. paper).
  1. Racism—United States. 2. United States—Race relations.   I. Title.
  E184.A1G566 1997   96-39653
  305.8'00973—dc21   CIP

For the scholarly community of colleague-friends
who made this volume conceivable

TABLE OF CONTENTS

Acknowledgments

These essays would not have been possible but for the many and extensive discussions with valued friends—in person, over the telephone, across cyberspace. Regular conversations with Tommy Lott made me rethink, redirect, and refine many of my arguments. Howard McGary encouraged me to clarify points large and small. Visits to and by Paul Gilroy opened up insights otherwise hidden from view. Henry Giroux's invitations led to reviewing both Cornel West's and Dinesh D'Souza's books and his incisive comments on my drafts dramatically improved them. Naomi Zack's invitation led to the writing of the article on mixed race, as did Renee Schroff's to an article on crime and preferences, and Lewis Gordon's to the meditation on Fanon. I benefited greatly by presenting ideas on affirmative action and class to a group of colleagues—faculty and students—in the School of Justice Studies at Arizona State University, especially from comments by Michael Musheno. Leonard Harris's helpful comments on "Hate, or Power?" led me to revise it more than once. Herman Gray, in reviewing "Taking Stock: Counting by Race" for *Cultural Studies*, made especially helpful suggestions that led to considerable revision of that essay. (Herman's suggestions, it turns out, were more useful to me than to the journal, for though the essay was accepted for publication I found myself more quickly able to publish the piece in this collection than in *Cultural Studies*. Nevertheless, I appreciate also the critical assistance and encouragement of its editor, Lawrence Grossberg.) Cedric Robinson and Nahum Chandler offered insightful comments on an earlier draft presented at the Warwick University Conference on Race and Modernity organized by Abebe Zegeye and Julia Maxted.

Sally Merry gave me the idea about the framing force of bureaucratic forms that I incorporated into the essay on the census, "Taking Stock." I would not have been able to complete this paper without the incredible archival skills of Barbara Lammi, who made it possible for me to make sense of the scattered and inconsistent historical data on racial categories in the census. Vikki Bell prompted me to rethink what I was up to in the Fanon essay, as did presenting it to an audience at San Francisco State University at Anatole Anton's invitation.

"Between Blacks and Jews" grew out of my participation in the Workshop on Black-Jewish relations at Harvard University, directed by Skip Gates. I am grateful for the opportunity to have been party to the often scintillating exchanges among participants in the workshop. In particular, two years of group meetings enabled extensive discussions with Laurence Thomas and Adam Newton from which I have benefited immeasurably.

My colleague Pat Lauderdale offered me a sociological compass I would be loathe to leave at home in any social storm. His insightful comments on earlier drafts of nearly all these essays reduced the probability of embarrassment. If there still be cause for embarrassment the fault is mine alone, due perhaps to not having yet learned to read the compass.

Pietro Toggia provided wonderful research assistance while pushing me to define my views more clearly. The book would never have been completed but for the terrific skill of Kay Korman, my administrative associate, and the supportive staff of the School of Justice Studies as well as Sam Michalowski, whose combined efforts and boundless humor make administrative duties seem neither administrative nor duty-bound. Janet Soper of the Publication Assistance Center, College of Public Programs at Arizona State University again left no stone unturned in producing incomparable camera-ready copy, helped immeasurably by my research assistant Ruth Butler (wordprocessing) and by Pietro Toggia (producing the indexes). I am grateful also to Jayne Fargnoli, the initiating editor on this book, for trusting me so quickly, and to the staff at Routledge, especially Alexandra Mummery and Ronda Angel, for easing me so effortlessly through the production process, and to my friend George Lipsitz for saving me from embarrassment.

Alena and Gaby, still the source of so many thoughts, repeatedly renew the critical spirit, their combined good sense driving me to distinguish good ideas from bad, fresh stories from foul. They continue to suffer through my silences, my absences, and my flights of rhetorical fancy, only bringing me, like Maurice Sendak's midnight baker, back to dawn's earth with a loving and laughing bump.

Introduction:

The Racial Fabric

Between January 1995 and October 1996 over one hundred largely black churches throughout the American South were set alight in arson attacks. Little notice was paid publicly or politically until a widely publicized arrest on June 10, 1996, for a fire set a few days earlier in Charlotte, North Carolina. A white girl of thirteen from a wealthy suburb neighboring the church admitted sole responsibility. At the time of her arrest the local police declared that the fire she had started was unrelated to any other, and that she had not been racially motivated but was a "seriously disturbed" girl involved in teenage satanic activity. The same day two black churches were set alight in Greenville, Texas. Three men—two white, one Hispanic according to reports—were questioned and released for lack of evidence. Greenville has been the heart of Texan Klan activity historically;

twenty years ago a sign welcoming people to town read "Home of the blackest land and the whitest people."

President Clinton finally moved the spate of fires to the center of national attention, declaring them the work of "racial hatred." Indeed, the fires seemed to be shades of the South in the sixties: black citizens repeatedly under attack, apathy among nonblack citizens, denial of racism by at least one local police force, overzealous FBI agents stereotypically pursuing church members as culprits, belated public commitment, and an apology by a president. There may have been no racial motivation in the Charlotte case, but the lack of concern about almost thirty fires previous to that one may have suggested to a teenager disturbed enough to want to torch a church that black in this case is better. As it turned out, a few days after the teenager's arrest, a Charlotte police representative admitted that the teenager "harbors ... anti-African American beliefs." Law enforcement failed to understand the complex dimensions of racial configuration, reflecting a broader social failure to comprehend the complexity of racial matters.

On May 8, 1996, the South African Parliament voted to adopt a new constitution, among the most progressive in the world, thus finally bringing apartheid to a formal close. A day later, F. W. de Klerk, former South African President and then Deputy President in the government of national unity, announced that he and the Nationalist Party he headed were withdrawing from the government. They planned to fashion a robust opposition party in South Africa's fledgling democracy. Within a day the South African stock market lost 1.5 percent of its value. In recent history, South Africa has revealed to America that race crosses borders and oceans even as it is transformed by that crossing. South Africa's experience suggests that the global frame in which race operates today, in the United States as elsewhere, needs to be reconceived. Why does the peaceful resignation of the former scion of South

African political life—to form a democratic opposition in a transformed, a "new," society—cause such consternation in its capital markets?

The answer is all about race. Whites, for all of their former sins, are seen in South Africa, as in the United States, as the guarantors of stability and political rationality, of peacefulness and law and order; blacks represent just the opposite. So whites removing themselves from direct power suggests to rational self-interested investors that there will be a slide into contentiousness and chaos, into instability and insecurity. If the church arsons seem like racism as usual, the South African political economy signals its new form.

The church burnings symbolize—and actualize—contemporary conditions of black-white relations in America. White anxieties about uselessness, social dismissal and alienation, economic vulnerability, social decline, black advancement, and equal opportunity are expressed variously. For example, white religious groups are beginning to stress the rash of suspicious fires at white churches throughout the country, while two black men have been charged in the arson of a black community church the men had been contracted to restore in a town called, ironically, Whiteville. At the extreme, whites' anxieties are expressed by attacking a welfare state perceived as "black," in concerns over a public culture increasingly dominated by blackness, and in a resentful politics charging reverse discrimination. Thus, the "new" American racism is not unlike, and not unrelated to, the deregulated market-driven racism of the South African case. In both, longstanding and questionable presumptions about white rationality and black irrationality combine to produce painful personal and socioeconomic consequences. White greed and fear are hardly rational motives, dominated as they are by racist stereotypes. An unmitigated drive to profit mixed with paranoia frames stock market, cultural, and political practices in the United

States as in South Africa. The racialized results read like business as usual.

As the millennium closes we tend to live in sprawling cities, and these cities are related more and more not just to other cities in our nation-state but to other cities globally. (The economy of Los Angeles, for instance, ranks eleventh among the *states* in the United States, an indication of the growing power of global cities.) In modernist political economy, urban environments represented the mark of the modern, of industrialization and technological prowess, the pull off the land, and the nexus of migratory patterns set off, but hardly containable, under colonialism. In the postmodernizing political economy, the city is increasingly global, constituted by the flow of capital, economic and social, the crossroads of manifold and transnational mobilities. In that sense, the city conjures up dramatic dangers, offering a palette of once unimaginable possibilities.

These possibilities and problems have emerged out of postwar shifts in political economy; that is, in the mode of capital accumulation (as David Harvey demonstrates) that resulted from another technological revolution (being on-line increasingly symbolizes for the late 1990s, it seems, what mainlining or being on LSD did for the late 1960s). Attendant to these changes are less visible shifts in relations between capital and labor, economic and political power, and social self-determination and its relative loss. The shifting concerns about race, politics, and culture have to be read in the context of these structural transformations in the United States from a manufacturing economy to a service economy (global financial services at the high end, social services at the low); from a global power to a global partner; from a presumptive (indeed presumptuous), homogenous, military-industrial complex to a complicated, heterogenous, multicultural hybrid; and from a social order in which work was work and the rest leisure to one in which finding work that pays a living wage is work and play is big business, which we increasingly work to afford!

The past thirty years or so have witnessed the evisceration of the American working class, so much so that it's not too extreme to think of the destruction as the outcome of a collusive and well-coordinated attack, especially during the 1980s. In the first half of the twentieth century, deep struggles occurred between capital and labor, commercial interests and strong unions. Labor's power, such as it was, began to erode at the apex of the success of the Civil Rights Movement for reasons at least partly related to local racial dynamics, but also to international economic shifts. What emerged was the erosion not just of the power of the working class in the United States, but the erosion of the U.S. working class itself.

The traditional class formation of capital and labor has transformed: now we have a growing but still small body of the very (and increasingly) rich; an associated professional service class (doctors, lawyers, accountants, mutual fund executives); a middle class of technicians, managers, middle-level professionals, and academics most of whom find it harder to maintain their position in very competitive markets; and a fading working class and the (desperately) poor that includes those characterized as the underclass, the working poor, minimum-wage service workers, the retired working class, and the underemployed. The major manufacturing centers of urban America have watched their manufacturing bases dissipate: from the mid-1950s to the mid-1980s New York, Philadelphia, Chicago, and Los Angeles—among other cities with significant if not majority non-WASP working- and middle-class populations—each lost approximately half a million manufacturing jobs. The U.S. working class, along with its associated labor "difficulties," has been moved offshore to other parts of the world where labor costs are cheap, where labor reproduction costs are minimal for U.S. capital (consisting for the most part of a now threatened foreign-aid budget), and where production can be moved elsewhere swiftly when labor "problems" are present. Nike, that quintessentially American company, leads the field in the global labor safari.

One indication of the demise of the traditional working class is that an increasing share of non-executive manufacturing positions that require some technological skill are being cornered by those with college degrees in engineering and the like. A sign of the tenuous condition of the middle class in America is that middle-level professional jobs requiring considerable skill (e.g., computer programming) likewise are beginning to be shipped offshore where both direct and reproductive costs are significantly smaller. From 1968 to 1994 the top 20 percent of American households increased their share of aggregate income from 40.5 percent to 46.9 percent, from roughly $74,000 to roughly $106,000, an increase of 44 percent after adjustments for inflation. The bottom 20 percent saw income increase by a meager $500 or 7 percent (roughly $7,200 to $7,700). These class shifts from the prewar period to the present are exemplified by attendant shifts in electoral politics. Here "the new South" and "Reagan Democrats" have become the significant factors, alongside the supposed declining significance of the black vote.

Since the late stages of the Reagan administration, the U.S. economy has shifted from its traditional dependence on housing construction and on real estate investment. After the stock market plunge in October 1987, the value of housing stock dropped significantly, following on the heels of its sharp inflation in value in the early 1980s. Confidence in housing and real estate waned as investments deflated dramatically (tied to changes in the tax code that precluded deduction for owning a second home). These and falling interest rates prompted acceleration of investment in the stock market. The anonymity of stock ownership distanced investors from the plight of the corporation's workers. It thus accelerated alienation from and lack of empathetic interest in the plight of working class and poorer citizens. Stockholdings were considered a profit making venture, to be bought and sold according to fluctuations in the market only. Indeed, stocks are rarely held long enough to warrant a lasting interest in the lives—the working and living conditions—of the faceless players who produce wealth. By contrast, interest soared in those fronting the organization. Little resistance faced massive increases in chief executive compensation packages, now totaling more than $20 million per annum and in the most notorious instances accounting for 200 percent more than the annual compensation of the corporation workforce. Chief executives take credit for corporate well-being, happy to see corporate profits grow by an average of 13 percent per annum and to watch their stock value soar, but they are quick to request worker givebacks to achieve their profitable ends and to blame worker inadequacy or intransigence when profits drop and stock values plummet. It is this alienation effect—prompted by the shift from investment in housing stock to the faceless stock market, and coupled with the recent programmatic dismantling of welfare assistance stretching back to the New Deal—that has exacerbated the growing income gap in the United States and the increased vulnerability and erosion of the working class. It has had dramatic effects on the prospects for black citizens, aiding the rise of at least part of the black bourgeoisie while braking the prospects of the black poor and working class. Advertising, aimed overwhelmingly at the middle class, intensifies the experience of alienation through its stereotypical representations.

Unlike traditional immigrants, African Americans are the only group members who, in fashioning a middle class, have been forced to face the coterminous configuration of a lumpen class, a graduation and degradation of simultaneous sorts. It's as if the consolidation of a substantial black middle class has been constrained by the weighted handicap of their "brothers" and "sisters," a pulling back as there is a surging forward, an informal (and so supposedly unobjectionable) restriction on Abel for the plight of Cain.

More visible than such structural dynamics—indeed, helping to hide them from view—are deepening racial divides. Race seems to be tearing our social fabric. It is everywhere—on the street and at work, on the radio and television, in just about every magazine and at the movies, at schools and colleges, in the playground and on the playing field. And, of course, it's on the internet. A month or so ago I happened upon a public policy discussion list engaged in a heated exchange about the virtues and vices of affirmative action. One discussant, signing off under the pseudonym "John Knight," insisted upon attributing to affirmative action what he perceived as the decline of the United States over the past thirty years. Affirmative action, our beleaguered Renaissance man insisted, has been the cause of soaring divorce rates, declining SAT scores, depressed wages, debilitated worker productivity and competitiveness, and job loss to the tiger economies of Southeast Asia and the hungry economies of the developing world. That's quite a burden to bear. Race not only matters; at times it seems to be all that does.

Race has become a touchstone. Sewn over the centuries into the seams of the social fabric, the idea of race (or, really, the ideas, for they are multiple) furnishes the terms around and through which a complex of social hopes, fears, anxieties, resentments, aspirations, self-elevations, and identities gets to be articulated. It's not that race, for instance, is isomorphic with class, nor simply that class is articulated as race. Rather, classes themselves are now racially fractured. Racial configurations cut across class, rendering even intraclass alignments ambiguous, ambivalent, and anxious. This social fracturing makes any policy consideration concerning race, especially policies that are racially explicit, fraught with the difficulties of fervent commitment and equally fervent denial. Such policies become difficult to negotiate, compromising to defend, and apparently easy to denounce but not so easy to renounce. The racial considerations attendant on any social issue—the racial dimensions and determinations of it, when explicit and overt—obscure most other considerations; and the racial formulation or effects of a policy drown out any other articulation or implication. These difficulties are further magnified by the variability of ethnoracial reference, the slipperiness of racial formation and reference, and (yet) by the overarching reduction of racial complexity to white and black, if not by whites tending to equate race with "the black condition."

A widespread view, especially among white Americans, is that racism would disappear if everyone simply ceased making (so much of) racial references. This vision strikes me as a contemporary version of those treatises on "the negro problem." Just as there never was a "negro problem"—only problems that whites took upon themselves to have with blacks (D'Souza [1993, 551] still thinks there is "a black problem")—so there is no "race problem," only difficulties that blacks and whites project they will have with each other. It's curious that racial referencing should become the dominant concern among whites at the moment whiteness ceases to be a racially invisible category. The discomfort with racial categorizing is not just with being identified as racially dominating; it is in being thrust into the glare of its own making. By rendering whiteness visible as a racial category, whiteness has been unveiled as increasingly irrelevant, as out of control in both senses. Whiteness thus becomes a victim of its own fabrication. Self-defined for many years as the residue of all the identities it took itself not to be, all those it excluded as abject, whiteness is now revealed as a leftover identity. And leftovers no longer sell in an economy of throwaways.

The conceptual and causal direction between race and racism, I suspect, runs mostly in the opposite direction. If, when, and as racism recedes (which is not to say that it is receding), race and racial reference will lose significance. I am not committed to the view that race can have no independent and sustainable value without racism. It is conceivable that it might, but I doubt so much would be made then of racial belonging. In any case, the conceptual relations between race and racism are more dialogical and dialectical than the baldness of the counterproposition would have them. The point, nevertheless, is that we should exert our social energies to contesting the power of *racisms* rather than in finding ourselves offended by *racial* (self-)identification.

In this volume of essays, I'm concerned to show how race is written into daily lives and experience in America, to demonstrate how it is a fabrication of and about the modern American subject. Throughout U.S. history, race has always been a central strand of state administration; a silent (and sometimes not so silent) barrier to kinship and adoptability; a condition of advancement and advantage, of power and privilege; and a mark of preference and improvement, of intellectual prowess and jury participation, of law's empire and social injustice, of ethnic excludability and historical denial, of social invisibility and sociospatial segregation. It has been so whether explicitly invoked or silently, invisibly evoked. This is a reality that the U.S. Supreme Court has denied in rendering unconstitutional all newly created voting districts that effectively lack white majorities.

These essays are a mix of popular and theoretical reflections. My purpose is to render readily accessible theoretical analyses regarding racial subjects—key topics around and about race and the racializing of social subjects in America. I take the primary title, "Racial Subjects," from the introductory chapter of my earlier, more sustained, and unapologetically theoretical book, *Racist Culture* (1993a), thus linking the more popular style and accessible themes of this collection of essays to the theoretical framework articulated in that earlier book.

Each essay in this volume was written independently of the others, though there should be an overall order and coherence to the book's thematics. In the first essay, "Hate, or Power?," I argue against the conception of racism as hateful expressions, a view widespread throughout popular discourse, suggesting that racism is better understood as exclusionary relations of power. Having set this conceptual background, I trace the history of changing racial categories over two hundred years of U.S. census-taking in "Taking Stock: Counting by Race," arguing that the state employ racial classification only to track historical discrimination. Relatedly, in "Made in the USA: Racial Mixing 'n Matching," I analyze the experience of and current interest in mixed race and the "one-drop" rule through the prism of Public Enemy's "Fear of a Black Planet." This is followed by reflections in "In/Visibility and Super/Vision: Fanon and Racial Formation" upon the social and philosophical twists of racial and (en)gendered invisibility by excavating their articulation in Frantz Fanon's work.

The conceptual framework laid out in the first four essays orders my discussion in the following four essays of the dilemmas faced by the new black public intellectuals, focusing in particular on Cornel West ("Whither West? The Making of a Public Intellectual"); of race and the law in the wake of the O. J. Simpson trial ("A World of Difference: O. J.'s Jury and Racial Justice"); of relations between blacks and Jews ("Between Blacks and Jews"); and of affirmative action in the context of the tension in contemporary political discourse between education and crime as affirmative action is reshaped by and reconfigures our political economy ("Crime and Preference in the Multicultural City"). I close the book with a critical discussion of Dinesh D'Souza's (1995) fatuous declaration of the "end of racism." In "Wedded to Dixie: Dinesh D'Souza and the New Segregationism," I argue that D'Souza articulates and rationalizes the vision of a newly emergent segregationism; that is, a racialized segregation no longer legally sanctioned in the public sphere but rampant in the informal, privatized, and market-driven one.

There is no single problem of race or racism. The problems that fall under the category of race, and the variety of racisms, are wide-ranging, dynamic, multiple, and numerous. So any claim to having a single solution to *the* race problem" or *the* problem of racism," just like any claim that we have come to *the* end of racism" (which end? which racism?) is necessarily misleading.

I avoid suggesting a single generalized "solution" to racism. Racism ranges across the social space, a hybrid mutation of social life, embedded in expressions large and small that often are socially legitimate. Any effective contesting of racisms must assume specific counterexpressions in direct or indirect response to the racist expression addressed. The range of topics covered in these essays—dealing with discrimination and racial categorization; with racial namings and racist exclusions; with the intersection of race, ethnicity, class, and gender that cuts across political economy, law, and culture—necessitates responses specific to the issue(s) at hand.

I doubt that the racial categories "black" and "white," subject to some facade of liberal progressive logic, are about to disappear, and I have argued at length elsewhere that liberalism is implicated historically in racist culture. So I want to emphasize here the distinction with which I concluded my book *Racist Culture*: between the sort of nonracialism widespread among whites and the form of praxis I will call here counterracism (emphatically, a counter *to* racism not a reverse discrimination), which is committed not only to transform the significance of racial categories but to contest the exclusions of racist practices.

Sometimes I suggest a mode of countering in response to the line of critical argument I address in a particular essay. In this spirit, I try to avoid clichéd platitudes, like "Learning from the past we need to remain critically vigilant, willing to interrogate our work as well as our habits of being to ensure that we are not perpetuating internalized racism" (hooks 1994, 182), or broad generalizations like "we must admit that the most valuable sources for help, hope and power consist of ourselves and our common history" or "we must focus our attention on the public square—the common good that undergirds our national and global destinies" (West 1993a, 11). Such expressions should be avoided especially in the absence of site- or expression-specific responses to racisms. These clichés are relatively benign. The recent spate of terribly bigoted biases, analytic and prescriptive, that we have witnessed lately is not, and is implicated in the deterioration of conditions of civility and safety facing all those considered nonwhite. I am expressly committed then to contesting claims such as "Policies based on white guilt and reverse racism have failed" (Taylor 1992, 358) and "what blacks need to do is to 'act white'" (D'Souza 1995, 556).

Exposing an expression as racist may sometimes suffice as contestation. The exposure may be enough to make its perpetrators sufficiently self-conscious to limit expressing themselves openly in racist fashion. Yet more will be required: a special, ongoing, and thoughtful commitment in the face of repeated, insistent, and self-righteous racist expressions. In response to the church burnings, for example, the Anti-Defamation League (ADL), a leading Jewish association in America, set about collecting funds to be donated exclusively and completely to rebuilding the burned churches. Belatedly, the Christian Coalition rushed to assistance also. Ironically, on the same day the ADL announced its campaign, the overwhelmingly white Southern Baptist Convention, the largest American Protestant denomination, announced an aggressive campaign to convert Jews. This violates an implicit agreement among Christian organizations to discourage efforts to convert Jews in the interests of interfaith dialogue.

I have left the conclusions to each line of argument in each of the essays, rather than pulling them into a single compilation at the book's conclusion, thus maintaining the coherence of the essays even as they overlap and intersect. Accordingly, they can be read discretely even as I have endeavored to make them cohere within the overall structure of the book.

So, effective counter-to-racist commitment (here's a generalization, paradoxically) has to be site specific. Perhaps it is for this very reason that antiracist sloganeering and generalizations come over as so clichéd. On this score, then, I want to insist on a counterracist nominalism. Take any generalization regarding responses to racisms and its limits become quickly apparent. "We need more education." Well, yes, but of what sort? "We need more black faculty on campuses." That too, of course, but this guarantees very little by way of undoing or restricting racist expression in contemporary university settings. I can think of any number of people of all sorts of backgrounds I'd rather have as colleagues than Alan Keyes (or Alan Kors, to be "equal opportunity" about it), Ward Connerly, Robert Woodson, Dinesh D'Souza, or Leonard Jeffries. By contrast, I'd be happy to share intellectual space with Glenn Loury, for his positions strike me as keenly constructed, thoughtful, nuanced, complex, and usually well argued, even as I often disagree, sometimes strongly, with what he says. What about the generalization that "We need to equalize school spending for black children and white"? Now we're getting somewhere, as I argue below, for this addresses some important underlying conditions for racist expression, though it hardly exhausts the issue. Going to the foundations at one level, it barely scratches the surface at another.

Where I do make an occasional policy-oriented generalization, I limit it to a response to some identifiable expression of racism.

Here I offer my generalization as a way of excavating the territory of response or of mapping the area of anticipation. The generalization is intended then to scout the space of viable counter-to-racist commitment, opening, by promoting, public discussion about contextualized boundaries, limits, and the effectivity of dereified racializing expression and deracializing practice.

Most responses to racism fail in application to distinguish between individual and institutional considerations, even if they do so by definition. Some suggest the necessity of individual transformations (e.g., find a friend of another race, stop stereotyping, prevent prejudice) while ignoring policy considerations. Others focus solely on policy proposals (e.g., promoting or restricting affirmative action, housing or employment discrimination, racially fashioned voting districts). The complexities of racisms, their malleability and transformability, suggest that they need to be repeatedly confronted on the individual and policy levels.

Consider the difficulties posed for inner-city dwellers by the "concentration effect" identified in considerable detail by urban sociologists. The concentration effect exacerbates the products of a racially exclusionary poverty by concentrating them in a containable space easily avoidable by those not so confined. Conservative commentators largely emphasize the pathological character of the racialized poor as the overriding causal consideration in extending their poverty. So the concentration effect is not just spatial; it is also ideological. Those left or pushed into that container space are defined as having all the pathological characteristics supposedly acquired by virtue of being so concentrated. Indeed, ideological containment assists in isolating the racially identifiable threats within the space of containment.

We desperately need to combat the concentration effect through crossracial and transracial counter-to-racist coalitions, people not just seeking to understand each other but also working together on specific occurrences of bank redlining, the abandonment and defunding of particular inner-city public schools, and the proliferation of racist stereotypes in cartoons, movies, advertising, newspapers, and magazines. These coalitions must define specific ends—policy, political, and personal—worthy of being pursued with a view to untying threads in the knot(s) of the unholy trinity of those most basic conditions of racialized experience: residential segregation, racially patterned educational differences in input and output, and discriminatory joblessness with its disturbing discriminatory effects of violence, crime, and heightened police surveillance. As with a combination lock, which to open one must know the right numbers in the proper sequence, so here too we will fail to make any appreciable inroads in countering racist expression unless we can determine how discrimination in any one of these three areas exacerbates discrimination in the other two.

Contexts change, and with them strategies of response. At the risk of sounding clichéd, in turn, I close this introduction to racial subjects in the spirit of Fanon, with the call to continue counter-racist contestation. A closing and an opening; an ending and a beginning:

A Luta Continua ...

HATE, OR POWER?

In the past decade or so, racism has been popularly conceived of as hate. Public institutions such as universities have constructed hate-speech codes and state criminal codes have introduced the category of hate crimes. Media reporting on "racist incidents" in the public sphere—on college campuses or in shopping malls, in the United States or in postcommunist Europe—speaks almost exclusively of them as the expression of hate.[1] The Florida hate-crimes statute, typical of state laws that have become increasingly popular throughout the nation, makes possible (without requiring) the imposition of harsher penalties whenever a criminal offense "evidences prejudice based on the race, color, ancestry, ethnicity, religion or national origin of the victim." In *Mitchell v. Wisconsin*, the Supreme Court unanimously affirmed the constitutionality of such enhanced sentences.

This conception of racism in terms of hate did not always exist: in the 1960s and throughout the 1970s, reference to hate was largely absent. This absence was not due to the relative absence of or silence about racist "incidents" during the decades: the former, after all, was the decade of Civil Rights struggles and Black Power, the latter the decade of the Soweto uprising and the instigation of apartheid boycotts. It was the period of affirmative action and the charge of reverse discrimination.

We should be careful, however, not to erase the conceptual history that conflated hate and racism by simply insisting that racism's genealogy is limited to the decade that produced the claim to "the end of history" (the 1980s). The explicit public use of the term "hate" to characterize racist expressions emerges in direct response to the recognition of the return of visceral racism in the 1980s. This return has had much to do with the way in which the public rhetoric opened a space—a "window of opportunity," as the jargon would have it—for the reemergence, the reinvention, of exclusionary expression. Thus we find not only the collusive racializing by social science and by the media of the so-called urban underclass and its perceived habituation to drugs, welfare, teenage pregnancy, and crime, but also the strong administrative attacks on affirmative action—first by William Bradford Reynolds in the Reagan administration and then more widely by others, including a majority on the Supreme Court bench. This period has witnessed, in addition, the undertaking to license private discrimination—that is, the rise in nongovernmental commerce and employment, private educational institutions, privately sponsored parades, and the like.

The genealogy of racism as an expression of hate can be traced to the decade that produced the "end of ideology" thesis (the 1950s), and specifically to the way such social sciences as social psychology, sociology, anthropology, and economics initially constructed an understanding of racism once they fully recognized, and named, the problematic phenomenon. Racism was formatively understood in the 1950s as a prejudice, as an irrational premodern bias based on arbitrary and scientifically vacuous distinctions between biologically conceived racial groups.[2] This picture has been subjected recently to scathing attack by critical theorists. It nevertheless remains the view that misleadingly underlies the popular (mis)understanding of racist expression as hate speech, and of racist injustice as hate crimes.

Understood in this way, we can begin to see what such a characterization leaves out, what it refuses to acknowledge, how it silences effective counterracist strategies. The first point to notice is that the concepts of "hate speech" and "hate crimes" make racist expression turn on a psychological disposition, an emotive affect(ation), a dis-order—and so as ab-normal and un-usual. Racist (and sexist) acts are thus transformed silently into emotive expressions, into crimes of passion.[3] We tend, if not quite to empathize with the agent of a crime of passion, to discount the crime in the calculus of wrongs, to downplay its wrongfulness. Thus, at the extreme, the philosopher Michael Levin has questioned what he takes to be the imputation of specialness to racist crimes by virtue of their racist nature, insisting that racism adds nothing to the particular nature of the crime; that a lynching, say, is wrong because it is murder and no more wrong because it is the murder of a black person. What is dismissed in this characterization is the terror visited on the group, in light of which its members may feel especially terrified and the daily life of the group's members threatened.

More generally, expressions of hate encourage their dismissal as abnormal, not the sort of undertaking ordinary people usually engage in, the irrational product of warped minds. This reduces all racist expression to a single form: What is not reducible to hate is not criminalizable; perhaps it is not even racist (or sexist), for it fails to fall under the reductive characterization of racism (or sexism) as hate. Therefore it need not be considered serious or be taken seriously. Thus too, understanding racism (or sexism) as hate prompts the clichéd response that "all you need is love." Or, as Benjamin DeMott (1996) has characterized it in a scathing critique, if one makes a crossracial friendship racism will evaporate.

Racist expressions, however, are various—in kind, in disposition, in emotive affect, in intention, and in outcome. Moreover, racisms are not unusual or abnormal. To the contrary, racist expressions are normal to our culture, manifest not only in extreme epithets but in insinuations and suggestions, in reasoning and representations, in short, in the microexpressions of daily life. Racism is not—or more exactly is not simply or only—about hate. The refusal by a landlord to rent to or an employer to hire black people (at least for certain public positions—for waiters rather than dishwashers, say) because of the projected effects on business has little to do with emotion; nor is it irrational. It *is*, nevertheless, racist. Similarly, for a department chair to remark to a black interviewee that she clearly is capable of teaching a course on "Afro-American" thought despite nothing in her record indicating any interest or expertise in African American studies may involve prejudgment. But it is the prejudgment of normal inductive reasoning and not necessarily the prejudice of affective—hateful—animosity. Actually, the interviewer likely will claim to have the best of black interests at heart.[4]

What unites these cases as racist is the fact that they involve race-based exclusions (or inclusions) putatively licensed by (claimed) racial membership. It presumptively sets apart group members and groups, treating them stereotypically as alike and different from those perceived not to belong to the group, thus reducing individuals and their racial group to a fixed and devalued understanding of possibility, propriety, and acceptability. It follows that in many instances the perpetrators of what counts—

or at least should count—as racist or sexist expressions, including crimes, are not moved by hatred. The union or club rule, explicit or implicit, that excludes black or Jewish membership need not be predicated on hate, but on the preservation of economic advantage or the status of white members in control of the rules. What these expressions are all about, then, whether in a particular instance they involve hate, is *power.*

Power is control (at least potentially) over another person or over resources, and often over the person's relation to resources. Power is thus the capacity to effect an end. Racist expression is the assertion of power by perpetrators who often otherwise lack it, or it is the maintenance of relations of power, to remind an individual or class of people who it is that occupies the position of power. Such expressions therefore involve the assertion of selves over others constituted as Other in a space of diminished, threatened, or absent control. In this sense, racism is (or becomes) normal: it is endemic, if not quite pandemic, in social formations of disparate, discordant degrees of socioeconomic power and powerlessness. The relatively powerless, or those who perceive their power as threatened, resort to asserting themselves over those who are—who are *created* as—more powerless than they. More precisely, then, racist expressions may serve ideologically to rationalize relations of domination, or they may serve practically to effect such domination by defining its objects and subjects. So these expressions may be taken as the condition of domination and subjection, the mode and fact of racialized oppression.

Racist (and often sexist) exclusions (and inclusions) are done not only for the sake of gaining or maintaining power in economic or political or personal terms; that is, power is exercised in the promotion and execution of the exclusions, whether intended or not. So racist (or sexist) exclusions need not be sought only instrumentally to control the socioeconomic resources. They may be sought also for the recognition of some imputed value in the exclusions themselves, or for the sake of power itself. Concern among racists over recognition was a significant feature (among others) of racist expression in Nazi Germany, as it was also in apartheid South Africa, and I suspect it remains a principal consideration in personal attacks by neo-fascists and white-power thugs on Turkish immigrants in Germany and on blacks or Asians in the United States. This suggests that the proper yardstick against which to assess the degree of racist (or sexist) exclusion, its depth, is not simply the level of inclusion or access to social resources. It is, rather, the fuller measures of incorporation into *and* influence upon the body politic, whether economically, politically, legally, or culturally.

Although racist expressions are predominantly expressed by those who wield power, it is both conceptually possible and empirically evident that members of dominated racial groups can promote racial exclusions of nonmembers. While Louis Farrakhan's Nation of Islam may not formally exclude white membership, the language of its leadership hardly encourages white inclusion. Power, of course, is relative and variously expressed. A man who can attract a million men, give or take a few, to the nation's Capitol steps wields more power than many American Jews though his power is predicated on blacks' general lack of it. Given that the dominant, by definition, control the resources and social structures from which exclusions are made, racisms are largely, if not altogether exclusively, expressions from dominance. This further suggests two reasons why resistance to racisms is so often, if not predominantly, cultural. First, the production, expression, and appeal of culture cannot be controlled as easily as material resources. Second, to wrest control over one's culture is to pry loose the hold over naming and (self-)representation. This is a first step to self-determination, for it enables one to assert power over self-definition. And it is a necessary condition for taking command of the power to rationalize actions, conditions, and relations, for representation is always mediated by the prevailing discursive culture.

It might be countered that characterizing racist expressions in terms of hate has the pragmatic virtue of enabling a counter to be mounted where there might otherwise be none: in the law, by way of regulations and codes. It is much more difficult to criminalize or otherwise to regulate racist expressions of (imposed) power, not least because relations of power *are* so socially usual, common threads of the fabric of our social formation. Restricting the regulation of racist expressions to only those that are hateful, however, comes with a heavy cost. For one, it encourages us to think that the range of racist expressions—or at least the range that is intolerable—is thereby exhausted. (In this sense, it makes little sense to substitute for the designations "hate speech" or "hate crimes" the terms "racist or sexist speech or crimes" while leaving unchanged the conceptualizations they signify.) The couching of racism as hate limits response to the reactive. If the primary object of concern is hate, then we are reduced to waiting for the occurrence of hateful deeds, for how else do we recognize racism? This reduction encourages the removal of non-hateful racist expressions from the realm of political contestation. It effects this eviction by silencing the historical record of racialized injustices, by wrenching contemporary manifestations of racism from the long list of historical exclusions in terms of which such expressions are best understood.

By contrast, understanding racisms as relations of power leads us to acknowledge their diffusion throughout our culture and the history of their production. It underlies such expressions not as the idiosyncratic excesses of pathological individuals, groups, or societies, but as the (much more disturbing) normal manifestation of modern rationality. To challenge this demands far more vigorous proactive campaigns; in some fundamental ways, a cultural sea change. It requires not just that the relatively powerful see the constructed Other as like them, nor simply that those in positions of power cease explicitly to engage in "othering." It necessitates rather that those occupying any position of power be open to the deep and abiding influences of those deemed Other, of "the Other's" values and commitments. It requires that the society not just acknowledge "incidents" or "events," but that it engage in dialogic exchanges, taking seriously—and being moved by—the positions and ideas of those who have been marginalized; that those in positions of relative power be open, in theory and practice, policy and social structure, to the transformative implications of those over whom they exercise power.

Conceived thus, recourse to the social technologies of repressing "hate crimes" or "hate speech" appear not just inadequate but paradoxical. These technologies find their rationale in the hope that deterrence will be effected by extraordinary punishment of racist crimes. But if hate crimes or speech are the irrational products of pathologically disturbed persons it seems fanciful to expect potential perpetrators to engage in a rational calculus of the likely outcomes of their expressions. The likely effects, rather, will be to turn true believers into martyrs among fellow travelers, and capricious actors into sacrificial lambs in the eyes of true believers. Only those deeply committed to retribution for its own sake, victims of such crimes and their supporters alike, will gather much satisfaction from the punishment; the rest of us will take solace only that the racist criminal will be less able to perpetrate acts of this kind in the future. We can take no solace from perpetrators being free, even if punished, to discriminate again.

We—especially the racially dominant but also the racially marginalized—thus need to address more vigorously and dialogically than we have what it is in our culture and the history of its production that enables racializing categories to take hold. We have to address how it is that racializing categories can promote and characterize social relations of power and exclusion to license violence against the marginalized. Of course, there is a sense in which it is better to have hate-speech codes and hate-crime legislation: better pragmatically for those who are objects of such speech and deed when weighed against the absence of any other mode of response. Nevertheless, it would help to reconceive hate crimes and hate speech in terms of what they actually are: violent acts of imposed power over those *this* culture and its members continue to marginalize as racial Others.

I am not thus arguing that those who commit racially prompted injustices go unpunished; quite the contrary. I am suggesting rather that they be dealt with as not simply harming a particular individual or society abstractly, but also as harming the entire group—the body of particular people—with whom the object of the injustice is identified. In this sense, racist wrongs are wrongs, as the Ku Klux Klan Act of 1871 has it, against an entire class of people. And for such wrongs, perpetrators are to be held to standards of "strict liability." If we can do it for products, why not for people? Perhaps, then, we—again, collec-tively—will come to see racist injustices as wrongs against human-ity, and will treat them with the degrees of severity they deserve.

The invocation of humanity here—in responding to racist marginalization, objectification, and harm—is not meant to rein-state the essentialized abstraction of a universal and, thereby, to license a racializing reversal (that is, if a harm is to humanity, then whites must be harmed and this is what renders racist expression wrong). Rather, it is to promote a pragmatically grounded solidarity, a recognition that the specificity of the harm to individual black persons as black is a harm in which, but for their resistance, individual white persons are implicated. In this sense, it is not insignificant—indeed, it is deeply significant—that crimes against humanity are committed invariably by the relatively powerful against the powerless, articulated or picked out usually in class, gendered, and ethnoracial terms. It must be stressed also that in a deeply racist society, nonracial social institutions become implicated in the extension of racialized marginalizations. Transforming racism from "hate crime" to "crime against humanity" is designed, then, to shift philosophical ground from the narrow psychologism of offensiveness to the multiplicities of individual and institutional marginalizations, and from the abstracted limits of nonracialism to the situated revisability and resistances of counter(-to-)racist pragmatics.[5] "Humanity" here, then, stands as a trope of antiracist solidarity, and a normative standard of what postracist social relations might aim for and effect.

TAKING STOCK:

COUNTING BY RACE

3

Modern social subjects have become unself-conscious in establishing racial characteristics. They take for granted the recognition of racial difference: they make racial claims, assert racial truths, assess racial value—in short, create (fabricate) racial knowledge. In this sense, racial knowledge is integral to the common sense, to the articulation, of modernity's self-understanding.

Knowledge production, and this is especially true for social knowledge, does not take place independent of social circumstance. The production of knowledge is sustained and delimited by political economy and by culture—by its own and by that of the society more generally. Productive practices act upon the epistomological categories invoked, informing the knowledge thus produced, imparting assumptions, values, and goals. These categories that frame knowing, in turn, order their users' terms of articulation, fashioning content of the known and constraining what and how members of the social order at hand think and what they think about. The grounds of knowledge, accordingly, offer "foundations" for the constitution of social power (Habermas 1988, 272).

What I am calling "racial knowledge" is defined by two principal features. First, such knowledge assumes as its own the modes and premises of the established scientific fields, especially anthropology, natural history, and biology, but also of sociology, politics, and economics. This scientific cloak imparts to racial knowledge seemingly formal character and universality, authority, and legitimation. Racial knowledge acquires its apparent authority by parasitically mapping its modes of expression according to the formal authority of the scientific discipline it mirrors. It can do this—and this is its second constitutive feature—because it has been historically integral to the emergence of these authoritative scientific fields. Race has been a basic categorical object, in some cases a founding focus, of scientific analysis.

A few instances, both historical and contemporary, of this interweaving of race and science will suffice. There exists, for one, a long-standing partnership in the production of racialized social relations and exclusions in the late nineteenth and early twentieth centuries between the state and racializing eugenic science throughout Europe, the United States, and Latin America. More recently, there has been a rearticulation of these racialized presuppositions, not only in terms of sociobiology but more insidiously (because of its more direct practical effects) in celebration of the possibilities for social engineering of the new biotechnologies.[1]

Historically, this racialized concern with the body is anchored in physical anthropology, the racial presuppositions of which have assumed the status of "givens" in the field. The seeming

RACIAL SUBJECTS

inescapability of physical anthropology's racialized presuppositions was brought home to me recently. The university that pays my way sponsored a colloquium series on "The Origin of the Human Species." I was struck by how deeply the participants, all renowned proponents of competing theories about human origins, have assumed the racialized language of eighteenth-century anthropology, renewing the commitment to (mis)measure human skulls as a way of determining racial difference, and endorsing once again facile presumptions that the difference in size between a Wilt Chamberlain (the 7 ft. 2 in. black basketball legend) and a Willie Shoemaker (the 4 ft. 11 in. white champion jockey) is somehow racially significant. In lieu of an extended rebuttal, I will simply ask: What, then, is to be made of the difference in size between Bill Walton (the 7 ft. 1 in. white basketball legend) and Tyrone Bogues (the 5 ft. 3 in. current black basketball dynamo)? Carleton Coon's legacy has a longer reach than I am want to leave unchallenged.

Epistemologically, power is exercised in naming and in evaluating. In naming or refusing to name, existence is recognized or refused, meaning and value are assigned or ignored, people and things are elevated or rendered invisible. Once defined, symbolic order has to be maintained, serviced, extended, operationalized. In this sense, the racial Other is nominated into existence. As Said makes clear in his book *Orientalism* (1978, 31–49), the Other is constituted through the invention of projected knowledge. The practices of naming and knowledge construction tend to deny any meaningful autonomy to those so named and imagined, extending over them power, control, authority, and domination.

As I have suggested, science is implicated deeply in this process of racial nomination. At a more practical and direct level, the U.S. Census has served to weave racial categorization into the social fabric, blending scientific strands with public policy threads. After all, the census is an exercise in social naming, in nominating into existence. The wiser governing powers appear about those they nominate as subject races, the less will their administrative rule require raw force. Racial governmentality thus requires information about supposed racial natures: about demography and economy, housing and education. Information thus has two meanings: detailed facts about racial nature and the forming of racial character. The census has been a formative governmental technology in the service of the state to fashion racialized knowledge—to articulate the categories, to gather data, and to put them to work. Individuals and interest groups, in the United States and elsewhere, have lobbied the state regarding the promotion or dismissal of some racial category, thereby mediating or delimiting the hegemonic imposition and diffusion of state categories. Here, the state agency serves, as Stuart Hall and his collaborators (1978, 57–62) put it, as "primary definers." Individual or interest group intervention serve at best as "secondary."[2]

FORMALIZING RACIAL GOVERNMENTALITY

Racial governmentality is defined and administered by means of forms (pieces of administrative paper). Bureaucratic forms reproduce as they reflect racial identities, distributing them throughout the culture. Forms accordingly are both about form and content, ordering as they inform, as they call for and proffer data. Because form and content are so seamlessly merged in the bureaucratic document, forms offer to modern state governmentality—to bureaucratic rationality—its ideal technology. The positivity of data collection hides from view (in the form of the form) the axiology of presumed value, those suppositions of order and determination; it covers them up in the name of the practical and the given. And this capacity to veil presupposed value is enabled by the apparatus of forms through their archi-te(x)ture, so to speak, for the form embeds its determining and shaping capacity behind the surface positivity of its projected mandates: to collect data, to codify, to structure sameness for the sake of policy and common practice. In this sense, forms are the concrete product and application of the applied sciences of "Man" that emerged as the new episteme in the eighteenth century.

Thus, the form is in*form*ational, reproductive of a social formation as it institutes and applies its assumptions. The form speaks in behalf of repeatable social practices (*administrology*) by offering data in support. To the extent that the data—the field of collectible information—can be *form*alized (and by virtue of being in*form*ation it is already to some extent formalizable), the knowledge they purport to re-present acquires the status—the authority—and so the legitimation of science. It is with reason that statistics and forms emerge more or less coterminously. Forms presuppose the givenness, the absolute positivity, of the data to which the form extends logic, order, structure, coherence—in short, *form*.

*Form*al identity is identity conceived, manufactured, and fabricated in and through forms. It is rigid, static, at least insofar as it is intra-form(al), limited in its life to the parameters of the form and the bureaucratic rationality that the form informs. The form, and the identity prompted and promoted by the form, is regulatory and regulative. The form furnishes uni*form*ity—regularity, repeatability, reiterability, predictability—to identity, rendering it accordingly accessible to administration. In short, it provides governmentality with everything that amounts to knowledge in the scientific-technical mode necessary to administration. The form is the technology of scientific management par excellence.

The form offers insurance against the risk of un*form*ed—that is, an*arch*ical—social practice and life, a hedge against (or at least a circumscription of) future uncertainties and open-ended possibilities by restricting unfettered possibility to the predictability of inductive probability. Unformed anarchy is regulated by the constraints of the form. Conformity and the uniformity that are both its products and presuppositions are manufactured by silencing and rendering invisible or placing outside the margins of the form the data of pure heterogeneity.

In the case of identities, the de*form*ation of identity created or crafted through the technology of the form does not necessarily turn on a (philosophically or scientifically) realist understanding of identity—that is, that form(al) identity fails to capture the fixed and transhistorical truth of lived or experienced identity, its irreducible heterogeneity. Rather form(al) identity necessarily presupposes the static nature, the unchangingness, of identity as such, and so freezes what is historically in process, in trans*forma*-tion. So form(al) identity—and this is especially true for identity fabricated through census forms—always lags behind the more transitory nature of lived identity. The form is always already too late. For by the time the form appears, lived identity has altered; or it captures only a partial (a limited and biased) aspect of that lived identity while silencing all other aspects; or, again, even having captured something of that lived identity, the form fails to respond to transformational pressures because they are unrecognizable outside the parameters of the *form*alization that the form entails.

The form, then, like those employed in the census that speak to identity, always lags behind the complex negotiations of identities and (self-)identifications in everyday experience, even as it serves in part to shape and to fix those identities and identifications. In the case of the census count, there is a commitment to re*form*ulate categories better to capture the power of the name—to reflect interests, to shape identities, and to fix identification anew. To open up the form to renewably open-ended self-identification would quite literally undermine—de*form*—the very nature of the form, its administrative purpose, for it would at once remove the categorically reiteratable in*forma*-tion—the identity of information via categorization—that it is the mandate of the form to make available. Categorization extends to otherwise randomly collected data its identity, transforming discrete bits of data into information.

The U.S. Census serves, and was initially designed to serve, state interests, functioning to furnish information crucial to state revenue collection, and to distributional and voting purposes. But the census has also always had an ideological mandate; namely, to articulate, if not to create, a national profile, a mapping of the nation's demographic contours. I examine the practical intersection of social science, state-directed social policy, and racialized discourse by focusing on the ways that U.S. Census counts throughout their history have helped to fashion and to fix the racializing of the U.S. body politic. The census has worked thus to draw racial lines around and within the society, reifying as it reflects prevailing racialized common sense.

TAKING STOCK

A national census, by all accounts, is a stocktaking of the country's human assets, of the state's population capital. Accordingly, the census uses social science both functionally and ideologically. Functionally, it employs social science (and puts social scientists to work) to observe, define, oversee, and assess shifts in population (Conk 1987, 159). In this sense, the census promotes a sophisticated intersection of space and time. It maps the geographical contours of population distribution, fashioning a social understanding strongly predicated on historical records. So, ironically, a census is always too late, tied to past reports of social division and diffusion, presupposing categories crafted from the material of past records (Cohn 1987, 231–32).[3]

In the United States, the national census is as old as the republic itself, mandated decennially by the Constitution primarily for the purposes of voting district apportionment and of distribution of federal resources among states. But beyond these crucial administrative mandates, the census has functioned also to secure recognition and material benefits for groups otherwise ignored.

Ideologically, the census is a kind of "collective self-portrait" that serves to invent and to renew—to reimagine—the national identity (Starr 1987, 19). The U.S. Census has always racialized this national image: both in its imagined (pre)formation and in its statistical (re)creation, the racial Us and Other are produced and defined by the census, as it reflects and refines the racialized social formation.

In the name of an objectivity that claims simply to document or to reflect, the census of racialized social categories and groups purports to count without judging, to photograph without transforming. The census reflects the racializing categories of social formation that it nevertheless at once reifies, which it reproduces as it creates and cements as it naturalizes. This process of objectified nomination thus fixes (at least temporarily and tenuously) what are at best racial fabrications, for racial categories are at once creations from whole cloth and threads integral to—constitutive of—the prevailing sociocultural fabric. The snapshot of the national profile freezes momentarily into givens, thereby objectifying, the racializing categories it at once assumes and fashions. This body count, authorized by state mandate and its legal instrumentality, thus offers racialized categories the mark of respectability. It thus enables these indices of otherness, apartness, and fracture to extend over, to seep silently into, the social concepts and categories of the nation that are not so straightforwardly racial, especially those of class.[4] A national census profiles the laboring classes, mapping their regional availability, providing a snapshot of capital's labor needs.

The administrative mandate of the U.S. Census was racialized (just as it was engendered) from its inception. In 1787, the Constitution required the census to distinguish between "free white males," "free white females," "all other free persons" (by sex and color), "untaxed Indians," and "slaves." "The slave," presumed silently to be black, was defined as three-fifths a person for the purposes of resource allocation.[5] (Given that the Declaration of Independence opens by declaring all "men" equal, this implies, if it did not assume, that slaves—black slaves, to emphasize the point—were assumed not to be "men," that is, not fully human.)

It may help to group the racial categories employed in the two hundred years of census taking in this country into five periods. The first period runs from 1790 to 1840 during which the initial categories are baldly fashioned, framing the premises for all future conceptualization. The period offers no instructions as to the categories' definition or scope. The second period runs from 1850 to 1880 during which precise categories were streamlined as a reflection and in the expressed service of (racial) science. The third period spans from 1890 to 1920 during which categories first covered all of settled America (Lee 1993, 76) and responded to the significant thrusts of (im)migration. The fourth period covers 1930 to 1970 during which racial distinction in the United States began to proliferate against (or in spite of) the assimilationist grain. The fifth period includes the U.S. Census counts of 1980 and 1990 significant for transforming the presumptive basis of category formation from "objectively" given constructs to "self-identifying" ones.[6]

The first formal U.S. Census, in 1790, employed the initial constitutional categories, later qualified only by age for whites in the counts of 1800 and 1810. In 1820, the category of "Free Colored Person" was introduced and qualified by gender and age, though the age distinctions differed slightly from those categorized as "white."[7] In 1830, age categories for "whites" were multiplied, and gender and age distinctions were introduced for "slaves" reflecting those of the "Free Colored Persons," even though "slaves" were listed prior to the latter category. The only novelty introduced in 1840 was to invert in the inventory the order of appearance of "Free Colored Person" and "Slaves." Yet, as more black people gained freedom, the census was invoked

RACIAL SUBJECTS

Figure 1. Census Categories from 1790 to 1990
(Compiled with the assistance of Barbara Lammi)

1790	1800	1810	1820	1830	1840	1850	1860	1870	1880	1890
Free White Males & Females	Free White Males & Females	Free White Males & Females	Free White Males & Females	Free White Persons	Free White Persons	White	White	White	White	White
All Other Free Persons, Except Indians Not Taxed	All Other Free Persons, Except Indians Not Taxed	All Other Free Persons, Except Indians Not Taxed	All Other Free Persons, Except Indians Not Taxed							
Slaves	Slaves	Slaves		Slaves	Slaves					
			Free Colored Persons	Free Colored Persons Gender Age	Free Colored Persons					
						Black (B)	Black	Black	Black	Black/Negro
						Mulatto (M)	Mulatto	Mulatto	Mulatto	Mulatto
										Quadroon
										Octoroon
								Chinese		Chinese
										Japanese
								Indian		Indian

1900	1910	1920	1930	1940	1950	1960	1970	1980	1990
White	White	White	White	White	White	White	White	White	White
Black (Negro or Negro Descent)	Black	Black	Negro	Negro	Negro	Negro	Negro or Black	Black (or Negro)	Black or Negro
	Mulatto	Mulatto							
			Mexican						
Chinese	Chinese	Chinese	Chinese	Chinese	Chinese	Chinese	Chinese	Chinese	Chinese
Japanese	Japanese	Japanese	Japanese	Japanese	Japanese	Japanese	Japanese	Japanese	Japanese
			Filipino	Filipino	Filipino	Filipino	Filipino	Filipino	Filipino
			Hindu	Hindu					
			Korean	Korean			Korean	Korean	Korean
								Vietnamese	Vietnamese
								Asian Indian	Asian Indian
								Guamanian	Guamanian
								Samoan	Samoan
						Hawaiian	Hawaiian	Hawaiian	Hawaiian
						Pan Hawaiian			
Indian	Indian	Indian	Indian	Indian	American Indian	American Indian	Indian (Amer.)	Indian (Amer.)	Indian (Amer.)
						Aleut		Aleut	Aleut
						Eskimo		Eskimo	Eskimo
	Other	Other	Other Races	Other Races	Other Race	Etc. (Inc. Asian Indians)	Other (Specify Race)	Other	Other Race
									Other API

ideologically to shore up the institution of enslavement. Thus, as William Petersen notes (1987, 230, n. 90), the 1840 U.S. Census "measured" insanity and idiocy, claiming to show the percentage of blacks suffering both conditions to be greater in the North than in the South. These "facts" were then used to license the argument that though blacks were at ease with slavery, they were clearly incapable of adjusting to freedom. The argument and the data supposedly supporting it were vigorously challenged by Edward Jarvis, a Massachusetts physician supported by the Massachusetts Medical Society and the American Statistical Association, who demanded that the many miscalculations be formally corrected. Instead, John Calhoun, then Secretary of State and so in charge of the census, censored the critique and persisted in invoking the figures in support of slavery. A separate study conducted by Dr. James McCune Smith for a convention of free black Northerners found that eight towns in Maine where thirty insane black people were claimed to be institutionalized had no black residents at all. Moreover, Aptheker (1974) reveals that where the census had reported 133 black patients in the mental institution of Worcester, Massachusetts, they were all white, consistent with the nineteenth century tendency to identify idiocy and blackness.[8]

Instructions to census takers were initiated in 1820, though instructions regarding race first appeared for the 1850 census. Lacking explicit definitions of the racial categories, the census relied in its first half century on establishing the racial body count upon the "*common* sense" judgments, the (pre)supposed views, of its all-white enumerators. Persons were racially named, the body politic measured, and resources distributed based on prevailing racial presumptions and mandated fractional assessments. The society was literally marked in black and white.

From 1850 on, increasingly fine distinctions began to appear for those considered "nonwhite," and the growing complexity of

RACIAL SUBJECTS

these distinctions seemed to require issuance for enumerators of instruction schedules concerning the racial categories. Thus, in 1850, under the leadership of U.S. Census Superintendent, J. D. B. De Bow (for whom "the negro was created essentially to be a slave"), enumerators were asked to mark the color of "Free inhabitants." They were to do so by leaving the space under the heading "Color" blank for "whites," while "carefully" marking others as "B" (for "Black") or "M" (for "Mulatto"). Slaves were to be counted separately, and their color indicated also.

These categories informed a significant Californian case, *People v. Hall*, in 1854. In 1850, the Californian legislature had passed (in an act regulating California criminal proceedings) a clause prohibiting the court testimony of a black, mulatto, or American Indian person directed against a white defendant. Hall, a white man, had been convicted of murder because of witness testimony by a Chinese man. Hall appealed his conviction on the basis that the Chinese belonged with American Indians to a common Mongoloid race, and so the testimony of the Chinese witness was inadmissible. Appealing to the Bering Straits theory of American Indian migration and invoking the most vituperative antiblack rhetoric, the California Supreme Court upheld Hall's appeal and vacated his conviction (Renoso 1992, 833). The heart (not to mention the mind) of whiteness, it seems, is naturally set apart from the heart and mind of an othered and singular "nonwhiteness."

In 1870, further distinctions were introduced into the census: "Chinese" (largely because of the importation of coolie labor in the West) and "Indian" (marking the policy shift to removing American Indians to reservations). The new instructions cautioned enumerators to take special care in reporting "Mulatto (including quadroons, octoroons, and all persons having any perceptible trace of African blood)." The reason? "Important scientific results depend upon the correct determination of this class." By the count of 1880, the request for information about "Indians" had become more specific. The instructions for 1880 specified Indian division between tribes, and insisted on listing whether the person was a "full-blood" of the tribe or mixed with another. If mixed with "white," the person had to be marked "W" (a concession reflecting the presupposed closeness in the "great chain of being" between "Europeans" and "Indians"); if mixed with "black," he or she had to be marked "B"; and if mixed with "mulatto," he or she had to be marked "M" (indicating the overriding presumption of "black" otherness). Tribal adoptees were to be racially marked as "W. A." ("white adopted") or "B. A." ("black or mulatto adopted"). Moreover, enumerators were instructed not to accept answers that they "know or have reason to believe are false," indicating the continued power of racial definition vested in the hands of all-white enumerators.[9]

The instructions for the 1890 count reflected not only the rapid diversification of the U.S. population, but the intensifying administrative concern (in the face of this expanding diversity) with racial distinction, hierarchy, and imposed division. Thus, while the categories for "white," "Chinese," and "Indian" remained unchanged, explicit and superficial distinctions were introduced between "black," "mulatto," "quadroon," and "octoroon." "Black" was to refer to any person with "three-fourths or more black blood"; "mulatto" referred to those having "from three-eighths to five-eighths black blood"; "quadroon" to those persons having "one-fourth black blood"; and "octoroon" to those "having one-eighth or any trace of black blood."

In 1900, these distinctions began to collapse in the wake of the widespread social belief that "black" was any person "with a single drop of black blood" (Davis 1991, 5). So "black" was indicated on the instructions as "a negro or of negro descent." Ten years later the category "other" was first introduced. Anyone not falling into the established census categories was to be

RACIAL SUBJECTS

marked as "other," and his or her race (assuming of course that it was identifiable) to be listed there. The reintroduced definitions to distinguish "black" from "mulatto" shifted. They began visibly to reflect the struggle to balance blackness with the self-evident effects of miscegenation. Thus, the category "black" now "include[d] all persons who are *evidently* full-blooded negroes," while "negro include[d] all persons having some proportion or *perceptible* trace of negro blood" (my emphases). In keeping with the common comprehension of race but serving also to cement it, race was conceived (in a confused mix of the literal and the metaphorical) as blood, a confusion that necessitated reducing the basis of distinction between "black" and "negro" to nothing more than the enumerators' perception. This necessary, and necessarily reductive, recourse to appearance in racial designation predates the 1950 Population Registration Act of the South African apartheid state by almost half a century.

No changes were made to the racial categories for 1920. However, the 1924 National Origins Act, strongly promoted by the eugenics movement in the United States and sponsored by Senator Albert Johnson, president of the Eugenics Research Association at Cold Spring Harbor, Long Island, cut immigration. Immigrants from those countries already represented in the U.S. was cut to 2 percent of their numbers already residing in the U.S., as determined by the 1890 U.S. Census. Difficulties soon arose in determining the figures on national origins, so that by 1929 a flat cap of 150,000 immigrants per annum was introduced, 71 percent of whom were to be from Britain, Germany, and the rest of Europe. Japanese immigration was restricted completely (Gossett 1965, 406–07).

By 1930, the prevailing institutional mandates of racialized segregation and immigration restriction had prompted seemingly precise specifications for reporting race. Enumerators were required to enter as "Negro" any person of "mixed white and

Negro blood" irrespective of how small "the percentage of Negro blood." Moreover, a person "part Indian" and "part Negro" was to be listed as "Negro unless the Indian blood predominated and the person is generally accepted as Indian in the community." Similarly, someone of "mixed white and Indian blood" was to be counted as "Indian, except where the percentage of Indian blood" was deemed very small or the person was generally considered white in the community. In general, any "racially mixed person" with white parentage was to be designated according to the race of the parent who was not white; by contrast, "mixtures of colored races" were to be racially designated from the father's race, "except Negro-Indian." For the first time, also, "Mexican" was introduced as a separate *racial* category, and defined as "all persons born in Mexico, or having parents born in Mexico, and who are definitely not white, Negro, Indian, Chinese, or Japanese." In the next count, however, partly in response to objections by both the Mexican government and the U.S. State Department, "Mexicans" were to be listed as "white" unless they were "definitely Indian or some race other than white." While the concern by 1940 with racial purity may have been waning in the wake of Aryanism, the concern with the growing ethno-coloring of America seemed to demand a way of keeping whites separate and distinct.

This trend toward introducing ethnoracial categories while looking for ways to maintain a majority of whiteness continued unabated through the 1970 census. Accordingly, in 1950 the category of "Filipino" was introduced under the section on "Race," while American Indians were listed according to "degree of Indian blood: full blood; half to full; quarter to half; less than one quarter." The mid-century romance with the automobile prompted these odd metaphors, reminiscent of gasoline gauges, reducing in this instance American Indians to objects. This calculus was presumably tied to the New Deal undertaking to reestablish tribal administrative authority. Blood counts would provide the insidious technology for determining the range of bureaucratic control: the "purer" the "blood" the less assimilable and so the more they were to suffer governmental imposition. To illustrate just how far the concern with the racialized body count was carried, enumerators were warned, in an implicit nod to the intersection of race, class, and gender distinction, that "knowledge of the housewife's race tells nothing of the maid's race."

In 1960, new categories were added to the already accepted categories of "white," "Negro," "American Indian," "Japanese," "Chinese," and "Filipino": "Hawaiian," "Pan Hawaiian," "Aleut," and "Eskimo." The earlier addition of "Other" (that is, un/ specified racial categories) was replaced by "etc.," as though the imperative to racialize had assumed the naturalism of iterative ordinariness. Instructions to enumerators stated that "white" was to include "Puerto Ricans, Mexicans, or other persons of Latin descent" unless such persons were "definitely Negro, Indian, or some other race." Southern European and Near Eastern nationals similarly were to be classified as "white," while Asian Indians were to be deemed "Other."

By 1970, "Pan Hawaiian," "Aleut," and "Eskimo" were eliminated from the section on "Race," but "Korean" was added and "Other" was reintroduced with the explicit instruction to specify race. Those of supposedly "Latin" descent were asked to specify their place of origin or specify their descent as either "Mexican," "Puerto Rican," "Cuban," "Central or South American," "Other Spanish," or "none of these." At the same time, those responding to the question of race as "Chicano," "La Raza," "Mexican America," "Moslem," or "Brown" were to be classified as "white," whereas respondents listing "Brown (Negro)" would be considered "Negro" or "Black." Even as the census had begun to reflect the insistence of black-consciousness that "Negro" give way to "Black," there was an insistence upon the loaded distinction between brown and black, between (in census language from 1930 to 1960) "non-Negro" and "Negro." Somehow the so-called "browning of America" was lost in reaffirming the long-standing distinction between white and black, a sign perhaps of things to come. Andrew Hacker (1991) may yet be right, though for reasons he scarcely touches upon, that in the United States there are "Two Nations, Black and White, Separate, Hostile and Unequal." The seeming liberalization and loosening of racial classification that began tentatively in the 1970s (was it ever more rigorous?) was nevertheless overshadowed by the continuing imposition of narrowed racial designation—most notably, as "white" or "black"—standing silently behind the nuance of racial self-naming.

These transformations in race designation were carried forward into the 1980 U.S. Census in a way that altogether undermines any crosscensus comparisons. Most important, the census introduced the standard of racial *self*-identification that had begun in the early 1970s to be assumed in almost all fifty states. For census purposes, however, the injunction to declare oneself racially as one chooses was circumscribed. Respondents were still required to choose from *given* designations, a mix of traditionally racial, ethnic, and national categories. Thus, the primary categories of the 1970 U.S. Census were supplemented by the addition of "Vietnamese," "Guamanian," and "Samoan," while "Eskimo" and "Aleut" were reintroduced. "Black" became a primary designation, though "Negro" was retained as an alternate reading. Similarly, those previously identified as of "Spanish" origin or descent could now also choose to identify themselves as "Hispanic" (but notably not Chicano or Latino). To all of this was added a general question about ancestry, requesting information about ethnic/national descent. Included among the examples cited were "Afro-American," "Jamaican," "Nigerian," "Venezuelan," and "Ukrainian." Where "mixed race" persons had

RACIAL SUBJECTS

difficulty placing themselves, enumerators were instructed to report the mother's race/group, and where this was unacceptable, to list the first race cited. For the Spanish-origin question, if someone reported mixed parentage with only the second parent identifiable as "Spanish/Hispanic" (e.g., Italian-Cuban), enumerators were instructed to void the "Spanish/Hispanic" designation.

Whatever happened to the right of self-identification to *refuse* to identify oneself racially? The denial of such a right implies (if it does not presuppose) that race is a primary, indeed, a primal category of human classification, one so natural to the human condition that it can be ignored only on pain of self-denial. Underlying the imperative of racial self-identification is the presumption of naturalism: one is expected to identify oneself as what one "naturally" is (Goldberg 1993b). The democracy of self-naming is undermined by the authoritarianism of imposed identity and identification. Those resisting literally become the new "Others."

This apparent paradox of racial self-naming highlights the tensions faced by any nation committed to a racial numeration. The technology of counting can impose categories of identification or it can allow completely open self-identifying responses. The former will furnish a set of consistent categories and a statistically manipulable data base. The latter won't. Nevertheless, at best, the former will seriously undercount; at worst, it will have little objective reference to the nuances of people's felt identities. For example, on the basis of national origin and native language reports in the 1930 census, there were an estimated 200,000 Spanish speakers in New Mexico (roughly half that state's population). But the census count in 1930 listed only 61,960 for the category "Mexican." For the overwhelming majority, the category did not apply.[10] Unfortunately, unrestricted self-identifying responses will be statistically useless, for there is unlikely to be any categorical uniformity. Social identities, in other words, belie simplicity, and bureaucratic-statistical requirements (elevated by managed multiculturalisms) simply serve to enforce the racializing imperative of the census.

In the most recent census, these categories and their ordering again were redefined, if not exactly refined. Thus, the 1990 form asked respondents, under the heading "Race," whether they were "White," "Black or Negro," "American Indian," "Eskimo," "Aleut," or "Asian or Pacific Islander (API)," or "Other race (list)." "API" was specified as including "Chinese," "Filipino," "Hawaiian," "Korean," "Vietnamese," "Japanese," "Asian Indian," "Samoan," "Guamanian," and "Other API" (which was presumed to include "Cambodian," "Tongan," "Laotian," "Hmong," "Thai," and "Pakistani"). There was a separate question for those declaring "Spanish/Hispanic origin," reflecting the political history of nervous uncertainty (if not outright insecurity) over the racial identity of those so self-identifying. Respondents under this category were asked to distinguish whether they were "Mexican, Mexican-American, or Chicano," "Puerto Rican," "Cuban," or "Other Spanish/Hispanic." The latter included "Argentinean," "Colombian," "Dominican," "Nicaraguan," "Salvadorean," and "Spaniard." Although these categories were listed as "racial," they included a confused and confusing intersection of those deemed traditionally racial with national and ethnic configurations. The conceptual and political tensions in and between the categories was exacerbated by the appearance of a final question asking all respondents to list their "ancestry or ethnic origin." Examples on the form included "German," "Afro-American," "Croatian," "Cape Verdean," "Dominican," "Cajun," "French Canadian," "Jamaican," "Korean," "Lebanese," "Mexican," "Nigerian," "Ukrainian," and so forth.

These elastic racial, ethnic, and national characteristics mean, as the U.S. Census Bureau (1990, 2) readily admits, that "Data on race and Hispanic origin ... are not totally comparable between censuses."[11] Thus, the comparative group size of "Whites," "Blacks," "Hispanics," "Indians," and "Asian or Pacific Islanders" is misleading, precisely because the categories include nonracial subdivisions; while affirmative action policies based on these numbers will have unfair outcomes or be open to odious manipulation. The publicity in the 1980s surrounding the movie *Soul Man*, about the faking of ethnic identity to benefit from an affirmative action program, portrays one such move.

Categorical self-identification provides opportunities for movement by groups as well. Some native Hawaiians want to reclassify their group status from "API" to "American Indian," a concern motivated by solidarity, common struggle, and historical accuracy, but also because "Some colleges and the Department of Education have minority scholarships that you get through your status as Native American."[12] Moreover, though claims based on crosscensus comparisons may properly indicate population trends, they also may not. For instance, explaining the doubling of the "Asian and Pacific Islander population" in a decade strictly in terms of "a high level of immigration" may be misleading precisely because some of those counted as API in 1990 were not so counted in 1980. Indeed, no separate API category was included in the 1980 U.S. Census, only many of the ethnic/national subdivisions grouped under this rubric in 1990 (all of the categories in 1990 exemplifying "Other API" were missing in 1980). Some may object that nothing much is added by the introduction of the general API category. However, its presence at a time of heightened concern over group identity no doubt prompts the possibility of a self-identification otherwise discouraged—that is, silenced.

Similarly, from 1980 to 1990, there was a projected increase of 53 percent in "Hispanic origin population (of any race)." Part of this increase can be attributed to the introduction of new explicit subcategories like "Colombian," "Dominican," and so on. By the same token, the increases in the "American Indian" population (including "Eskimo" and "Aleut") of 70 percent from 1970 to 1980, and of 40 percent from 1980 to 1990, turned not only on categorical introductions but upon the reemergence of "Indian-consciousness," the drive to reidentify with Indianness in the face of the assimilative and integrative imperatives of hegemonic U.S. culture. Accordingly, the reported increase of 41 percent from 1982 to 1992 in the number of "Hispanic" doctorates (compared with a 19 percent drop in doctorates for blacks) fails to taken into account the related increase in the number of people primarily identifying themselves as "Hispanic," an identification prompted both by the emphatic appearance of the administrative category and the general social emphasis on ethnic particularity.[13]

The shifting politics of (self-)identification prompted and reified by the history of the census raise deep difficulties for any social science relying unproblematically on crosscensus population group comparisons from census reports on "Race and Hispanic Origin." Davis, Haub, and Willette (1988, 3), for example, report more than a 200 percent increase of "Hispanics" in the United States from 1950 to 1980, projecting estimates for the nonexistent data from 1950, 1960, and 1970. Similarly, Linda Chavez (1991, 104) acknowledges that "Hispanic" earnings in the southwestern United States in 1989 were still 57 percent of non-Hispanic earnings, just as they had been forty years earlier in 1959 (found by comparing earnings of Mexican-origin males in 1959 with that of "Hispanics" in 1989). Thus researchers can create a history by estimating the count for a category which did not exist at the time. In this sense, "Hispanics" is the only group in the United States fashioned retroactively, as a political response to a problem of political economy, namely, the command of economic resources, the demand for political representation, and the projection of a unified consumer body. ("Asian

RACIAL SUBJECTS

Americans" perhaps fits this account also, though in slightly different form and for different purposes.) The mix of legal and bureaucratic technologies reduces the nuance of experienced identity to the certitude of categorical identity. For instance, Teja Arboleda's maternal grandparents are European, his father's mother African-American, and his father's father Filipino/ Chinese. He is listed as white on his birth certificate. In responding to the 1990 Census, he refused to complete the ethnic/racial section. On the basis of his name, skin, and hair color an enumerator marked him as "Hispanic."[14] So much for the (pre)supposed correlation between race and I.Q. driving the agenda of *The Bell Curve*.

While crosscensus comparisons concerning racial data need to be approached with analytical sensitivity, such comparisons need not be dismissed out of hand. William Julius Wilson (1989), for example, in his justly influential study, *The Truly Disadvantaged*, uses data reliant on the race reported in various census reports. Wilson is concerned mostly with black-white comparisons, and though the census racial categories concerning blacks shift over time, the shift is largely within the category and so the effect on black-white comparisons is minimized. Wilson is generally sensitive, also, to nuances in the category "Hispanic," differentiating it from data reported under the category "Spanish-origin" (though he equates a U.S. Census Bureau report on urban poverty based on 1970 Census "Spanish origin" figures with 1980 figures on "Hispanics") (Wilson 1989, 58–59; also see 23, 31, 37, 65). Enough, however, about these administrative technologies. The underlying question is why we are concerned at all with counting by race.

COUNTING BY RACE

This line of analysis demonstrates that one should be deeply wary of drawing any intracensus implications based on racial categories. The categories are figments of an overrationalized bureaucratic imagination, and their implications are likely insidious. The 1990 Census, for example, reports that the population of "Hispanic origin" is greatest in the South and Western United States (California, Arizona, New Mexico, Texas, and Florida). But people collected under "Hispanic origin" in the southwestern states differ, often dramatically, from those in the southeast and in the large eastern cities like Washington, Philadelphia, and New York. Indeed, interests, culture, almost anything, causes racial identification counts of "Hispanics" to differ regionally. It is for this reason, perhaps, that contemporary census documents, in speaking of racial categories, commonly refer to "Race *and* Hispanic Origin" (my emphasis). The category "Hispanic" is an imposed one: it others as it unites, marginalizes as it generalizes, stereotypes as it aggregates. It purports to categorize identity for an entire subcontinent (and beyond) in the age of globalization and flexible accumulation, just as it seeks to create—to fabricate in the economic imaginary—a supersubject, a target market that abnegates the specificity of its constituents. It is a category that becomes fixed in the public mind—becomes a given of common sense—through sociostatistical profiles, the "objective" realism of numbers, and the reality of tables, charts, and comparisons.[15]

More insidiously, these racialized politics of numbers and the numerical politics of racial naming and placing must be comprehended in the context of their primary legislative mandate. The point of the census in U.S. history was to manage effective resource distribution and voting access. These economic and political mandates in the United States have always been deeply racialized, and the apparent contemporary democratizing of census self-identification serves only to hide from view newly framed racialized tensions that remain as managed as they always were. "Hispanics" may catch up with "Blacks" in their percentage of the U.S. population by the end of the decade and may pass them by the first decade of the next century. But this "fact" is as much a fabrication of racial designation as it is of demographic growth.

"Hispanic" was crafted as a nonracial term to cut across racial designations, yet in its generality it has served, and serves, as a new racial category.

Racializing the body count in this way has, as always, significant implications for voting rights. The voting rights of blacks are now guaranteed (in more or less complex ways) by the Fifteenth Amendment (1871), and by the 1965 Voting Rights Act and its 1982 amendment. One of the ways to dilute blacks' voting rights, perhaps one of the only permissible alternatives now, is to set them against "other" statistically dominant "minorities," minorities whose racial configurations are precisely ambiguous. Blacks are marked hegemonically as politically and socially liberal (and in the 1980s liberal came to be cast as literally un-American); whereas those configured as "Hispanic" (and perhaps also Asian American) are often cast as socially (and perhaps economically) conservative.[16] In the equally fabricated tensions between liberals and conservatives that characterize U.S. politics, the drive to bring those referenced as "Hispanic" under the "right" wing is under way (just as the New Deal and Great Society Democrats sought to capture the black vote). A social statistics that purports to report the truth underpins the new racialized dynamics. This new dynamic may be fueled, paradoxically, by the very instrument designed to democratize the social body count, namely, racial self-identification.

A key implication drawn by the state from the Civil Rights Movement and independence struggles of the 1960s is the importance of self-naming. Imposing names on groups and individuals was a significant social technology of control under cultural colonialism and racialized domination. The formal introduction of self-identification as the standard of group definition in the 1970s reflected the apparent drive to democratize sociopolitical institutions in the United States. Nevertheless, the parameters of self-definition have never been open-ended, for the state has always furnished the range of available, credible, and reliable—that is, of licensed and so permissible—categories in which self-definition could occur. Simultaneously in the 1970s, the overwhelmingly white-faced image of the United States was becoming dramatically shaded. There is a sense, then, in which the nominal politics of Hispanicizing is serving to soften, if not to undermine, this racial transformation. In census terms, "Hispanic" is only ambiguously a racial category, placed alongside, as an additive to, "Race." It is thus, at once, racialized and deracialized. "Hispanics" may now be white or black, where they once were certainly deemed "nonwhite" (George Bush, remember, in a televized family profile before the 1988 election, referred to his grandson, whose mother is Mexican, as "the little brown one"). In the past, the boundaries of blood counts were quite rigidly policed, evaded by some through "passing," though only at considerable psychological cost. Now this restriction has given way to a licensed and encouraged passing via redefinition; that is, a restructured white identity at once referencing as it passes over racialized difference.[17] This restructured racial identity reflects material interests. Examples include the intersection of race and class interests around "Mexicans" in the debate leading up to the Congressional vote on NAFTA, reading Mexican businessmen as white and the Mexican poor as not, and the ongoing debate concerning extension of health care to "illegal aliens." The census promotion of "Hispanic" while censoring categories like "Chicano" or "Latino" reorders the structure of whiteness as it strictures the boundaries of blackness.

We find in the example of the census, then, a technology that has racialized the social fabric and reflected the distinctions alive in the general culture. This bureaucratic document, distributed decennially throughout the population with a strong request for response, provides to the cultural categories it disseminates the imprimatur of official approval. Via the limits that census forms place upon self-identification and self-understanding, they serve also to endorse, to reify, and to normalize the categories found in the general culture. The census count, thus, naturalizes this national profile, authorizing the prevailing language of imposed identity and identification, licensing it in the name of the law and the state—from the constraints of which there is no escape.

There is a sense in which the census categories are as significant in their silences and exclusions as they are in their categorical inclusions. Two illustrations will suffice. As Dvora Yanow (1993, 16–17) perceptively states, an alphabetical listing of categories or names would signify a commitment not to differentiate irrelevantly between the entities listed and would be a commitment to treat all equally. The ethnoracial categories throughout the history of the census, however, have never been alphabetically ordered. Indeed, invariantly, "whites" have been listed first. "Whites" are never subdivided for the purposes of enumeration in the way "nonwhites" always have been: there is never a census concern to enumerate the ethnic subdivision of whites in the way that the census count has obsessed over those deemed not white. "White" is the only category that remains formally unchanged throughout the two-hundred-year history of the census count. It is undivided, nonpolarized, without distinction, and virtually without qualification. Nor, as Yanow observes, does the listing follow a historical logic, for then "American Indians" would be followed by "whites" (or perhaps even "Spanish") and so on. Rather, the categories are listed in terms of dominance, "white"; prevailing otherness, "black" (De Tocqueville's "Two Nations"); and then in terms of the hierarchy of being and degrees of alie/n/ation, qualified by this duality of imposed color.

The second significant silence concerns Jews, who are listed nowhere in the history of census categories. For one, there is no question concerning religion, either under "Race" or anywhere else. As Sharon Lee (1993) notes more generally, the absence of apparent curiosity concerning religious affiliation has a good deal to do with the controversy over the constitutional distinction between church and state. This explains the absence of Judaism as a category, not that of Jews, or Jewishness, to sharpen the contrast between religion and ethnoracial identity. This silence presumes Jewishness away as an appropriate racial designation, denies the possibility, post-1980, of Jewishness as a racial self-identification, rendering such a response abnormal even as it delimits its possibility. A defense of this absence cannot claim that Jewishness is not properly a *racial* category, for neither is "Hispanic." In addition, as I have argued in *Racist Culture*, to say "Jewish" is not a racial category is historically false; and if it weren't, this could count as a reason to silence all racial classification. Of course, it could be that this absence results largely from the reticence of prominent Jewish lobby groups to reinvoke a painful history of exclusionary categorization in and by the law, in which marking off was done to promote a final solution. But this possibility speaks only to the postwar absence of the categorical presence, and addresses not at all the relation between the categorical absence of "Jews" from the first-century-and-a-half of census enumeration and the history of American anti-Semitism.

The silence concerning Jews becomes even more significant when one considers that "Hindu" ("Hindoo") was included as a racial category in the census counts of 1930 and 1940. This inclusion assumes added significance due to a recent racial discrimination appeal to the Sixth District Court of Appeal. Dale Sandhu had been ruled ineligible by a Superior Court judge to bring a claim against Lockheed, his former employer, stating that his layoff had been prompted by racially discriminatory animus. Lockheed argued that, as someone of East Indian origin, Sandhu was considered "Caucasian" by the law, and so his argument failed to have standing under the California Fair Employment and Housing Act. But, appealing to the appearance in the 1980 census of the category "Asian Indian," the Appeals Court ruled that Sandhu was "subject to a discriminatory animus based on his membership in a group which is perceived as distinct." Similarly, recent jury discrimination suits have turned on demonstrating a significant disparity between the racial composition of a jury pool, or jury and alternates, or jury foreperson, and the racial composition of the jurisdiction in which the jury trial is located as measured by the most recent census tract count.[18]

One can only conclude that racialization is a deep historical reality of this social structure perhaps too readily called "America," so deep perhaps that its design strikes one as purposeful, or at least as the outcome (if not so readily as the instrumentality) of purposeful institutionalization. In the face of overwhelming evidence of a racialized social structure, the continued insistence on implementing an ideal of color-blindness either denies historical reality and its abiding contemporary legacies, or serves to cut off any claims to contemporary entitlements. This latter silence is effected by insisting that we interpret our social arrangements afresh, divorced from their modes of initiation, (re)production, and emergence. Such historical silencing freezes into place the "given" racialized conditions that their invocation in the face of this silencing—from the margins by the marginalized—necessarily wants to place in question.

This, then, becomes our dilemma: We (the People) hold out the ideal of color-blindness in the Constitution, Bill of Rights and Amendments, and in the Civil Rights Acts. No sooner is this done than these founding laws are racialized. To institute the ideal, racialized categories have to be invoked to rectify past injustice and present legacy. Two implications immediately follow. The ideal becomes racialized; that is, tied to its history, deidealized, necessarily unrealized. Yet, at once, given the historicity of racial categories—given their own formative conditions—the terms of racial fabrication themselves change, marking social formation anew. The census, I have argued, plays a central role in this process. Political technologies like the census accordingly render "race" natural, making it appear that the race naturally characterizes social formation. This naturalism freezes the prevailing terms of social relations into natural givens, seemingly inevitable and unchangeable.

To demonstrate, as I have, that racial terms are transformable does not alone undo the marking of social formation by race, for the new terms may serve simply to re-mark social relations, thereby recoding social exclusion and exploitation. As this recoding renews racialized social structure and relations, it ties present racial formation in a superficially apparent similitude to the past by hiding from view its transformed signification—its codes, meanings, and significance. Race today seems just like race last century, or last decade. The U.S. Census Bureau now recognizes that races are not the same, indeed, they warn us not to make crosscensus racial comparisons. Confusion may be the death knell of counting by race.

So, why count by race at all? Racial counting, it seems, sharpens the paradox: we're damned if we do and damned if we don't. I want to suggest that insofar as the paradox is of our own making—"our" at least in the sense of "our society" collectively—it is ours also to undo. To this end, I want to identify some reasons why in the race to count we cannot (and should not) but count by race.

First, race codes past *and* present discrimination, offering a rough and ready indication of opportunities that were (un)available at different moments in time. It serves as a "measure" therefore of the sorts of odds against or under which middle-class black persons, say, attained or retained their middle-class status; or of the degree to which poorer blacks have been denied socioeconomic mobility, or the degree to which just trials by jury are denied those in this country not white, male, or wealthy.

Counting by class doesn't quite do, for we know not only that it undercounts the racially marginalized, but also that it benefits the whitened marginalized at the expense of the black. In any case, if we want to determine whether there has been any improvement among those discriminated against for the color of their skin, we need to count the poor by race (however problematically defined), and race by wealth. Second, it follows that if we are committed to some form of compensatory justice, and of programs that facilitate compensation, we need reference groups. Given that much discriminatory exclusion has been effected in terms of racial definition, a racial count referenced to the sorts of groups racially excluded in the past becomes crucial. Third, we need—again, paradoxically—to count by race in order to undo racial counting.

This latter suggestion prompts a twofold strategy. Looking back to relieve the past, racially defined injustices and their consequent inequities, the injunction is to count by race—primarily, that is, in terms of "blacks" and "whites," but also in terms of "American Indians." Latter-day "Hispanics," "Asians," and "Pacific Islanders"—whose racial experience in or at the hands of this country qualifies them for compensatory justice—will count on this mandate as not-white; historically, that is, as "black." This suggestion is meant to apply only for administrative technologies of counting; I do not mean to undermine the importance of multicultural histories like those that have begun recently to be narrated. Looking forward, by contrast, and enjoined by a rough motivational mix of color-blindness and democratic self-definition, the implication is to encourage open-ended (I am prompted to add open-faced) self-identification. The undertaking here is to undermine the social control of racial naturalism. Promoting open-ended self-identification takes us beyond the insistence on reified racial categories required by managed multiculturalism and the bureaucratization of diversity. From the point of view of bureaucratic manipulation and control, counting by properly open-ended self-identification is statistically useless. But that, precisely, is its virtue.

So race is to be counted only where it signals class exploitation and exclusion—past, present, and predictably future. Where race indicates a class that is socially, politically, and economically marginalized, there is a need—if justice is to be served—to identify members, not to ensure their social distance but to promote programs to facilitate their self-defined (that is, autonomous) self-development. In that sense, taking stock is not a matter simply of making a body count but of making the numbers count, defining where we have been, where we are coming from and now are, and where, dialogically conceived, we see ourselves headed.

Made in the USA:

Racial Mixing 'n Matching

> Man you ain't got to
> Worry 'bout a thing
> 'Bout your daughter
> Nah she ain't my type
> (But supposin' she said she loved me)
> Are you afraid of the mix of Black and White
> We're livin' in a land where
> The law say the mixing of race
> Makes the blood impure
> She's a woman I'm a man
> But by the look on your face
> See ya can't stand it.
> —Public Enemy, "Fear of a Black Planet"[1]

Americans are trying to understand that racial purity is a thing of the past. There was a time, of course, and not so very long ago, when prevailing sentiment would have racial purity as the wave of the future. Conventional wisdom denied that racial purity was nothing more than a thing of the imagination, a scientific and social, political and cultural narration. The United States, perhaps more than other countries, has begun to realize this, but continues to deny the deep implications this realization has for the racializing project. For racial purity is an expressed commitment now of only the fringe right and the racializing project is advanced more acceptably in terms of mixed race and multiculturalism.

We are, in the words announcing *Time* magazine's special issue in 1993 on "The New Face of America": the "World's First Multicultural Society." This characterization reifies yesterday's common sense as it announces tomorrow's. For it silently denies the heterogeneity that so clearly marks human histories as it reinstates racialized characterization as the grounds of today's multicultural commitment.[2] Mixed race provides the metaphorical anchor for multiculturalism. But the racial mix of this multicultural condition, not to put too fine a tautological point on it, is still the mixing of races. Race is equated now with culture, and it is simply reshaped, rather than dissolved, in unconsciously illicit acts of miscegenation. And what may be socially illicit becomes electronically conceivable as test tube babies are produced by a Hollywood computer program where humans in the flesh fear to tread.

In its fall 1993 issue on multicultural America, *Time* invoked Hollywood's special effects program, Morph 2.0, used to create Michael Jackson's transformation in the *Black or White* video and the robot of *Terminator 2*, to "predict" computer-graphically the ethnoracial[3] outcome of progeny from mixed marriages between seven diverse men and women. The special issue was titled "America's Immigrant Challenge," perhaps explaining the total absence throughout of American Indians, including their omission from *Time*'s computer graphic experiment. Indigenous people were once more effaced in a silent extension of the doctrine of discovery: empty lands for the taking.

It should come as no surprise, then, that *Time* chose for its mixing and matching experiment the least diverse-looking representatives, across ethnorace not to mention class. Lest anyone objects that these are naked headshots (what can they say about class?), hairstyles are something of a class giveaway. Progeny were projected by a "straight 50–50 combination of the physical characteristics of their progenitors." Although *Time*'s editors admit that "an entirely different image" could have been produced by an input of different percentages, they fail to acknowledge that an even percentage split also involves choices (even as such choices are claimed to be circumscribed by the limits of the computer technology) and so they presuppose value assumptions, for human beings are hardly symmetrical within morphological traits. Halving the difference between straight blond and curly black hair does not give you straight blond hair, at least not nonpresumptively. And genetically, there is no literal halving of the difference between (more-or-less) "black" skin and "white," whatever these phenotypical hues signify.

I am going to argue that this "new face of America" is being colored with the revitalized cosmetics of the racialized condition. The transformations in the body politic are being marked anew by reconfigured racial categories. Thus the challenge to the project of racial purity in the celebration of mixed-race identities is at best ambiguous, (re)fixing the premises of the racializing project in place as it challenges that project's very terms of articulation. I interrogate the possibilities and limits of mixed-race formation through the examples of category construction, focusing on the recent fashioning of "Hispanics," the creation of "Coloured" identity in South Africa, and the moral panics prompted in relation to crossracial adoption.

FASHIONING MIXED RACE

To comprehend the transforming continuities of the racializing condition (in this apparent epistemological rupture between yesterday's common sense and tomorrow's) and the implications it suggests for (re)conceiving the body politic, we need to understand the location of the concept of "mixed race" in the racial project.

The dominant account is that racial distinction in the United States—in contrast, say, to Brazil—always has been simply between white and black. This view is accurate only in the sense that since its founding moment white-black divides have dominated U.S. racial formation and the prevailing racial narratives recounted about America. Nevertheless, the history of racial categorization in this country indicates a need for a more complex and nuanced account, as revealed by the census material discussed in the previous essay.

In "Taking Stock: Counting By Race," I showed that distinctions began to appear in the U.S. Census enumeration in 1850 for those considered "nonwhite." This reflects the emerging social acknowledgment of miscegenational progeny, suggesting gradations in color-consciousness. (For a summary of the U.S. Census history regarding mixed-race categories, see pp. 35–46).

> Man calm your ass down, don't get mad
> I don't need your sistah
> (But supposin' she said she loved me)
> Would you still love her
> Or would you dismiss her
> What is pure? Who is pure?
> Is it European state of being, I'm not sure
> If the whole world was to come
> Thru peace and love
> Then what would we be made of?

To summarize: until the mid-nineteenth century, formal racial designation in America was fixed in black and white, driven no doubt by dominant strands in racial theorizing coupled with prevailing popular racial sentiment. From mid-century, finer "mixed-race" distinctions appeared reflecting the tension between the promise of abolitionism, Reconstruction, and the attendant freedom of association, on the one hand, and state and populist suspicion about the outcomes of racial mixing, whether social or sexual, on the other. With the commitment to segregation in the dying decades of the nineteenth century, the one-drop rule developed along with a renewed insistence on the reductive and essentializing binary between black and white. After World War II, as the social movement for Civil Rights and desegregation gathered steam, "mixed-race" (self-)consciousness reemerged in light of splintering racial conceptions and growing hybridities, antiracist movements and postcolonial commitments, anxious insecurities amidst calls to black-consciousness and black self-sufficiency as well as white resentments.

> Excuse us for the news
> I question those accused
> Why does this fear of Black from White
> Influence who you choose?

The general category of "mixed race," then, and the specific subcategories of racial identity it licenses, were admitted into racial configuration as a way of cognizing the social and techno-logical complexities of racial designation, experience, and enu-meration. This belated cognition, however, continued to rest on (more precisely, in) racial terms. Thus, "mixed race" may seem adequately to capture prevailing demographic heterogeneity, but it does so only by silently fixing in place the racializing project. It naturalizes racial assumption, marking mixed-ness as an aber-rant condition, as transgressive, and at the extreme as purity polluting. "Mixed race" may seem to offer exciting proof positive that a deep social taboo has been transgressed, that racial disci-pline and order have been violated, that liberty's lure once again has undermined the condition of homogeneity by delimiting the constraints of the hegemonic. Yet it at once, and necessarily, reimposes the racial duality between blackness and whiteness as the standard, the measure, of mixed-ness.

> Man c'mon now, I don't want your wife
> Stop screamin' it's not the end of your life
> (But supposin' she said she loved me)
> What's wrong with some color in your family tree
> I don't know

There are serious implications, political as much as social, of remaining tied to the racializing project. Investing in the category of mixed race, giving it equal time in the media mix of America, serves to extend insidious possibilities to etherealize the deep historical divisions of wealth and power that continue to be effected and exercised under the sign of race, to license a politics of competitive division in the face of purportedly scarce social resources. Three examples will suffice to illustrate the material implications of this project.

POLITICS AND THE POWER OF MIXED RACE

"Hispanic"

The hybrid category "Hispanic" in the ethnoracial imagination of American social life is little more than a quarter-century old, fashioned in popular discourse in the late 1960s but introduced formally into the census count only in 1980. Two related questions arise. First, why was it now deemed necessary to introduce a new category? Second, why this category in particular?

There is a certain obviousness in the response to the first question. From the 1960s on, there was an audible increase in Spanish-speaking people tracing their origins to south of the border. This group, however, was becoming increasingly diversified even as it was united broadly by a common language and religious denomination. Thus, it consisted of inhabitants of the formerly Mexican territories (or their offspring) as well as more contemporary Mexican (im)migrants; the post-1950s influx of expatriate Cubans; and the postcolonial, cold war, and late capitalist migration from Puerto Rico, the Dominican Republic, El Salvador, Nicaragua, Venezuela, Guatemala, Argentina, and the like. "Mexican" had been counted in the census, off and on, since the territorial contestations of the late nineteenth century. Historically, the Hispaniola influence on the far west is now part of its legend, linking local Californian history to Mexican history, revealing the contingency of border determinations and making more complex the political culture of border crossings. It is, of course, the rapid growth of a population identified first by language and only second by geographical origination that rendered evident the "need" for a new and separate category, one linked but no longer reducible to Mexican relation. It was a

"need" prompted and promoted by politically conscious representatives of the newly identified and identifying group, a group
raising questions about the naturalism and scope of racial definition as it re-cognized itself, at least in one self-formulation, as "La
Raza."

Census history indicates a long-standing if checkered U.S.
perception that those of Mexican origin are white, tying Mexican
history to its European legacy. Indeed, even indigenous and
mestizo identities are whitewashed under the prevailing span of
the Bering Straits theory of migration. The diversification of
Spanish-speaking (im)migration to the United States over the past
thirty years, its ethnoracial heterogeneity, revealed the limits of
continuing to count Spanish-speaking people as "Mexican" while
it also implicitly challenged the propriety of conventional racial
counts.

So, why then the category "Hispanic?" Why a category so
obviously tied linguistically and historically to European identification, if not identity? For one, the category renders explicit the
historical influence of Hispaniola throughout the continent,
linking contemporary migration to the United States from Latin
America to European migration historically, and European discovery and settlement of America to that of the Americas more
broadly. At the same time, invocation of the category "Hispanic"
implicitly encodes linguistically referential racial formations
from the nineteenth century on, while it silently acknowledges
the formal and degrading restriction of Spanish—and more generally non-English and non-Northern European—people in the
history of U.S. immigration.

The category "Hispanic" thus problematizes certain prevailing
assumptions about racial definition and formation. "Hispanic"
becomes not so much a third race, a category of mixed race—black
and white melding into brown—as an evidencing that race is
politically fabricated and contested, that the very conception is

elastic and transformable. The category "Hispanic" is recognized by the ethnoracial technology of the census as white, but the nervous insecurity of this recognition is reflected in the qualifications about when to count "Mexicans" or "Hispanics" as black. At the moment of dissolving whiteness in America, a category is fashioned to extend America's tie to Europe, and so by way of standard racial logic to whiteness. This formulation neatly resolves two potentially conflicting concerns. On the one hand, the dominant interest is in having America remain a "white" country, one "European" in racial if not geographic definition; on the other, an interest group is formed around an identity determined as "white" because of the benefits that flow from this association and the disbenefits, symbolic as much as material, that attach to blackness.

Accordingly, under the sign "Hispanic," hybridity, or mixed race-ness, has come to challenge the one-drop rule prevalent almost throughout the twentieth century. Nevertheless, the category of "Hispanic" remains vested, if somewhat ambivalently, in the (ethno)racializing project and its attendant assumptions, interests, powers, and payoffs. It is the product of, as it reproduces, an economy predicated on necessarily creating new markets and new consumptive subjects; of a politics of shifting alliances and social values where cultural values and commitments are seen as "natural" hunting grounds for conservative votes.

So, "Hispanic" is a population category as manufactured and as mixed in its extension as "black" was from its inception. "Black" was created initially in the name of the project of racial purity. "Hispanic," by contrast, was crafted to cut across racial designations, to reflect (ad)mixture. In its generality, however, "Hispanic" serves silently to reify a new racial category, to extend the project of purity, even as it is a product of mixture. Mixed-race

RACIAL SUBJECTS

or transracial hybridity opens its (self-)referents to the shifting interests of those in control of the categories.[4]

"Coloureds"

A second example reveals how the undertaking to undo the insidious consequences of the racial project via mixed-race hybridity impales itself on its racializing assumptions. This concerns the constitution of "Coloured" in South Africa, that category of mixed-race formation in terms of which apartheid was defined.

When the Dutch invaded the Cape of Good Hope to settle it in 1652, they were greeted by indigenous San and Khoi-Khoi (still referred to in the local vernacular as "Bushmen" and "Hottentot"). The story goes that desire got the better of these European men who arrived without European women, and offspring of mixed race quickly followed. Shortly before the British took over colonial rule of the Cape at the turn of the eighteenth century, the Dutch settlers had become so concerned with diminishing racial purity and the "curse of bad blood" that they moved to circumscribe miscegenation. The challenge of desire to the purity imperative was renewed with the Boer trek northward to escape British colonial rule in the 1830s, for the white trekkers quickly met other indigenous ethnic groups, variously defined as "African," "Black," or "Bantu." Constrained by no law other than that perceived as God's, white men once more imposed themselves upon black women. The resulting population was considered of mixed race. Along with Malaysian coolie laborers brought to the Cape in the late 1800s, they were nominated "Coloured" before the close of the nineteenth century.

People designated "Coloured" have always had ambiguous status in South Africa, with telling social, political, economic, and psychological effect. The designation itself presupposes the stark disjunction between unshaded white and black as the norm.[5] The apartheid state formally instituted the category "Coloured" in the late 1940s and 1950s, outlawing mixed marriage and intercourse, while defining the (existing or future illegal) offspring of inter-racial relations and their progeny as "Coloured." Definition of the racial terms that constituted apartheid's self-conception was offered first in the Population Registration Act of 1950 and was tightened in later amendments. So, "White person" came to be defined as:

> a. In appearance obviously is a white person and who is not generally accepted as a coloured person; and b. Is generally accepted as a white person and is not in appearance obviously not a white person. (*Population Registration Act* 1950)

To prevent the appearance of a tautology (a white person is one appearing white), the definition of "white" necessarily presup-poses and explicitly invokes as its point of reference (as it con-ceptually must) the category of "Coloured" (that euphemism in the South African vernacular for "mulatto" or "mixed race"). The definition of "Black" or "African" (or "Negro," for that matter) likewise invokes the category of "Coloured." The inevitable failure of the imperative of purity is that it predicates the defini-tions of the principal racializing project categories (black, white) upon the conceptual implications of "mixed race." Absent such predication, the categories of racial purity run the apparent danger of conceptual and referential emptiness.

The horrifying effects of apartheid's schema of racial classifi-cation were especially felt by those suffering reclassification (usually from "white" or "European" to "Coloured"; or "Col-oured" to "Non-European," "Bantu," "Native," or "African," and ever so occasionally and begrudgingly from "Coloured" to "white").[6] Mixed race thus came to mean mixed status: fewer rights and a more tenuous social position than whites, but significantly better conditions than those faced by the over-whelming majority of "Africans." With ambiguous status, however, came also the problematic ambiguity of political posi-tionality and social identity. In the wars of position and maneuver that have marked South Africa at least since 1960, the prevailing concern of those defined as "Coloured"—who suffered this question more than did those categorically shaded more lightly or darkly than they—has been where they stand. Political ambiguity and ambivalence (a taste of power, however marginal, has its lures) was the configuration of mixed race. Indeed, the shifting fabrication of mixed-race status enabled (in many ways, was designed to promote) marginalizing alienation at the center of racial definition.

The laws of South Africa restricting intermarriage and miscegenation were repealed in the 1980s and 1990s. And yet, in the drive to configure an identity within racialized space—a space that dominated, if not exhausted, the range of available identity formation in South Africa—many South Africans have identified as and with the commitments of "Coloured." There is, in some nonreductive sense, a "Coloured" constituency and a "Coloured" vote, "Coloured" interests and "Coloured" concerns. There is, in an important identifiable sense, also a "Coloured" language and perhaps a "Coloured" culture.[7]

But beyond this, and more problematically, those identifying as "Coloured" have promoted forms of exclusion vested in identification with their category. The University of the Western Cape (UWC) was founded by the designers of apartheid as an institution for the separated higher education of Coloureds in South Africa. In the late 1980s, the university managed to redefine itself under astute leadership as the intellectual base of the African National Congress (ANC). Taking advantage of the liberalizing trajectory, UWC instituted in real terms the ANC's commitment to nonracialism, transforming an institution designed to circumscribe the possibilities of mixed race into one in which races would mix. However, the discursive arm of apartheid is considerably longer than this enlightened image would have it. A student survey conducted at the university in 1991 revealed that an overwhelming percentage of those students considering themselves "Coloured" not only wished to maintain racially segregated dormitories (with Coloureds especially kept apart from those deemed black Africans), but insisted that UWC remain a "Coloured" institution, run by and for those deemed racially mixed in kind and culture. Gone in name, the separateness of apartheid lives on in legacy, disciplined by the normalized shadow boundaries of mixed-race definition.

> I've been wonderin' why
> Peoples livin' in fear
> Of my shade
> (Or my hi top fade)
> I'm not the one that's runnin'
> But they got me on the run
> Treat me like I have a gun
> All I got is genes and chromosomes
> Consider me Black to the bone
> All I want is peace and love
> On this planet
> (Ain't that how God planned it?)

Mixed-Race Adoption

The politics of racialized mixed status are not nearly so formalized elsewhere as they have been in South Africa. Beyond the southern tip of Africa, therefore, the implications of mixed-race formation are played out more explicitly in the informalities of broader sociocultural sites than they are formally in the law, political institutions, and governmental technologies. This is exemplified by crossracial adoption in the United States. The debate around racialized adoption in America is in many ways complex, and I do not mean to belittle the complexity of the issues. Mixed-race considerations add considerably to this complexity, in ways that reify as they are meant to dissipate the racializing project in America. Such considerations in adoption are a tug-of-war between the liberalizing imperative to pay no heed to race in placing adoptive children and the racializing insistence on prioritizing it (a position held, for instance, by the National Association of Black Social Workers [NABSW] which advocates that black children be placed only with black parents). Usually the latter wins out: most public and private adoption agencies in the United States make race one of their primary concerns in placement (a condition the U.S. Congress has been moving recently to restrict).

This resort to race has special, and especially troubling, implications for children defined as racially mixed. While logically it may seem to imply that their pool of potential placement is enlarged, the history of racializing insists that mixed-race progeny are nonwhite (the one-drop rule). If, for argument's sake, one accepts the NABSW argument that black children placed with nonblack parents will necessarily lose the sustenance of black culture in bearing the heavy nihilistic weight of racism with which their blackness will necessarily burden them,[8] mixed-race children with any black background will be affected also. (If the argument holds for black children, perhaps it holds for all defined as nonwhite; the same form of argument is forwarded by many American Indian groups.)[9] Thus the pool of placement in the case of mixed-race children is restricted to that for black (or in the more general case, for nonwhite) children. But, it is open to whites to object to such restrictions on placement because it necessarily withholds from mixed children their white cultural heritage. The logical consequence of this line of deeply racialized analysis is that mixed-race children be adopted only by mixed-race parents, and perhaps most awkwardly only by parents of the precise racial mixture as themselves. The fact that nobody baldly claims this (or, I hope, believes it) testifies only to the poverty of such restrictions' racializing premises.[10]

Perhaps a future adoption standard conceived in the name of heterogeneity (and reflecting a changed commitment to advancing the interests of parentless children rather than the conflicted concerns of parents and a racialized adoption market)[11] will be represented in the willingness of adoption agencies to place a white child with willing black parents (just as we might talk about the desirability of whites choosing to move into, without taking over, black neighborhoods). At the same time, nonblack parents adopting African-American children, as perhaps generally, have a responsibility to convey to their children in sensitive fashion the breadth of African-American history and the richness of African-American culture. This would require turning the racializing paradigm on its head.

> Excuse us for the news
> You might not be amused
> But did you know White comes from Black
> No need to be confused

CULTURAL HYBRIDS, MIXED RACE, AND HYBRID CULTURE

Why, then, is it necessary or desirable to create a mixed-race identity, given that mixed race-ness denies race any status but construct? Two sorts of answers come to mind. First, in a society where race is important and the one-drop rule carries weight, those not "pure" black or white (whatever significance is invested in this formulation) are alienated not only from socially dominant (read white) concerns, but also from dominant black ones.[12]

Racialized discourse is complex. Darker black people—"real blacks," on the racist presumption—have sometimes tended to dismiss lighter blacks. And maybe the pecking order of hues plays havoc in relation to African authenticity, too, for Africans come in all shades of "black/brown," to quote Clinton (that is, George, the original funk man, not the free-riding blues brother in the White House). There has been a long history, in the name of racist commitments, of elevating lighter blacks over darker ones (Spike Lee problematizes this interestingly from the internalized perspective of blacks in *School Daze*). These racially discriminating tensions between light and dark are predicated in turn around ambivalences about mixedness, purity, preferential treatment, and passing. So the conception of "mixed race" is fraught historically with political ambivalences, tensions, nuances, and

RACIAL SUBJECTS

ambiguities that most commentators on the subject, including Naomi Zack (1994), largely pass over in silence.

The second answer to the question might run as follows. Mixed race will create solidarity between mixes of any and all "designated" racial groups. If this is a viable answer, then the common historical experience that is to serve as the glue for a mixed-race identity can only be a history of oppression. In the U.S. experience this would return us to the racial category "black," which must be understood as overdetermined—internally differentiated, based on a variety of experiences of exclusion and oppression. A conception of blackness that fails to acknowledge such differentiation among "blacks" is determined essentially; it is fixed fully and without distinction by dominant, imposed, and exclusionary racist discourse.

All this points to a central dilemma facing any conception of mixed race. If those committed to mixed race were prompted to give up any underlying biological insinuation in their conceptions of race, thus restricting race to a cultural conception historically conceived, mixed-race hybridity could become significantly more challenging and in an interesting way. For mixed race then is conceivable explicitly as nothing more nor less than mixed culture, and cultural heterogeneity is the norm rather than the exception it is made out to be on the assumption of ethnoracial purity.

Here's a thought experiment regarding just such questions about culture and race. Ask yourself which of the following performers and groups are white, black, or mixed: Aerosmith, Alabama, Apache Indian, the Beastie Boys, Hootie and the Blowfish, In Living Color, Lenny Kravitz, Markie Mark, Parliament Funkadelic, UB40. Are their names real pointers? Could you answer just from listening to their music? In both cases the answer is no. Cultural heterogeneity has become almost all there is. There was a time when, for some, group formation was considerably more localized and inward-looking than is now generally the case.[13] Now, the insularity and isolation necessary to sustain homogeneity constrain cultural possibilities and are maintained only by the force of imposition. In modernity, the myth of homogeneity becomes nothing other than a narrative cultural members fashion for themselves in fabricating a binding identity.

Thus, the normalcy, the seeming "naturalness," of racial fabrication is at once fixed in place and challenged by the admission of mixed race-ness. The assumption of mixed race upends, as it extends, the racializing project. If, in the social formation of (post)modernity, there is no escaping the confines of race, standing inside the mixed condition of hybridity confronts the proponents of purity with a telling query: How indeed do you know you're not mixed?[14] That it should not matter reveals that the project of racial purity is nothing but political (self-)assertion. For instance, Italian Americans are treated by City University of New York as a protected minority, subject thus to (quickly fading) benefits in terms of hiring, promotion, and institutional resources.[15]

The cultural assumption that now resonates in racial definition nevertheless presupposes yet another circuitous commitment. For it necessarily presumes cultural ownership by racial members. The claim of cultural property—"this is my (or our) culture"—artificially fences off cultural production as it polices the conditions of cultural consumption and exchange.[16] While one may pose the question of cultural ownership generally, it becomes especially fraught with respect to racially identified culture. The problem of owning cultural artifacts via forceful, coerced, or commodified appropriation is exemplified in the history of colonial museums. Static ownership of cultural artifacts is hardly synonymous with the experienced dynamism of cultural belonging. But beyond this, what makes a racialized culture mine or yours? Mere racial belonging? Attributed belonging or a sense of belonging? As far as I can tell, my cultural commitment is closer to Nelson Mandela's than it is to Norman Mailer's, to Toni Morrison's than to Helen Suzman's. I have been characterized, among other things, as white, European, Anglo, Jewish, and African American. What racial culture, exactly, is mine? Or to which do I belong?

I do not mean to deny the existence of, say, "black culture." Quite the contrary. "Black" in this context refers pragmatically to a history of experiences that "blacks" have suffered and enjoyed, have been subjected to (in both senses of subjection) precisely as black. Black racial identity is coercive, no doubt, in part because identity formation is coercive by necessity. Blackness has been produced in coercive circumstances, and it can express itself coercively. But it is also a self-fashioned identity that is deeply meaningful, in nonexclusionary ways, to many people—and deeply meaningful to some of us who engage those so self-defined. "Blacks" may signify an imagined community; but it is an imagined community I cannot imagine living without. Ironically, because of this history of subjection and responses to it, there is a sense in which black culture, a culture deeply informed by its own history, now stands as vibrant, dynamic, and desirable, whereas what may be called "white culture," if it exists at all, is expressed only tenuously. The history of racist culture has prompted self-defining cultures of resistance that at once challenge racialized parameters as they are partially defined by them. White culture, such as it is, defines itself not against that which it is not but as that which is insular and homogeneous. White culture has tended to become (if it was not always) a decadent culture, for the most part static, nostalgic, retrospective. Its romantic retrospection is tied to a historicism that displaces any historical memory of racialized terror with Disneyesque dehistoricized theme parks. What energy white culture has, it acquires from (as it denies) the racialized cultures of otherness.[17]

Again, if the racialized conditions of cultural belonging could be established,[18] what, then, would a culture of mixed race be? Neither white nor black, I think, but some hybrid mix of multiple components that, catalytically, generated something significantly and dynamically new. However, as the examples of "Coloured" in South Africa and "Hispanic" in the United States have revealed, racialized products of cultural bricolage are not beyond the constraints of cultural exclusivity and exclusion, of derogation and dismissal. The ambiguity that threatens the racializing project, inherent in the relative lack of mixed-race racial definition, promotes the alienation of mixed-race members. To group formation, racial characterization adds the fabrication of naturalism, the fixed and fast insinuation of community insider and outsider. In qualifying hybridity, it delimits the (al)chemical dynamics of cultural transformation by giving in to the racializing presumptions of ownership and selectivity, of purity and homogeneity, of the dangers of pollution.

At best, then, the condition of mixed-race formation constitutes an ambivalent challenge to the racial condition from within the fabric of the racializing project. It tugs dangerously at the limits of the racializing discourse it at once invokes, straddling ambiguously the sites of double-consciousness, rejecting as it defines itself in and through racial terms, dismissing as it reifies the racial project. Nevertheless, if we play up the mixing at the expense of racial matching, we begin to see that an insistent hybridity dissipates the political persistence of purity, if not the project of racial formation *tout court*. At the limit, the cultural imperative to renewed and improvisational hybrid mixing implies renunciation of the racial matching and definition reflected in the reification of the nominal case: whiteness, blackness, "mulatto," "Coloured."[19] The reiterative revisability of hybrid heterotopias confronts the command of homogeneity with the material and discursive conditions of its horizon, exploding the confines of fabricated racial identities again and again into something new.

In this sense, the multicultural babel that makes up the United States, a babel constituted emphatically out of already produced multiplicities, becomes a historically fashioned microcosm of an unfolding world and an experimental space for hybrid formation and transformation capable at least in principle of testing the limits of the political technologies of identities. Yet there is a practical qualification. Such history-effacing will (expressed in the Madison Avenue injunction to "Just Do It") must be made to carry, and not so silently as we have become used to, the historically directed imperative to counter racist exclusions (or as a counter-T-shirt so eloquently puts, to "Just Undo It"). The marvels of "mutant power" and "monstrous cyborgs" to make new identities should not be allowed to erase the need to resist the exclusionary legacies of past or present ones. In this fashion, "Made in the USA" may come to stand for racial dissolution through mixing rather than the racial fixing of matching, of a naturalized racial fraternity. That is a social story we need to imagine, fashion, and narrate—repeatedly.

Besides the optimism of identity (re)formation, however, the (dis)rupture of Public Enemy's rap emphasizes that the play of textualized theory should not be allowed to drown out the call to resist and to transform the marginalization in economic and sociopolitical power con-figured and en-gendered by racial formations. I have argued that such marginalization may be advanced as much in the name of mixed-race formation as in the purportedly pure. This makes race matters significantly more complex either than racists or simple-minded nonracialists would have them. There are no conceptual guarantees. Langston Hughes, rapping in the 1920s, poignantly offers a sense (a sense

at once ethical as it is oedipal) of just how complex race matters—
pure, simple, or mixed (up)—really are in his poem "The Cross":

> My old man's a white old man
> And my mother's black
> If I ever cursed my white old man
> I take my curses back.

In/Visibility and Super/Vision:

Fanon and Racial Formation

5

For
Isidore Goldberg (1916–1995)
who taught me about speaking truth to power

The complexities of race I have mentioned in previous chapters are explored with some subtlety by Frantz Fanon, who dissects tropes of visibility and invisibility. Metaphors of visibility and invisibility pervade Fanon's body of work. This perhaps is to be expected. His corpus is concerned primarily with interrogating colonialism's expressions of and resistance to such metaphors, and thus overwhelmingly with addressing the shifting and complex questions of "the color line." The title of Ralph Ellison's justly famous novel, *Invisible Man*, indicates that the realities of dominant racial definition are all about the lived implications of visibility and invisibility. Whiteness has long been characterized in terms of light and learning, blackness in terms of darkness and degeneration. Accordingly, visibility carries with it connotations that tend to be appealing, even intoxicating—access, opportunity, ability, in short, power; and invisibility has tended to connote absence, lack, incapacity, in short, powerlessness.

Social invisibility, Lewis Gordon notes (1995), manifests in not being seen: A child, whose hand is always up in response to the teacher's question, is never called upon; people in moments of distress or emergency are overlooked while others deemed more important or worthy are tended; wrongdoing, no matter how extreme, goes unrecognized because those suffering aren't those one recognizes (as people, as kin, as important) though one expresses horror when the same condition confronts "one's own." Invisibility also happens when one does not see people because one "knows" them through some fabricated preconception of group formation. As Ellison writes (1972, 273–75), Faulkner's screenplay for *Intruder in the Dust* reveals in exquisite detail the lengths to which a white Southerner would go to reproduce the "negro" of his imagination when the black man he stumbles into one night fails to replicate his preconception. These examples reveal that invisibility is enabled by racialized characterization. Race hides those it is projected to mask and illuminates those it leaves unmarked. It demarcates all race marks in shades of black and white.

Fanon's clearly self-conscious use of the conceptual apparatus of visibility and invisibility is remarkable for its nuanced excavation of the prevailing meanings signified by the social experience of in/visibility. He offers a strategic understanding of how visibility and invisibility can be used contextually for contesting oppressive racial conditions. Fanon's comprehension that visibility *and* invisibility are contextually valuable—that tension links their sometimes affirmative and sometimes negated value—is tied inextricably to his radically antiessentialist and nonreductionist metaphysics, ontology, epistemology, and politics.

I am concerned in this essay accordingly with two related pursuits: to examine the complexities of racial formation (understood in antiessentialist and nonreductive terms), and to do this through a reading of Fanon's analysis of how race contextually orders the visibility and invisibility of social subjects.

Readings of racial conditions that reify race in fixed and unchanging terms presume that racially coded invisibility is restrictive, that it essentially, and so necessarily, delimits possibility and opportunity. On these assumptions, visibility is taken as a virtue, a norm of whiteness amid the night of blackness. Visibility, then, always should be pursued, protected, cherished; invisibility is to be avoided, derided, denied. Fanon illuminates the limits of this prevailing picture with an antiessentializing reading of matters racial. He does so by demonstrating that politics and epistemology, metaphysics and culture, psychology and technology, ontology and medicine, and the racial and gendered dimensions of social life are deeply intertwined.

MASTERING SURVEILLANCE

Underlying Fanon's analysis of visibility and its delimitation stands the Hegelian concept that human beings assume self-consciousness in and through recognizing themselves in those they recognize to be their others. "Man," writes Fanon, "is human only to the extent to which he tries to impose his existence on another man in order to be recognized by him" (Fanon 1968, 154). Recognition both presupposes and reinforces the light of human worth, respect, and esteem. Self-consciousness requires recognition by the Other, indeed, it is an imposition upon the Other, and thus presupposes the Other's existence though not the Other's equality. But one's visibility is predicated also on the assumption of self-determination. Being recognized, whether as self-conscious or as Other, and thus being visible, requires that one be outside the Other's imposition, free of the Other's complete determination. To establish self-consciousness, then, to be free, one paradoxically has to engage the Other in combative conflict, to risk one's freedom, to place one's very life—one's humanity—in question.

It follows that visibility and invisibility are not simply states or conditions of being. Rather, they characterize, express, reflect, or they are the effects of strategic relations. As such, visibility does not necessarily advance the interests or well-being of those deemed visible, nor does invisibility necessarily constrain or delimit satisfaction of one's interests. Constitutive or reflective of strategic relations, visibility and invisibility each can serve contextually as weapons, as defensive or offensive strategy, as a mode of self-determination or denial of it.

It is true that invisibility may manifest for the most part as powerlessness. The tension between visibility and invisibility is indexed intricately to, and mediated by, the intersection of multiple subject positions and identity formations, among which the complex mix of ethnoracial, gendered, and class situations, definitions, and expressions mostly dominates. So, poor black women are likely the most socially invisible in societies where poverty, blackness, and women historically mark the depths of powerlessness. Under some conditions, nevertheless, invisibility can actually be invoked to advance power, personal or political, or as an expression of power itself. As Fanon observes, "The colonized exerts considerable effort to keep away from the colonial world not to expose himself to any action of the conqueror" (Fanon 1970, 111). Invisible to the colonial conqueror or the racially dominant (the phantom of paradise, as Luis Bunuel once put it), the colonized effectively can delimit the power of the colonizer or racially domineering over their lives; from sites of invisibility they are able thus to ignore or to contest colonial or racial control.

Lewis Gordon (1996) astutely characterizes the sadist and masochist in terms of their personal control or lack over their in/visibility. The sadist is one who "takes advantage of the invisible dimension of himself as seer to deny the fact of his being seen." The sadist is a subject, before whom all others are objects. *He* defines the terms of engagement, invoking the possibility of his invisibility—a possibility that depends on his capacity to control his self-definition—to order the conditions of relation. Able for so long to determine the terms and conditions of racial definition, whites were able until recently to appear as though racially unmarked. Race marked the other, objectified them as they were racialized. But blackness as a project—a projection of—the white imaginary is a condition of invisibility, a mode of being unseen because unseeable (of not *being*, precisely, at all) (Gordon et al. 1996, 2–3). Ellison's haunting admonition (1975, 3) captures this in short: "I am invisible, understand, simply because people refuse to see me." The black body, as unseen, is reduced to—is the standard for—anonymity (Gordon et al. 1996, 5–6): "*They* are all alike in their blackness, I'm unable to tell them apart." So *they* can be treated as all alike, theoretically and practically, aesthetically and morally, historically and politically.

By contrast, *racially* invisible—the ghosts of modernity, whites could assume power as the norm of humanity, as the naturally given. Unseen racially, that is, unseen as racially marked—or seen precisely as racially unmarked—whites could be everywhere. The evasion of marking, however, becomes by way of a negative dialectic a mode of demarcation. The author of racial law, as of law in general, is at once above it but bound by the terms he is committed to establishing. The expression of power is its delimitation. This delimitation marks the racial condition of the masochist's formation. Seemingly in control of the terms of racial definition, whites necessarily depend for their racial power on being recognized as white by the Other defined in racial terms precisely as black. Thus whites require recognition qua white by those whose very human existence they deny. And this is characteristic of the masochistic condition as Gordon (1996, 5–6) defines it: the masochist is one who "throws himself into the gaze of others while denying their otherness." Thus whites, set as sadists by way of their invisibly predicated self-determination and definition, reduce themselves to masochistic self-denial in terms of their self-proclaimed invisible otherness.

The colonial condition offers a limit case of racially encoded sadomasochistic relations. Colonialism renders invisible the lines of power and control both within the colony and especially— through the spatial and administrative technologies of distancing—between absent colonizing power and people and their colonized counterparts.[1] This sadistic invisibility makes possible the partial hiding from view of the source of characteristic control, domination, degradation, and oppression that is the mark of the colonial. The fabricated fact of invisibility, worked into the condition of coloniality as it underpins it, renders that condition seemingly natural and so inevitable, a law of racial nature, the natural state of the world. Hidden from view, blind to the world and to themselves, colonizers transform self-determining subjects into objects, and naturalized objects into colonial subjects, into subjected peoples. Colonialism "succeeds" thus to the extent its social relations of power remain invisible, so long as their presumed naturalism goes unchallenged. Paradoxically, the colonizer masochistically strives for recognition as dominant and powerful; he requires recognition from an Other he fails at once to recognize. Striving for the anonymity of invisibility, the colonizer is desperate at once to be visible. Recognized yet unacknowledged; acknowledged yet unrecognized. Subject but not object; objectified yet not subjected. The colonizer im*pales* himself on the whitened lance of his own projection, driven there by colonial denial and colonized resistance, by the native's invisible presence and the colonized's presented visibility.

RACIAL SUBJECTS

Caught between administrative supervision and the Super Vision made possible by camouflaged invisibility, the colonized or racially marginalized strike back, resorting to the counter gaze made possible by colonial or marginalized invisibility to derail the surveillance necessarily predicated upon the premise of transparence and the perspicuity of appearance. As Fanon (1970) remarks, while analyzing what he calls "Medical Supervision" (109), "In the colonial situation, going to see the doctor, the administrator, the constable or the mayor are identical moves" (120). Such visits help administratively to transform the native into the colonized, self-determining people into colonial or racially marginalized subjects. The information licensed by medical, bureaucratic, political, or police visits fuel colonial, racialized governmentality just as the information they release is framed—it is ordered and fabricated—by the colonial or racial imperative.

RACIAL (MIS)RECOGNITION

Fanon points out that in the colonial situation (local or at a distance), the primary thrust of the Master in relation to the Slave is not for the sake of recognition but for work. The colonized are dehumanized, their humanity effaced, not simply for the sake of the colonizer's ego satisfaction but for the colonized's exploitation (Fanon 1968, 157). What colonialism and racial marginalization seek to hide from view, to render invisible about themselves, is the grounding fact of their possibility: that they are predicated only on force and fraud (Fanon 1970, 72). Hobbes, Locke, and Rousseau all exemplify their states of nature in terms of non-European states of being. The fact that force and fraud are the only virtues necessary in the Hobbesian state of nature (the state of "warre") reveals, rather, that a readier representation of the contractualists' "natural state" is not "the savage peoples of the Americas" and the like (Hobbes 1975 [1651], 187), but the colonial condition imposed by European whites (geographically or racially) upon those deemed non-European.

Colonialism and racial power are operationalized at both the material and the representational levels. Materially each seeks to strengthen domination for the sake of human and economic exploitation. Representationally they seek to sustain the identity of the ideological or discursive image each creates of the colonized or racially marginalized and of the depreciated image the latter have of themselves (Fanon 1970, 17–18). Marginalization, racial or colonial, thus undertakes at the latter level to extend and maintain a veiling, to effect a strategic invisibility of the marginalized: to maintain invisibility socially and politically so as to minimize the costs of economic reproduction and labor enforcement. Through normalization racial marginality can hide from view its constitutive forms of domination and exploitation. By making the relations and practices of dominance seem standard, normal, and given, marginality (colonial or racial) creates as "acceptable" its central social expressions of degradation and dehumanization, rendering unseen the fact that it makes people what they are not. Colonialism is quite literally untruth, an untruth that to sustain itself must be hidden from view. Fanon speaks of this as "the lie of the colonial situation" (109), a lie that infects the colonized who to survive find that they are "hardly ever truthful before the colonizer" (108, n. 2). One could easily extend the point to racisms more generally.

Like modernity, of which they are subset conditions, colonialism and racisms are conditions of extreme ambivalence (Bauman 1991) that impose a structure, an order of things, which they inevitably are incapable of sustaining. Drawn to an order, a scheme of classification, they at once cannot sustain because it is both misrepresentative and unrepresentative of a people the very being of which it negates, the colonial or racist condition faces (off) its impending disorder with differentiation and division, separation and subordination, manipulation and mystification—in short, with fraud and force (Fanon 1968, 59). It is in this sense that Fanon sees himself as engaged analytically, critically, in a form of *un*veiling (1970, 21).

Veiling renders black people invisible by controlling the dominant meanings and representations of blackness. Blackness accordingly is an artifact of whiteness (Fanon 1968, 12). It follows that the process of unveiling involves "humanizing" black people in the face of their being "racialized" (86), accurately reestablishing historical memory in the wake of its deformation, actively insisting that black being opposes its overwhelming erasure. "Face to face with the white man," Fanon writes, "the Negro has a past to legitimate, a vengeance to exact; face to face with the Negro, the contemporary white man feels the need to recall the times of cannibalism" (160).

Thus veiling and unveiling are qualified—indeed, conditioned—by the racialized metaphors of inking and bleaching (Fanon 1968, 34). Race extends visibility or invisibility to those it categorizes, and it may be used strategically to promote or deny recognition, social elevation, and status. Whites assume visibility in virtue, though often in denial, of their whiteness, and extend visibility to those upon whom whiteness lights, in recognizing the mulatto, for instance (43). Recognized as black, black people at once are made visible to be rendered invisible, to be "denegrified" (78). Fanon insists, rightly it seems to me, that this logic offers only a cruel choice to black people, only a deadly way out and that is into the white world: "Turn white," he writes, "or disappear" (71).

The white world controls and dominates, though that domination and control are fragile and tenuous. (Even the variety of black nationalisms and separatist projections are a reaction to the world of white standards and control.) So black people are faced with the dilemma that the principal mode of personal progress and self-elevation open to them is precisely through self-denial, through the effacement, the obliteration, of their blackness. They are predicated, that is, upon the possibility of rendering a significant feature of their self-definition invisible, if not altogether effaced. This invisibility, in turn, is effected through the necessity of recognition by whites, which is begrudgingly extended only at the cost of the invisibility of blackness. In other words, this "internalization—epidermalization—of inferiority" (Fanon 1968, 10) involves at basis a recognition of a person *as* white. This cognition at once denies whiteness as it extends it, and effaces blackness as it claims to recognize it (38).

Blackness is transformed into a fabrication of the white imagination: "I discovered my blackness, my ethnic characteristics; I was battered down by tom-toms, cannibalism, intellectual deficiency, fetishism, racial defects, slave ships, and above all else, above all: 'Sho' good eatin'.'" (Fanon 1968, 79). The product of all this is—the Negro! If black people, qua black, are wiped away, they are replaced by the figure of "the Negro." Invisibility becomes a response to this forced and fabled visibility:

> I am being dissected under white eyes, the only real eyes. I am *fixed* [Fanon's emphasis].... I am laid bare. I feel, I see in those white faces that it is not a new man who has come in, but a new kind of man, a new genus. Why, it's a Negro!... I slip into corners, I remain silent, I strive for *anonymity, for invisibility.* [My emphases] Look, I will accept the lot, as long as no one notices me! (82)

To which there is but a single conceivable response: "Since the other hestitated to recognize me, there remained only one solution: to make myself known" (81). Define oneself visibly to the world, or die.

This self-definition consists broadly in making visible what the invisible hides, and this "magnification" centrally involves, if it does not require, a form of historical excavation, an archaeology. Archaeology turns on not only uncovering the hidden and (purposely) buried, and so not only on making the unseen seen, cognized, and re-cognized; it requires also the extending of a logic of form to the uncovered, a different way of thinking about—quite literally, of *seeing*—it. "The white man was wrong, I was not a primitive, not even a half-man, I belonged to a race that had already been working in gold and silver two thousand years ago" (92).

This response to the logic of disappearance emphasizes a strand in the DuBoisian dilemma of double-consciousness: the impossible ideological requirement of the socially dominant that race be denied or ignored and the necessary psychosocial imperative that one is defined in good part by one's race. Fanon furnishes his own formulation of this racial dilemma over color blindness and color-consciousness: "In effect what happens is this: as I begin to recognize that the Negro is the symbol of sin, I catch myself hating the Negro. But then I recognize that I am a Negro. There are two ways out of this conflict. Either I ask others to pay no attention to my skin, or else I want them to be aware of it" (140). The dilemma, one America knows only too well because it helped shape it, is an inherent product of racist societies. *"It is the racist who creates his inferior"* (Fanon 1968, 65, emphasis in original).[2] In this sense, Fanon rightly sees that the underlying sources of racially prompted in/visibility lie in "social structures" (71). In the face of being confronted with the claim, which is shouted in his face, that his blackness "was only a minor term" (97), that it was "Nothingness," Fanon accordingly recognizes the contingent necessity of "standing inside"—of taking on—the "fact of blackness," of assuming "negritude" not as "Infinity" (97) but as the required mode of his lived experience:

> My negritude is neither a tower nor a cathedral,
> it thrusts into the red flesh of the sun,
> it thrusts into the burning flesh of the sky,
> it hollows through the dense dismay of its own pillar
> of patience.... (97)

The prevailing logic of whiteness, then—white mythology, as Derrida puts it—is to make invisible the visible and visibly threatening. The logic of negritude, by contrast, is to make visible (necessarily to itself, contingently to the world) what has been rendered invisible by the force of whiteness, by "colonial desire" (Young 1994). Making the invisible visible by its very nature is a *political act*, one that requires symbolic murder (Fanon 1968, 141). In this sense, the political schizophrenia of color-consciousness in a society that takes itself to be color-blind calls forth the drive to maintain alterity as a mode of making visible—the "alterity," that is, "of rupture, of conflict, of battle" (158).

THE WAR OF THE VEIL

The colonizer's or racially dominant's drive to unveil is the desire "to win the battle of the veil at any cost" (Fanon 1970, 32), to unmask and unclothe with the view to dominate, to exploit, to penetrate—in short, to satisfy every whim. Whites, notes Fanon, face the world with an acquisitive stance, from the viewpoint that the world belongs to them. It is this arrogant presumption, one arrogating the world to themselves, that underpins the commodification of human beings, that grounds slavery (Fanon 1968, 90). This drive in turn prompts local resistance. Thus, "the white man ... creates the Negro.... But it is the Negro who creates negritude. To the colonialist offensive against the veil, the colonized opposes the cult of the veil" (Fanon 1970, 32–33).

More generally, parameters and paths of resistance and emancipation are initiated by the forms that oppression assumes. Yet, once initiated, they are not limited by or to oppressive direction or determination. Even when the oppressed assume categories of degradation in the name of contestation, stand inside them as a place of combat, the categories assumed are invested with novel, resistant, redirected and redirecting significance, "a revision of forms of behavior," as Fanon puts it (1970, 33). The veil is assumed—taken on or discarded—as a vehicle of change, its significance not fixed but contextual. It acquires its value in relation to social, political, cultural, and economic demands it at once reflects and symbolically demands.

RACIAL SUBJECTS

The veil, in Fanon's analysis, is in part symbol for, in part effect of, the complexity and overdetermined formation that is colonialism. The veil is a cultural artifact, a mark of gender and ethnoracial identity, a site at which race and gender are ordered and mediated. There is nothing in the cultural fabric of the United States, historically or contemporarily, that carries the material symbolism for those not white in the way the veil has for women in colonized North Africa. This difference highlights that between a racial definition that is mainly cultural and one that is predominantly epidermal. Hence perhaps the double-edged value of "passing," in the cultural vernacular of black America.

On one hand, the veil represents the distance between colonized and colonizer, the wall between the "European city" and the "native city" (Fanon 1970, 37), between oppressor and oppressed, rapist and raped, between the obviously powerful and the seemingly powerless, between projections of the modern and the traditional, "the West" and "the rest." On the other hand, the veil stands for (as it at once enables) a space of self-determination, a possible realm—because unseen and so undisciplined and literally uncontrollable—closed to colonial penetration. Here the veil serves complexly to maintain mystery, refuse mastery, and hide history in a double-edged resistant refusal. Seeing but not seen, the veiled woman suggests the forbidden and impenetrable, a forbiddenness and impenetrability that "frustrates the colonizer" (29). "Thus the rape of the Algerian woman in the dream of the European is always preceded by the rending of the veil"—a violent violation and abject humiliation at once of the woman so treated and of the colonized generally (31).

The Western preconception of the veil is that its value is vested in traditional Islamic culture, representative of conservative, male-dominated constraints upon timid, unliberated women.[3] What Fanon shows by contrast is that the value of the veil is deeply contextual, that in Algeria at least, the necessity of the veil is linked directly to the spatial colonization of the city (Fanon 1970, 21). The European city surrounded the native city (just as the "white" city or suburbia surrounds what is taken to be the "black" inner city), the only opening from which was into the European (or white) orbit. The native city and its inhabitants (like "black" urban space), completely circumscribed, experienced colonial (or racialized) city space as a mode of domination, their movements controlled as their lives were confined, patrolled, and surveilled. The colonial (or racialized) city made the colonized (or racially dominated) invisible to itself; the native (or "inner") city enabled its people, quite literally at the heart of the colonial (or racialized) city, to be invisible to the colonizer. Within the kasbah, however, women were protected by the familiar space of the kasbah itself; outside the kasbah, the veil substituted for its protective mantle (37). Here the analogy with the racialized North American city breaks down (Brigham 1996): External colonizers are foreigners to be swept out in a way that the racially dominant likely cannot be. For the racially marginalized of the "inner" city there is nowhere to retreat, not least because the "inner" city belongs to them at best symbolically and morally rather than economically (and often not politically).

For the colonizer, the veil maintained the distance of order and the order of distance; for the colonized, the veil hid the threat of resistant disorder as it could protect native women from the European gaze and colonial desire (Fanon 1970, 22). Behind the safety of the veil matters of considerable import were conducted. Arms were hidden, transported across enemy territory, false papers delivered by a "woman-arsenal" (40, 43). The veil, as a form of camouflage, a means of struggle (46), "protects, reassures, isolates" (44). Contrast in this sense the Battle of Algiers with the March on Selma!

Colonialism accordingly involved an attempt to unveil women and thereby "save" them (from tradition, from their culture, from native men, from themselves), and thus to master them (28). Women's bodies as objects of desire and media of exchange were fought over and circulated among men, their unveiling pursued to promote penetration: "These test-women, with bare faces and free bodies, henceforth circulated like sound currency in the European society of Algeria.... After each success, the authorities were strengthened in their conviction that the Algerian woman would support penetration into the native society ... the flesh of Algeria [was] laid bare" (27). Transformed via unveiling into desirable commodities, women seemingly found themselves laid bare, objectified, *alien*ated. After the initial nakedness of unveiling, however, the unveiled woman assumed the stance, the disposition, of visibility; she took on and charge of the possibilities unveiling made available to advance anticolonial struggle. She became self-assured, determined yet self-controlled (44), a navigator and negotiator of the hazardous routes necessary for successful resistance to colonial control. The native woman made a strategic choice to pursue a self-determined undertaking to discard the veil for the sake of advancing a war of position and maneuvre against colonial settlement, domination, and penetration, thereby promoting a transformation in the disposition of the unveiled—a freedom, an unconfinement, a self-possession.

Thus, the veil contextually assumes significance in relation to the functions to be performed by veiling/veillessness, especially in relation to the body (47). Fanon characterizes this as the "historic dynamism of the veil" (48). In the Algerian struggle, the veil first served as a mechanism of resistance. By playing on the traditional rigid separation of the sexes, the Algerian woman could work behind the veil, doing things not otherwise possible or permissible precisely "because the occupier was *bent on unveiling Algeria*" (49, Fanon's emphasis). Later, once the colonial authorities had worked out the instrumentality of the veil in revolutionary praxis, it was abandoned in favor of a self-confident baring, a diversionary revealing still in service of struggle (49). After May 1958, as a response to the "modernizing" unveiling of women directed by the demands and forces of "*Algerie francaise*," Algerian women once again—and in the name of self-determination, of stripping the colonizer of his logic—donned the *haik* "but stripped once and for all of its exclusively traditional dimension" (48).

Analogously, the value and virtue of in/visibility are contextually determined. There are moments, for example, when those working for dramatic social transformation in colonial or racially marginalized conditions want their struggle to be invisible, unseen though not unfelt; there are other times when its impact is registered fully only when openly conducted and witnessed, where its effects are witnessed, visible, and registered in the media. There is here a question of authenticating what is made visible, and indeed of what is invisible or unseen but known. Obviously the battle over media representation and control is played out around this question. (Fanon writes at some length of the role played by the Voice of Algeria in authentication of the Algerian revolution [69].) By contrast, those combatting revolutionary or liberatory transformation—the Master, the dominant, the colonialist—want resistance to be squashed, and if not squashed they would prefer it to remain unseen. And then there are moments when they would have resistance public as a way of instilling fear and counteraction, as a mode of "legitimating" or rationalizing the full force of reaction.

VISIBILITY AND VOICE, STEREOTYPES AND SUPERVISION

Visibility may assume subtle forms. As with fear or expectation, one may read in people's faces a certain psychosocial state of being. One can remain informed of social conditions by keeping one's ear to the ground, so to speak, or to the radio; by watching the media or listening carefully to the underground network of information, word of mouth, or the whisper in the street. "The

Algerian who read in the occupier's face the increasing bankruptcy of colonialism felt the compelling and vital need to be informed" (Fanon 1970, 59). To escape the Master's misrepresentations, one needs to "acquire [one's] own source of information" (59).

Radio and television are technologies that can promote invisibility and produce depersonalization. As "the voice of the occupier," Fanon says, "the radio was considered ... a means used by the enemy to quietly carry on his work of depersonalization of the native" (Fanon 1970, 78, 79), extending "a daily invitation," as Fanon puts it, "not to go native" (55). Not unlike the veil, radio and television, technologies of governmentality both, nevertheless can be used to make visible from a place or position of relative invisibility conditions of oppression and liberation (66-67). "Buying a radio, getting down on one's knees with one's head against the speaker, was no longer just wanting to get the news concerning the formidable experience in progress in the country, it was hearing the *first* words of the nation" (77). So radio and television make the invisible visible via explication, obviating, reporting, renewing. Like the telephone, though more generally and more depersonalized, they could bring together those not only at a distance but those quite literally unaware of each other's existence or common plight, producing a new (self-)consciousness and a renewed commitment. "The Voice of Algeria, created out of nothing, brought the nation to life and endowed every citizen with a new status, *telling him so explicitly*" (80). Radio is also a means of revelation, or at least of concealing and revealing. Like the print press, radio, television, and now the computer superhighway can serve as a gauge of the horizon of possibility and probability, even as its parameters are subjected to governmental supervision, if not control. Where these technologies are under direct control of the dominant forces in the country—as they were in apartheid South Africa, for example—they serve not only as instruments of hegemonic oppression but possibly also as potential sources of information about and insight into the state, the oppressor, the dominant.

Fanon thus recognizes that the links between knowledge, power, and technology make available or hide from view information necessary to the promotion of different interests. Knowledge may be empowering, but power orders knowledge. Technology offers a medium for the dissemination of information but at once mediates the message. To inform is to give form to the empirical, to make visible the hidden and audible, the silent or silenced, just as it makes invisible the seen and inaudible the spoken. "The 'truth' of the oppressor, formerly rejected as an absolute lie, was now countered by another, an acted truth" (60). Colonial and racial governmentality are fueled in part by a rationality of distance and distantiation, and in part by a logic of close constraint. The situational possibility and interface of these modes of domination are made possible by technologies that produce invisibility. Yet this very invisibility can be invoked as a site of contestation, and these same technologies can be mobilized to effect sites of emphatic refusal and spaces of visible and visibly resistant presence, conceived as enacted truths of the oppressed.

Fanon's intricate phenomenology of invisibility invites an open-ended formalization of the modes by which in/visibility may be produced. These modes, Fanon suggests, may be class specific. In the case of a professional class, invisibility likely will be motivated conceptually, stripping people of their ethnoracial belonging or identity and causing intellectual and cultural alienation. In the case of labor, by contrast, invisibility is tied to racially prompted exploitation, and predicated upon racially explicit and contemptuous debasement (Fanon 1968, 159). This distinction suggests a broader one between invisibility vested in definitional determination, in conceptual considerations, on the one hand; and an invisibility necessary to the production of which is

RACIAL SUBJECTS

sociostructural architecture, on the other. Beyond this distinction, however, Fanon's detailed analysis reveals that neither form of the invisible can be promoted, let alone sustained, independent of the other. A person's or population's invisibility may emerge in some part or instance as an epiphenomenal effect of sociostructural arrangements, of political economy. Nevertheless, it is likely even then that a discourse of degradation or dismissal, of infantilization or ignorance, has been invoked also to prompt or promote, reify or rationalize the sociostructural disappearance in question. In any case, once invisible, it becomes that much easier in moments of structural transformation, restructuration, or socioeconomic rationalization, to take advantage of an invisible group, a "pathetic population," to satisfy structural imperatives like cutting welfare programs or slashing education for those unable to pay their own way, to cover their costs.

As a principal bearer of culture, of His Master's culture in the instance at hand, language purports to serve in a variety of ways to produce invisibility. First, language is claimed to carry the standards not just of *a* civilization, but of civilization as such. To say that a person is a great black poet/writer/doctor/intellectual subtly conveys hidden degradation, judgmentally qualifying both intellectual activity and blackness (Fanon 1968, 13, 14, 30). Beyond this, language (like radio and television) is a technology of governmentality, a means of domesticating the influence of the colonial occupier/master. The occupier's language—in Algeria's case, French; in South Africa's case, English and what became Afrikaans; in the American "inner" city, standard (non-)Black English—orders the anarchy, the lack of form, supposedly afoot in the preoccupied country or space. So language assists in the domestication of the native or racialized people and culture, imposing the order of the Logos upon the presumed flux of a people supposedly lacking rationality and the *Geist* of world history (Fanon 1970, 75). The Logos borne by European language is supposed to drag primitive society into the modern, the rational, the historical. Against this, the insistent use of native languages, mother tongues, and racialized vernaculars becomes not just simple individualistic means of resistance but the common voice of an emergent nation or culture bent on "unveiling itself" (75).

Fanon exemplifies this contrast in terms of the pull between French and Arabic, between different languages—one foreign and imposed, inserted with outsider imposition, the other local and indigenous; the one European and tied to—as it opened—European interests and networks, the other inserted into local Arabic concerns, considerations, even constraints (76). A similar point can be made within the historically contextualized contrasts of a single language in postcolonial settings, for instance, Afrikaans in South Africa. Conceived as the voice of the white marginalized at the turn of this century, Afrikaans assumed at the height of apartheid's power the status of the oppressor's language, an oppressive and oppressing language, silently directing commands to, and diminutions of, the oppressed black masses of that country, most visibly resisted in 1976. For many black South Africans since 1948, however, Afrikaans was learned circumstantially as the medium more necessary than English to negotiate the white world—often the world of work and political engagement, in short, the prospects for survival. It has transformed into something else in the postapartheid moment. Afrikaans has been taken up in South Africa's multilingual babel as part of a possibility of producing the new—a social and linguistical hybrid (a development that might bear interesting comparison with Black English in the United States). In this sense, multilingualism in South Africa serves not so much as an unveiling (which presumes something already there) but a novel creation, not a discovery but an invention, licensing new modes of being and expression, hence new possibilities (Parker 1996).

As the bearer of culture, language carries and conveys values, and these norms of conception and perception often stereotype, and in stereotyping render invisible, their objects of reference.

> One family in particular has an excellent reputation: "They're very black but they're all quite nice." ... The father was given to walking up and down his balcony every evening at sunset; after a certain time of night, it was always said, he became *invisible*. Of another family, who lived in the country, it was said that on nights when there was a power failure the children had to laugh so that their parents would know that they were there. (Fanon 1968, 116, my emphasis)

The invisibility stereotyping effects is produced because the person stereotyped emulates the anticipated reaction that the Master's stereotype projects. "In the end, Bigger Thomas acts. To put an end to his tension, he acts, he responds to the world's anticipation" (Fanon 1968, 99). Fanon likens the displacement of precolonial values by the Master's to a conquest: "it was 'the consequence of the replacement of the repressed [African] spirit in the consciousness of the slave by an authority symbol representing the Master, a symbol implanted in the subsoil of the collective group and charged with maintaining order in it as a garrison controls a conquered city'" (103).

This identification of values is produced through education: "The black schoolboy in the Antilles, who in his lessons is for ever talking about 'our ancestors, the Gauls,' identifies himself with the explorer, the bringer of civilization, the white man who carries truth to savages—an all-white truth. There is identification—that is, the young Negro subjectively adopts a white man's attitude" (Fanon 1968, 104). Claude Steele and Joshua Aronson (1995) have offered empirical evidence of such stereotypical reaction in black college students in the United States who, though at the top of their class when entering school, replicate and reproduce the prevailing expectation of them to fail and drop out. Cinema, too, is all about the employment of character types, at the extreme, of stereotypes. In striking contrast to Fanon's Tarzan movie experience (108), Spike Lee interrogates this emulation of the Master's stereotypes in his searingly brilliant film, *Clockers*. Lee has Stripe's brother, Victor, paragon of self-restraint and moral propriety, explode in violent anger and viciously murder the drug-dealing store manager of Ahab's, the local take-out joint.[4]

Black people accordingly are made invisible by and through stereotypical whiteness, as a result of "hallucinatory whitening" (Fanon 1968, 71). The mythical Negro is a savage-cannibal (145–48), a penis symbol (113). Like the Jew, blacks stand stereotypically for otherness, defilement, lack. They are conceived as communists, subversives, and radical revolutionaries (129–30), in short, as politically driven, evil incarnate, by nature immoral. "In order to achieve morality, it is essential that the black, the dark, the Negro vanish from consciousness" (137–38). Where the Jew in addition comes to stand for the figure of the exploitative and lecherous capitalist, the black man comes to represent the image of the criminal. "Both of us stand for Evil. The black man more so, for the good reason that he is black" (127–28). The generic invention of black people as inherently inferior (105) at once reduces them to silence, to nonexistence, literally and metaphorically to nothing (98–99). Once internalized, stereotypes may manifest incrementally as self-loathing, self-denial, self-effacement. Social science, especially ethnography, has helped significantly to shape these images of the racialized Other or Native, "putting the native in his place" (142), and thus transforming natives into the Native, the different into the racially degenerate, naive and needy, hopeless and helpless.

If stereotyping reduces black people to but dull shadows of themselves, then social structure hides them from view, erases them, almost altogether. In the postcolonial period, social

RACIAL SUBJECTS

structure has served silently to shift behind the veil of ignorance, so to speak, and so largely to silence concern(s) for (though not necessarily about) the racially marginalized. Fanon identifies how this came to pass at the very moment of anticolonial success. Historically, the Negro—steeped in the inessentiality of servitude—was set free by his Master. He did "not fight for his freedom" (Fanon 1968, 156). If anticolonial struggle was the fight for self-determination, for freedom as that most human of values (158), Fanon suggests that anticolonial (and counterracist) forces allowed the terms of their struggle—the standards and value of freedom—to be defined by the colonial Master (and the racist). "The Negro knows nothing of the cost of freedom, for he has not fought for it. From time to time he has fought for Liberty and Justice, but these were always white liberty and white justice; that is, values secreted by his masters" (157). The colonial Master, the generically white man, established values and standards others were expected always to (fail to) meet:

> The Negro is a slave who has been allowed to assume the attitude of a master. The white man is a master who has allowed his slaves to eat at his table.... The black man was acted upon. Values that had not been created by his actions, values that had not been born of the systolic tide of his blood, danced in a hued whirl around him. The upheaval did not make a difference in the Negro. He went from one way of life to another, but not from one life to another. (156)

Given liberty, black people failed in the pursuit of their freedom; extended justice, they were denied the opportunity to fail on their own terms—and so the possibility of self-determination and success. The transformation in and of values from those imposed to those driven by and reflecting self-determination and self-definition is a necessary condition of complete visibility. Denied self-determination, denied the freedom to choose one's principles, one is denied self-definition and so the visibility self-definition makes possible and marks.

Conceived in this way, the conditions for visibility suggested by Fanon continue to be eviscerated, eroded, and sometimes altogether absent from postcolonial contexts. Constraints upon postcolonial and antiracist struggle set by lack of institutional and structurally defined power extends invisibility of and to the postcolonial dispossessed and oppressed. I close these reflections by considering briefly some contemporary examples.

POSTCOLONIAL IN/VISIBILITY

In Australia, since at least the 1930s and accelerated from the mid-century, governmentality was concerned with the administration of all aspects of Aboriginal life. As Pat O'Malley shows, this governmental administration and control produced, as it presupposed, a form of projected invisibility. Invisible, Aboriginals safely could be ignored; visible, they could—they had to—be decimated (O'Malley 1995, 4). In the late 1950s, the area of Central Australia where many Aboriginals wandered was declared formally by the Australian State to be uninhabited, a "terra incognita" in the center of Australia. Earlier, the state had proscribed intermarriage even between "half-caste" and "full-caste" Aboriginals in the attempt to contain by circumscribing them socially and spatially, to set them apart so as to set them aside, to make them visible to—nothing but objects of—governmentality. Rendered instrumentally and institutionally visible to and through bureaucratic rationality, they were thereby made socially invisible, unseen literally and figuratively in the scheme of Australian social formation and self-identity, nonexistent in the order of the commonwealth of national identity or the "postcolonial" republic of ends. State mandates suggested eugenically breeding out "half-caste" Aboriginals through miscegenation with European Australians; "full bloods" in turn would die out naturally in the failure of evolutionary fitness. Assimilation and natural extinction through strictly enforced apartheid would breed the desirable end of Aboriginal invisibility, Aboriginals' "gentle genocide," as O'Malley puts it.

American Indians suffered a comparable fate in the state's expressed commitment to the logic of their disappearance. Consistent with the policy of assimilation, the intention of which was to wipe out all traces of Indian culture, the U.S. Department of the Interior as late as the end of 1930 was committed to implementing the especially pernicious "Bow and Arrow Ceremony." A representative of the department would appear in Indian country with a list of those to be granted U.S. citizenship. In the ensuing citizenship ceremony, candidates would be asked to shoot an arrow with a bow handed to them by the government agent. Pronouncing the arrow, supposed sign of the primitive past, as the person's last shot, the agent then handed the candidate a plow as a symbol of work, a purse as a symbol of saving and economic rationality, and a U.S. flag as a symbol of freedom. The ceremony obliged them to renounce their Indian names—the visible badge of their Indianness—in favor of assuming an Anglicized name. The policy of assimilation was played out through the instrumentalities of effacement, the culture of naming buried beneath the assimilative erasure of culture, American Indians whitewashed—made invisible—by the wave of a governmental form and the U.S. flag.[5]

Australian Aboriginals and indigenous American Indians suffered the extended effects of an earlier globalizing expansion. It should be obvious that globalization marks the social formation, structure, and culture not only of the (former) colonies and colonized in the wake of their independence. As Fanon suggests, globalization has had deep structural implications also for colonizing and dominant geopolitical powers. Thus Los Angeles, like other cities in the United States, has experienced dramatic shifts in its mode of structural reformation in the postcolonial period since World War II, and especially in the past twenty years.

Indeed, these shifts are linked to the postcolonial transformations globally that I identified in my chapter "Introduction: The Fabric of Race." The City of Angels has witnessed these transformations as visibly as any American city, and in its culture (and cultural industry) it has reflected (as it reflects upon) these changes for the rest of the country (and more imperially for the rest of the world).

The changes attendant to this broader restructuring are more obviously at play in Los Angeles than elsewhere. For one, across roughly the same period the city became identified with new waves of influx, migration, and immigration—and not just from across borders or seas but across the landscape of America (the lure of opportunity, leisure, and play long associated with the image of that city), thus magnifying its diverse character. The workforce of the city has become dramatically "Latinized," and its politics have shifted from what a short while ago was dominantly black-white to become increasingly diversified, hybridized, fragmentary, and fractured. The shrinking of traditional and "legitimate" opportunities gave way to the emergence of alternate economies (the creation of new opportunities in the face of their absence). So drugs and guns have manifested more visibly, but also new cultural forms have opened other(ed) economic opportunities, like gangsta rap and hip hop.

At the same time, there was a distinct and increasingly self-conscious shift to the privatizing of the public mandate and public services: You get what you can pay for.[6] In this sense, California's Proposition 187, which outlaws any social service provision (including nonemergency medical and educational services) to illegal immigrants and their children, is only the latest development in this logic of privatizing the health and educational costs of unskilled labor. Proposition 187, approved by electoral endorsement, has no design on ending immigration or the employment of immigrants, only for ensuring a continued source of "waged slavery" by refusing education to immigrants and cheapening labor by privatizing its associated costs.

The effect of all this is to render the population that "occupies" central and east Los Angeles *invisible* politically and economically, to be policed but not seen or heard (from), a population beyond the boundaries of the political imagination save as that unspoken reserve army of labor that keeps unskilled wages, and so the minimum wage, in check. Inflation is kept low on the backs of the unemployed also, for the unemployed tend not to vote while consumers stop by at the polls on the way to the mall (or these days at the mall). In this sense, the Los Angeles implosion in 1992 was neither a riot nor an uprising, neither an intifada nor quite a revolt, but an overflowing of anger no longer containable, at once self-defeating and other directed. This implosion can be understood thus as the bitter and pained insistence on visibility—"We are here, deal with us"—in the face of the logics and policies of invisibility.

The revolution, as Gil Scott-Heron once suggested, may not be televised, but Fanon hints that it will be deeply linked to technological innovation. Even he could not have predicted in the 1950s, however, that the deeper, unseen revolution would turn out to be an electronic one rather than directly political. Television and computers are its media, surveillance and supervision its mode, discipline its message, containment its effect. In this context, Los Angeles's implosion was about making public the privatizing of marginalization. Related to these deep structural shifts, as should be apparent and has been commented upon by many others, is the transformation in urban space that accompanied them: peripheral suburban spaces decentering the city and rendering the center marginal.

Obviously, the police loom large here both in terms of the apparatus of microdisciplines and as the general form of urban administration and supervision.[7] Helicopters and floodlights ensure the surveilled and supervised visibility of the racially marginalized population within their constructed confines the better to enforce their invisibility from without. Beyond the ghetto/*barrio*, out of sight, out of mind. Prisons pick up where the population fails to acknowledge its "natural" boundaries. California's commitment to prisons over public schools—privatize the latter while using public dollars for the former—is a renewed pledge to the politics of invisibility.[8] The crisis attendant on economic transformation and its political, legal, and cultural legitimation is being policed by a culture of imprisonment, a newly emphasized (if not exactly new) technology of invisibility and social disappearance. Prisons in the postindustrial social formation of postmodernity serve two logics. They fuel an extended economy searching for a jump start in the wake of the late military-industrial complex, due to base closings and plant layoffs. And they instantiate the logic of disappearance—the invisibility—of the racially marginalized, the unemployed and "permanently unemployable" population of the city and the state. In a single stroke, governors can assume the rhetoric of Caesar: Veni, vidi, ...

In the projection of white superiority and black inferiority, of white visibility and black invisibility, however, the fragility of masterhood is reflected and refracted. In this reflection and refraction there is to be found imprinted, much like a cinematic dissolve, hint of the insidious invisibility of white people. As the presumptive norm of racial power and elevation, the racial dimension of whiteness can be denied, or at least ignored. If race is Other, whiteness is invisible, the site of racial power and arrogance. While whites can cower behind the presumed invisibility of their whiteness, this paradoxically hides from view the vulnerability of whiteness and white folk. The presumptive invisibility of whites can be turned against them, their spoiled nature qua whiteness revealing a fragility at the heart of whiteness, their decadence a powerlessness that can be challenged. Invisible in terms of its whiteness, white power is viciously visible in conception and effect but fragile in application and self-absorption. As such, it can be confronted and condemned, resisted and restricted, diffused and defused.

If the complex state of social being is reduced now largely to the frame of political economy, then in societies marked exhaustively by commodification and race the poorest of the racially marginalized are reduced virtually to nothing. Even at these marginal extremes, however, moments exist—fleeting and unexpected though they may be—when this marginal economy may be invoked to stand outside, apart from, the spotlight of state surveillance and supervision, and so beyond its administrative governmentality. It is at these sites that modes of emancipatory resistance are fashioned, making possible moments of radical self-determination, effecting in short what Fanon calls freedom. Invisible at the margins, the marginalized can challenge and sometimes ignore visible power at the very visible and cumbersome center. Or they may appeal to a divided moral economy of the powerful, playing one representative off against another. In a passing reversal, the formerly invisible may become momentarily visible, while the formerly visible are frozen at the margins of their own fabrication. Examples abound: the Zapatistas in Chiapas, those fighting for freedom in South Africa in the dying days of apartheid, the racially marginalized of Los Angeles circa 1992, those carving out cultural hipness in a world where culture and hipness have become paramount.

In this sense, the struggle for visibility so insightfully and incisively interrogated by Fanon continues to be critically significant. It is, after all, the struggle for power, autonomy, self-definition. And it is, perhaps paradoxically and in the face of essentializing racial assumptions, a struggle for which the veil of invisibility can continue to offer strategic value. For invisibility can enable the marginalized even—indeed, especially—at the most depressing moments of degrading dismissal to advance their own sense of themselves, their own ontological commitments, their own frames of knowing and action, a self-defined politics and aesthetics, economy and culture. These are senses, the development of which are enabled by relative invisibility, that need not be implicated in that Hegelian drive to dismissal via recognition by the racial Other.

It is these dynamics of recognition and miscognition, of visibility and invisibility, in which contemporary black intellectuals are embroiled, especially as they become elevated through media(ted) recognition as public intellectuals. I address the particularity of these dynamics in the essay that follows.

WHITHER WEST?

THE MAKING OF A PUBLIC INTELLECTUAL

As a philosophical and political doctrine, liberalism is committed to individual liberties and the protection of privacy. The critical focus on liberalism, and the emergent interest in analyzing social identities since the 1980s, opened an attendant theoretical engagement in exploring the public sphere (Habermas 1989) and public culture (Black Public Sphere Collective 1995) as well as their influences on identity formation. In turn, these concerns and the material conditions they at once reflected and represented prompted a renewed interest in the conditions and commitments of the public intellectual.

Public intellectuals speak in, to, and about public spheres and public cultures, articulating a grammar of political morality (Brenkman 1995, 7) that challenges conformity and bias. Public intellectuals want to generate new ideas, to examine these ideas and their premises critically, and to weigh arguments on crucial issues regarding public well-being and democratic flourishing. They test the limits of the given, the prosaic, and the sacred; and they seek in an open forum to debate and deliberate about the least contested and most basic of social values with the view to promoting social involvement, social intercourse and transaction, coalitions across sometimes antagonistic social groups, mutual recognition and respect, civil agreement and acceptance, multiplicity and heterogeneity—that is, civic incorporation (Goldberg 1993a, 220-23) and public visibility.

Public intellectuals accordingly pose the difficult questions, speaking to a wide audience while avoiding orthodoxy of value and vocabulary. They enlarge a social, political, economic, or cultural issue so as to engage the public, to render it sufficiently general so as to *publicize* it—to make it a public and not parochial concern. Public intellectuals excavate local issues for their underlying general principles to effect local outcomes, challenging the powerful in the name of freedom and (in freedom's absence) of emancipatory commitment (see Said 1993; Becker 1995; Williams 1995; Giroux 1997).

For the past decade or more, Cornel West has been keeping us intellectually honest. He has an admirable ability to weave together a wide range of theoretical scholarship while showing how seemingly disparate (if not conflicting) views have compatible premises or purposes. He has been at the forefront of the related drives to make analysis of race and racism intellectually vital, especially in the humanities, and to emphasize the importance of interdisciplinary insight. He has deepened our knowledge of the range and limits of philosophical pragmatism by articulating its genealogy, of engaged theology by exploring its possibilities, and of critical multiculturalism by refusing to accept its silences. All this, and yet more, for West's appeal has turned upon a tireless capacity to renew, if only momentarily, a flagging faith and a hopeful confidence in the emancipatory project by mixing insightful intellectual critique with incisive social criticism.

The publication of *Race Matters* marked not so much a new direction for Cornel West (1993a) as a new mix: intellectual critic becomes unabashedly public intellectual; critical intellectual shows up as the social critic. Yet, in this new mix, in taking center stage in the public and not just the academic theater, Cornel West—like any public figure—is no longer so clearly in command of his meaning.[1] For public representation designed to intervene at the level of civic debate and public policy commands a certain language and style of analysis, and these are hardly value free. They pull at their users, dragging them *center* stage. If one chooses to stand on this political stage—and if one's book is to sell in the marketplace of popular policy analysis—one risks at least *sounding* centrist. Presidential hopefuls suffer this strategy only too well. As economic and cultural capital project the next fifteen-minute icon from which to generate soundbites and surplus value, critical language becomes muted, internalized, sometimes self-directed. The power of language gives way, if only silently and subtly, to the language of power, if not to the gaps between language.[2] Where the subject is race, the silences speak louder than words.

So this is West's dilemma, that of the critical intellectual turned public critic, as he sets out to offer a "balanced" analysis of the contemporary condition of America in racialized terms, of racialized America: to speak the language of truth to power as power speaks to truth!

Race matters, West suggests emphatically and repeatedly, and matters deeply to racialized America, but it is not all that matters, and certainly not all that serves to define the conditions of everyone who lives the racial condition, the matters of race in America. Racism is *a* determinant of the divide between black and white America, but it is one determinant among several, nor does it necessarily determine that divide in the final analysis. Any account that either elevates racism to the status of sole determinant of the conditions of blacks, and so also of whites, or denies its determinacy altogether, dramatically overstates the truth.

This much has been pointed out by any number of analysts, academic and public alike, though the mix may vary from one to another and the advice often goes unheeded, both in theoretical and in practical political analysis. Nevertheless, *Race Matters* makes formative moves in new directions, blending theoretical critique with more straightforward political commentary to fashion a cutting critical account of, and contrasting vision for, race in contemporary America.

West's framework is expressed in terms of a single critical principle: Black Americans face a nihilistic threat, a threat to their very existence that cannot be reduced simply to economic terms of material deprivation but which is more deeply experienced as an existential depression, a sense of self-worthlessness, and social despair (12),[3] and all of which prompt meaningless, hopeless, and loveless lives (14–15). This is an important point, for though figures show that about one-third of blacks in the United States now are considered members of the middle class, this membership is economically more tenuous than it is for nonblacks occupying the same socioeconomic positions. In any case the history and contemporary legacy of discrimination, struggle, and shifting ceilings leaves almost no black person, middle class or marginalized poor, existentially untouched. Public representation of blackness, the fabricated racial image, is still one of lawlessness and violence, of threat and pollution. A feeling of deep social and personal despair is a (psycho)logical consequence of this imagined, though imaginary, dehumanizing projection.

So, for West, the principal opponent of "black survival in America is not oppression or exploitation but the nihilistic threat" (15). It follows that the two prevailing but reductive paradigms for explaining the social situation of American blacks are both inadequate. Liberal structuralism reduces the condition of blacks to strictly economic terms and responds with more government programs and money; conservative moralism by contrast blames the victims, reducing poor blacks' current conditions to the impoverishment of values and moral degeneration. West criticizes the former for failing to comprehend that both structural programs and personal values are necessary to confront the nihilistic threat, that people must be encouraged not to give in to their structured circumstances. The latter position, he contends, reduces the culture of moral poverty to the level of personal responsibility, to the poverty of culture, and so fails to acknowledge the institutional implications of culture. For culture, argues West, is rooted in and distributed through such social institutions as families, schools, religion, and the media. Thus, the crisis of morality West acknowledges confronting black Americans is not so much a personal failing (though he thinks individual blacks also have to admit some responsibility) as it is an institutional one, pervading social culture.

If the history of black America has been one of struggling against not annihilation but "nihilism" (15), then the obvious question West must confront is why this threat is more pressing now than in the past, and more so for blacks than for others. He offers two reasons, though he focuses primarily upon the second. The first is that black culture and life have been pervaded by market forces and market moralities, by profit making and the pleasure principle, creating habits of consumption that undermine traditional morality and habits of the heart. Combined with the legacy of white supremacist beliefs, this pervasion of market forces prompts a nihilistic self-loathing among blacks, a deep existential angst, for blacks have to deny their identity, their very being, to operate in the world defined by the market. This in turn extinguishes the flame of hope, and dramatically shrinks the range of possible meanings black people can draw on, leading to a deep-seated and pessimistic rage (17–18).

Given that intensified commodification and the morality of the market are conditions also facing those considered and considering themselves nonblack, it is surprising that West says almost nothing about the way market mechanisms exacerbate white supremacy. If blacks suffer this commodified condition more intensely than others, the continuing legacy of white supremacy constitutes something like a multiplier effect on blacks' degrading and exclusionary experience (Goldberg 1993a, 91). These effects necessitate an analysis of how historical shifts in the modes of accumulation transform white supremacy, and how such transformations have served both to license and rationalize different exploitative practices in relation to whites and blacks. West was drawn for popular purposes to frame his analysis in existential terms, thus drawing the focus away from political economy and entailing that structural issues remain largely hidden from view.

The second reason West offers for why blacks face a more intense nihilistic threat is the "present crisis in black leadership" (15), both political and intellectual, and the underlying social irresponsibility of middle class blacks. Indeed, this argument goes much of the way in tying together the otherwise disparate essays in the book.[4] West places the emergence of the contemporary black middle class in the 1960s.[5] This emergence, he thinks, expresses an obsessive drive for status and an addiction to the stimulation of new commodities and experiences. The result is dramatic deterioration in personal, familial, and communal relations among African Americans, accompanied by a renounced moral commitment and reduced critical engagement in social causes (36–37). This atomistic individualism and self-serving egoism in turn pervade black leadership, middle-class movers who are left politically powerless and intellectually impotent.

Lacking the virtues of personal integrity, political savviness, moral vision, prudent judgment, courageous defiance, and organizational patience, black leaders are adrift from the communities they purport to represent. Their expensive clothes set them apart, symbolically and materially, from any organic links they might have with their constituents, just as the shabby dress of black intellectuals imprisons them in their academic ivory towers (38–40).[6]

West's critique nevertheless initiates and identifies an important insight. In the American social formation, formal political leadership tends to be from the wealthy and powerful down. Even if a leader emerges from a grassroots organizational setting, it takes capital to run a campaign, and time is taken up with the instruments of campaigning, electioneering, and governing. Prospective political leadership, like prospective leadership generally, therefore becomes consumed with and by those who have, or have access to, capital. Once in power, even a grassroots representative is pressured—by the interests of capital, by colleagues and their discourses, by forms of debate and representation, and by his or her own relation to and control of resources—to re-present capital's (now his or her own) interests. So, by process (one might say almost by definition), a grassroots representation, once it aspires to formal political representation from the inside, will very likely be sociostructurally transformed into the representation of capital's interests. West moralistically and simplistically dismisses the dress and culture of contemporary black leadership as a metaphor for this phenomenon.

In spite of this insight, West's two arguments nevertheless fail to sustain his claim that blacks suffer the nihilistic threat more than others. Absent the qualifier "black," both arguments apply to America at large. In one direction, West has overgeneralized the scope of the nihilistic threat, perhaps for rhetorical reasons, though it essentializes in its totalizing reference to "blacks" and "the black community." The nihilistic threat is perhaps less pervasive for relatively successful blacks than West implies. In the other direction, the weight of the nihilistic threat experienced by most blacks is sustained more heavily than West seems ready to indicate here by the legacy of institutional and representational racisms. It is at this intersection of race and class that the multiplier effects of economic exploitation and racist exclusion weigh most heavily.

West concludes this line of analysis by noting that black intellectuals have suffered more than others the professionalization of knowledge, the bureaucratization of the academy, and the proliferation of arcane jargon.[7] Again, he offers two arguments to support the charge. In the first instance, the American academy has become insulated from its social situation because of professionalization, thus both reducing the likelihood of radical political critiques and disarming the ones offered (41). But all this shows is that critiques by black scholars have suffered as those by whites have. (This also has the uncomfortable consequence of being self-referential: *Race Matters* may be implicated inadvertently.) To sustain the claim to intensified suffering, West assumes here what he has argued elsewhere (1993b), namely, that black scholars are more vulnerable in the academy than nonblacks.

This vulnerability seems to be the import of his second argument, for here West bemoans the poverty of black intellectual life. Citing no supporting evidence, he harshly dismisses black intellectuals who are independent of the academy—journalists, artists, writers, feminist groups—as "mediocre." Thereby, he offers no support to independent black intellectual culture. I suppose he is contrasting them to the likes of black modernity and the Harlem Renaissance (see Gates and West 1996; by contrast, see James 1996). He criticizes the general poverty of a self-sustaining support system for black academic intellectuals—a lack of interdisciplinary journals and magazines, for instance, critically analyzing black culture and its relation to American society (41–42). While the contributions of independent black intellectuals and support systems may offer less for structural reasons than one would wish, West unfortunately and reductively paints a large body of people with a single stripe, along with some important and fascinating critical work. He may be right in bemoaning the failure of "black" capital to furnish material support for critical black intellectual projects (sometimes capital represents just capital's narrow interests, period). Nevertheless, this is a dire circumstance generally faced by the left. Contrast the number and nature of magazines and journals on any library or store shelf funded by neoconservative foundations with those financially supported by critical concerns.

The conclusion to this line of analysis is marked by a further tension. West insists that both political and intellectual leadership need to be prophetic and race-transcending rather than race-distancing or race-embracing. Race-denying or race-distancing political managers and academics avoid representing black political or intellectual interests in the name of neutral political or academic representation (Tom Bradley, Wilson Goode, and the "mean-spirited" Adolph Reed are cited). The dialectically opposed race-identifying or race-embracing protesters (Farrakhan and Marion Barry, and much of Afrocentric thought) rhetorically reproduce the sort of racist hierarchical categories they so vociferously object to. By contrast, the race-transcending leadership of a Harold Washington or Jesse Jackson circa 1988, and of James Baldwin and Toni Morrison embody the virtues necessary to prophesy deliverance.

This tripartite typology (denying, embracing, or transcending racial appeal) is useful as a critical heuristic in the domain of social critique. West's commitment to race-transcendence is both morally and politically appealing, even if he does little more in filling out its content than mention some necessary components, a point to which I will return later. However, it may be misleading, and in a nontrivial way, to map a critique of intellectuals onto political leaders. For one, problems of political economy facing blacks today are significantly more complex than they were, say, even during the Civil Rights struggle. Perhaps the failure of leadership noted by West is a product not so much of class but of an insistence that the issues are singular, discrete, and homogeneous when they are disparate, heterogeneous, and irreducible. Also, it may be that once a resounding critical voice emerges these days, like a Cornel West, it gets corporatized. Agents take over, fees become exorbitant, contractual conditions mediate critical engagement and relation, rights are sold or withheld. The critical voice begins to quaver beneath the weight.

These demands necessitate that intellectual representation and critique be significantly more nuanced, and in many ways the record is more complex than West acknowledges here. It follows that West's somewhat snide slighting of black intellectuals, independent and academic alike, is not simply silly but counterproductive. It indiscriminately (and perhaps all too discriminatingly) undermines important critical work otherwise unavailable; it serves inadvertently to reify the judgment of the right that there but for affirmative action go white males; and it sounds awfully self-serving, even if unintentionally so. In short, while West's line of criticism seems designed to promote the independence—the racial transcendence, as the argument would have it—of his own critical voice, a reader unfamiliar with his earlier work may wonder what he thinks about the views generally represented as black neoconservative. It is with more than passing interest, then, that I turn to what West has to say about this subject, and about the related matter of affirmative action.

It is refreshing to find in *Race Matters* a candid critical reading of blacks' generally uncritical support of Clarence Thomas, and of the dramatic failure of black leadership in resorting to a bald racial (and blatantly sexist) appeal in promoting for Supreme Court justice a person whose expressed commitments were generally antithetical to the interests of blacks.[8] West succinctly pinpoints the vulgar racial reasoning upon which Thomas's campaign ultimately succeeded: the appeal to black (racial) authenticity (to which one might also add white guilt). This appeal effected the closing of black ranks behind Thomas's nomination by way of black male subordination of black women in the putative interests of the black community facing a hostile white environment (23–25).

This appeal to the rationale of black authenticity presumes a fixed essentialist conception of blackness, of who is really black. West contrasts this with a dramatically more appealing, historically based conception. Blackness consists in being the subject of white supremacist abuse *and* part of a rich culture and community struggling against this abuse (25–26). This raises a crucial question, namely, whether blackness can and does have any self-defined meaning beyond that crafted in response to white abuse. The conception of blackness as constructed rather than given is understandably reactive, for it is predicated largely upon the pervasive presumption of victimization. Elsewhere in the book, however, West suggests more affirmatively at least the potential for fuller black self-definition in extolling the virtues of, and need for, black self-respect and self-love. If the investment in struggle is what West means by blackness as a political category, then perhaps this imperative to promote and sustain black self-respect and self-love is what he intends by his repeated affirmation of blackness as an ethical conception.

Against this background, West identifies some acceptable features of black neoconservative critique: the rejection of victimization status for blacks, and especially identification of the breakdown of moral fabric and values among younger blacks.

Nevertheless, he is generally critical of the poverty of neoconservatives' oversimplified and truncated discourse. Thus, West notes the substitution by black neoconservatives of the appeal to nation for the appeal to race, of their appeal to their own victimization at the hands of liberals for liberalism's appeal to racial victimization, and most importantly the failure of neoconservatives to acknowledge the crucial structural features of poor blacks' socioeconomic conditions. Accordingly, West identifies the eclipse of U.S. economic predominance and the structural transformation of the U.S. economy as factors underpinning what he characterizes as the moral disintegration especially of poor black and working poor communities throughout the country.[9]

In addition, West allows himself a series of questionable analytical reductions. He attributes the poverty of black neoconservative analysis to being predicated narrowly upon a critical response to liberalism. In turn, he argues that liberalism restricts the cause of black poverty to racial discrimination. Moreover, West reduces the logic producing conservatives' own xenophobia, sexism, and homophobia to a psychologism; that is, to conservatives' quest for order. He is correct to attribute neoconservative analysis largely to reactions to its reconstruction of liberalism. Nevertheless, we cannot here fail to notice another tension in West's own analysis. He opens his book by bemoaning liberalism's economistic commitments in responding to racial discrimination. Thus, he rightly picks up on the ambivalence in liberalism between appeals to racial discrimination and appeals to structural conditions like class in accounting for the contemporary black condition (William Julius Wilson's vacillation over the last fifteen years or so being a case in point). West himself attempts to combine these explanatory elements in a complex mix, tempered by the addition of cultural considerations like the repeatedly noted flight of traditional morality. But, it must be asked, what's so great about "traditional morality"? This seems, as the slogan goes, as much a part of the problem as the solution. West suggests traditional morality is instrumental to warding off "self-hatred and self-contempt" (17). Yet traditional morality, recall, is as tied to racist, sexist, and homophobic commitments, as it is to love and respect (Goldberg 1993, chapter 2). Finally, West's psychologizing of neoconservative bigotry as an appeal to order fashions a further form of reductionism, presuming a singular logic to a broad set of expressions with complex motivations and reasons.

Moreover, West defends affirmative action programs against neoconservative attack, even as he identifies their limited value and effects. Far from reducing black self-respect, West argues that affirmative action has furnished a limited redistributive mechanism insufficient to do away with poverty or to effect equality. He recognizes that the mechanism has benefited middle-class Americans disproportionately (accordingly, he affirms his own commitment to a class-based policy of affirmative action); and while he recognizes the importance of affirmative action's role, he considers it largely to have been a reactive one. That is, affirmative action has worked mainly to ensure the inhibiting of discriminatory practices against women and people of color (64).

The swiftness of West's analysis here not only leaves him silent about the moral arguments sustaining affirmative action, he is less than careful in places. Though it is true that affirmative action may be contextually necessary to diminish discrimination (West insists that in its absence, racial and sexist discrimination would return with a vengeance), discrimination nevertheless has continued despite such programs. West also insists, again rightly, that elimination of black poverty is a *necessary* condition of black progress, but adds oddly that affirmation of black humanity is but a *sufficient* condition for black advancement (65). Of course, West may be suggesting, contrary to neoconservatives, that affirmative action has had more to do with affirming black humanity than eliminating black poverty; if so, I think he is largely correct. But, obviously, there can fail to be black progress in spite of black (self-)affirmation, for black persons may lose out still in the competition for jobs and resources despite equality of regard for them. After all, racist exclusion, or at least its legacy, may assume various forms. It is more likely that black (self-) affirmation serves rather as another necessary condition for black progress, without which such progress is unlikely to materialize but the presence of which alone does not guarantee (self-) advancement.

In spite of these gaps, silences, rhetorical overextensions, and miscues, the first five articles in West's book do seem to hang together. They offer a provocative and critical, if in places rocky, excavation of the contemporary state of black America; of the conditions of its emergence and problems, its poverty and the possibilities of political leadership; and of its occasional moral lapses and suspensions. The final three articles perceptively and in places challengingly spell out some pressing cultural problematics confronting blacks in their relations with nonblack Americans. Here, West develops three discrete though sometimes related analyses. First, he analyzes contemporary tensions between black and Jewish Americans, especially in the face of some current black anti-Semitism and Jewish antagonism to black interests. Second, he confronts the deafening silence by blacks and whites alike in addressing black sexuality, and the implications of this silence in and for racialized relations. Finally, West gives analytical voice to the youthful black rage expressed in response to the "absurd" conditions faced today by young blacks, and the importance of the figure of Malcolm X in articulating this rage. He insightfully interprets the analytical importance of Malcolm as encapsulated in the relation between black self-affirmation, desire for emancipation, deep-seated anger against a society seemingly designed to shut blacks out, and the looming probability of an early death.

Thus, *Race Matters* touches analytically upon virtually all the primary problematics pertaining to matters of race in contemporary America. Its shortness and breezy style all too luringly invite a quick and cursory reading. This is unfortunate, for such a reading would have one cast too quickly over and dismiss too readily some thoughtful, sometimes complex, and usually thought-provoking contributions. To address what West's account has to commend it, as a pedagogy about race and the production of the public intellectual and social critic, then, it is necessary to bring into sharper relief some underlying assumptions that silently frame his analysis.

Two fundamental assumptions structure Cornel West's analysis in *Race Matters*. Having rejected, early on, the deterministic structuralism of political economy and the finger-pointing moralism of cultural conservativism, West is left to embed his critique in a contrasting background communitarianism. Thus, he speaks of the "breakdown of family and neighborhood bonds"; of the "collapse of spiritual communities" that have "created rootless, dangling people" (5); and of the lack of "vital communities to hold up precious ethical and religious ideals" (37). This failure of community ties lies at the heart of West's attack on the black middle class, on the poverty of contemporary black leadership, and on the perceived absence of moral commitment, which he thinks has been swallowed by the unmitigated drive for personal achievement, egoistic self-advancement, and self-serving interests.

Philosophical liberalism is wedded strongly to a conception of sovereign yet atomistic and isolated individuals freely choosing their own commitments, endeavors, and actions. The space of the sovereign individual is taken to be protected by rights delimiting incursion by others, institutions, and the state. Communitarianism defines itself in terms of a critique of this liberal view of the self, holding that human beings acquire an identity through the historically defined communities to which we belong. Individuals' conceptions of the good—of what ought to be pursued as a matter of morality or value—are not self-defined so much as they are acquired by way of our necessary socialization in a community. Persons are situated in specific social contexts, sharing moral values, a common conception of the good, and mutual goals acquired in and through community membership.

Cornel West's critique of the state of black America, and of America more generally, then, is aimed largely at the failings of the liberal model and its political implications. The radical egoistic individualism of the black middle class, as of the middle class more generally, is cited as the prevailing cause and symptom of disintegration of a vital black community. This failure of community is considered in turn to underscore the dissolution of moral habits, virtuous relations, political resistance, and leadership. In short, the crisis in black America is part of the moral crisis of America more generally, its malaise a function of the economic advance of a few black middle-class *individuals* and the almost inevitable attendant moral, social, and political failures.

The second, though more silent, frame of West's analysis is derived from his repeated emphasis on self-love and love of others. The need for more love of self and others is called for as a contrast to the contemporary overemphasis on liberal self-interest and the absence of community that is the object of West's communitarian critique. What West means by this, as he sometimes says, is the Kantian imperative enjoining greater self-respect and respect of others. But this commitment to the language of love in racial matters carries with it another, more reductive implication, for it suggests that racist exclusion, invisibility, discrimination, and bigotry can be understood best in terms of the existential experience of hate. As I explained in my second chapter, racist expression is reduced to the offense of hate speech, racist violence to hate crimes. The power that is at the heart of any racist expression is reduced to the realm of offensive ideas, institutional exclusions are reduced to existential experiences like angst and psychological alienation, conditions of resistance are reduced to a stress on significance, hope, and the spirituality of psychic conversion.

These two framing ideas—communitarianism and a call for love—draw West away from a more radical focus on political economy and the continuing legacy of racist discourse. I don't mean to deny the necessity of community ties and psychological well-being, of communal regeneration and the defeat of the nihilistic threat, such as it is. Yet, as analytical frames they are reductive, and misleadingly so. Response to racism requires, minimally, not that my neighbors love me but that they treat me fairly and, as Bill Cosby put it, that they leave me alone. The socioeconomic plight of most black people in America today needs to be addressed not simply in terms of an antinihilistic need for community but, as West himself acknowledges, in terms of radically redistributive measures.

The radical critical voice of Cornel West we have heard over the past decade is still there, but it has been muted. Thus, his appealing identification of morally grounded multiracial alliances and coalition strategies is understressed. Thus, he quietly mentions, without elaborating, the importance of black cultural democracy and transracial relations, of grassroots organization and organic leadership, of public space and resource equality. These are central features of transformation, as too are hybrid postracial identities and pragmatic politics. Indeed, so much does West understress these considerations that he is almost completely silent about the content of these key modes of resistance and transformation. Just as he is virtually silent about the central matter of racialized power, so he says close to nothing about the scope, methods, and content of his prophetic framework;[10] about what antiracist coalition strategies might be effectively adopted; about the moral content of Jewish and black identities that would facilitate their alliance; about the political leadership needed (as opposed to the kind that is not); and most importantly about the ends toward which crossracial alliances and racially transcendent coalitions ought to work. Indeed, was he to stress throughout the radical, and radically antiessentialist, implications of hybridity that he mentions in conclusion, it would likely undermine the essentialist tug of the language West seems compelled, if only for populist reasons, to adopt.

I mention these silences for one gets the overwhelming sense from *Race Matters* that the silences are pregnant with significance. Confronted with a unique opportunity to speak to a very large audience about pressing racial matters all too usually swept aside in public discourse, Cornel West seems moved to adopt a set of terms widely circulating in the public domain even as he has critically rejected the presuppositions on which they are based. Caught between celebration (as of the second coming of the New York intellectuals in Berube 1995; Boynton 1995) and dismissal (by a displaced wannabe in Wieseltier 1995), public intellectuals are made these days by giving in to the dominant's nostalgic dreams or worst nightmares. West's critique is muted here precisely by assuming a framework of analytical concepts tied up intimately with the sort of philosophical liberalism he has criticized in the past, even as he has had the intellectual courage to identify its valuable elements. Thus, *Race Matters* teaches us all too clearly that the truths a public intellectual will speak to power are constrained, if not redirected, by the mediations power places before truth.

Today, when we so need critical public intellectuals, a Sojourner Truth or Frederick Douglass; a John Dewey, Ida B. Wells, or Antonio Gramsci; a W. E. B. DuBois or a Philip Randolph of our time, we create impossible demands: a public figure whose publicness is predicated on selling an impossible number of books, rushing about on speaking engagements literally every other day, and driving an elegant town car to a book cover photo session from the Platonic academy of Princeton (or more recently Harvard) to a rooftop high above the jazz streets of Harlem. That we have to be *told* the rooftop is in Harlem is hardly testimony to the power of the image in our culture, though it highlights a tension faced by West in representation. For the book cover, read against the reiterated fact that the background is Harlem, encapsulates the dilemma of the successful public intellectual in our time: What gets foregrounded against a fading background—the indistinguishable, blurred image of racialized urban blight and the *wealth* of culture to which it is tied historically—is the figure of the public intellectual himself, the accessible persona, the face of a media star. Most observers recognize him without knowing what it is he stands for, or against (see Reed 1995), without any understanding of the problematic he is trying, in terms not quite his own because he has been divorced from those, to call our attention to and about which he often has interesting, complex, and challenging things to say.

Cornel West owes us nothing. What he owes himself only he can determine. So I do not want to add my voice to those who say that Cornel West owes us a more sustained critical analysis of matters racial. But in trying to gauge whether we should head West at the urgings of this most informed of public intellectuals, it would be welcome help.[11]

BETWEEN BLACKS AND JEWS

7

Commentary on black-Jewish relations in America has tended to ignore the deep structural changes that have reordered the society in the second half of this century. These changes form the backdrop to the tensions that have become obvious recently. I discussed in my introduction the dramatic shifts in class formation over the last forty years. These shifts have been accompanied by changes in the positions, prevailing representations, and perceptions of blacks and Jews. I turn now to examine the increasing tensions between black and Jewish Americans against the backdrop of such structural shifts and in light of the ideological divides currently marking these quintessentially American groups.

Jews in the post-World War II period have moved largely from working and petit-bourgeois to middle-class and upper-middle-class status, a trajectory recent Jewish immigrants from Russia are likely to follow. The prevailing public perception of Jews, however, is that they have come to occupy positions of power and political control. The evidence is considered obvious. Jews in President Clinton's first administration, for instance, held all five leadership appointments in government concerned with economic well-being: Greenspan, Reich, Rivlin, Rubin, and Kantor. Leadership in the Department of Commerce, interestingly, was held by Ron Brown until his untimely death.

African Americans, assisted somewhat by the mixed legacy of affirmative action, have made it into the middle class in increasing percentages (now roughly one-third of black Americans) just as the middle class has undergone economic constraint. At the same time, the erosion of the working class into real poverty has effected disproportionately those characterized generically as nonwhites. One indication of this is that among the top eighteen most industrialized states in the West, the United States suffers the widest gap between rich and poor; only in Israel and in Ireland, where social services for the poor are much better, are children poorer. Nearly half of black American children now live in poverty. In the public mind of America, "black" and "underclass" have tended to become synonymous. Approximately a third of black Americans fall into the category of the truly poor, with black children particularly at risk. Affirmative action no doubt has assisted some blacks in securing access to middle-class benefits. Simultaneously, though, it has been invoked to rationalize abandonment of the truly needy: "If affirmative action has not helped you to get ahead, there's nothing more this society can do for you." Indeed, such arguments go, even that route to social access or security will be closed down in the name of race neutrality and color-blindness!

So, for Jews generally it has been a short, if bumpy, ride from Ellis Island to the America Medical Association, the American Bar Association, and Wall Street, perhaps but two generations long.

America has delivered on its billing as a promised land. For blacks it has been an endless and incomplete cliff side roller coaster through body-strewn landscapes from 1865 through 1964, and from 1965 to the checkerboard present. The landscape is littered with broken and half-kept promises.

The increasingly antagonistic relations between blacks and Jews now prevailing are in considerable part class-aligned. African Americans are the one group in the United States among whom the expression of anti-Semitism seems to have increased. This phenomenon is far from universal among blacks, and where it does occur it is education- and class-related. It is most notable among those with high school and perhaps some college education—the marginally or wishfully middle class, and especially and most visibly among activists who purport to represent this class. Anti-Semitic expression, the sort promoted by Nation of Islam representatives, resonates among poorer blacks in articulating Jews as exploiters of black powerlessness, as the cause of poor black plight—as absentee slumlords, exploiting bosses, appropriators of black talent. Middle-class black anti-Semitism among professionals and on campuses sees Jews as blocking black advancement—lording their power (in terms of executive, professional, or academic positions and academic capital) over blacks, self-consciously and self-interestedly resisting affirmative action.

By contrast, antiblack sentiment among many Jews has to do with faded Jewish engagement with less advantaged African Americans, commensurate with dominant class-defined Jewish interests. Middle-class to upper-middle-class Jews and lower-middle-class and poor black people tend to have little to do with each other: they live apart, work apart, pray and play apart, and die apart. Crown Heights, often held up as a place where blacks and Jews clash, is hardly a microcosm of African American–Jewish relations in America, for black residents of Crown Heights tend to be recent immigrants and Hasidim are not representative of

Jewish America in attitude, action, profession, dress, custom, or religious practice. Blacks tend to live within city limits, Jews now beyond them. These distances attest to the difficulty of generalizing about group relations, for the groups are more fractured and less homogenous—more internally diverse—than stereotyping acknowledges. Also, generalization is made more difficult by acknowledging that there are Jews who are black, African Americans who are Jewish.

The broad class distinctions between blacks and Jews, together with the associated perceptions and the sorts of intersections they promote (or restrict), have implications for prevailing representations of each other. In black anti-Semitism, "the Jew" comes to stand metaphorically for the figure of the capitalist, of capitalism, of prevailing social power ("the Man," Hollywood moguls, absentee movers and shakers), indeed, of whiteness itself. To risk overenlarging this point, there is an analogy to be drawn here with Marx's "On the Jewish Question," in which the Jew is identified metaphorically with generic religion and accordingly as the alienated figure of capitalism, just as modernist writers like Joyce, Pound, and Eliot invoked the figure of "the Jew" in their writing as the emblem of exile (Gluzman 1996). Jews are perceived and now mainly perceive themselves as white (a perception that grew notably out of their postwar identification as European and coterminously with their class elevation). African Americans who are Jewish by matrilineal line or conversion are viewed as black, as Jewish anomalies, as are the Falasha in Israel. Sammy Davis Jr. was hardly recognized as Jewish at all, while Rube Goldberg is presumed Jewish because of his paternal name. The power of the proper name is superseded or cemented by the cultural dominance of skin color.

Blacks accordingly are no longer positioned in Jews' social imaginary as fellow marginals and outsiders. Rather, Jews today think of blacks (qua black) as the anonymous wretched of the earth (at best to be helped and at worst to be ignored; paternalism or renewed invisibility) and as new competition for education, employment, and real estate (driving prices up, not down—now there's a change!).

Thus, the recent attacks by some visible blacks on Jews have involved a double movement. The attacks offer, first, a critique of whiteness for which the Jew is taken to stand. (This critique has become increasingly prevalent as Jews have assimilated, representing a curious redirection. As Jews become less Jewish by becoming more assimilated, more embedded in capitalist social formation, they are reified as more Jewish, as white capitalists—gold digging, conniving, self- and group-promoting, representative of and foreign to the American way.) Second, and simultaneously, there is an attempt to empty the category "Jew" of its historically fashioned identity content, to be replaced by what Zygmunt Bauman (1989, 45) calls "the metaphysical Jew." Here Farrakhan and followers talk dismissively of "the dirty Jew," "bloodsuckers" engaged in a "gutter religion," so as to be able to assume the mantle, to step inside the category, of "the true Jew," the "Israelites"; namely, to take on the paradigm of an oppressed, suffering, chosen people (see Early 1996).

Against this backdrop, African Americans and Jews (as Laurence Thomas [1995] has argued most forcefully) both claim a premium on historical suffering, perhaps with good reason. But the claim often crowds out acknowledgment of one another's (and others') historical experience. This introspective disposition is tied up with an introverted historical memory. It is hard enough for Jews to get Europeans and Euro-Americans to acknowledge their role in the historical allowance and production of the holocaust, and for African Americans to get white Americans to understand blacks' centrality in American history. Getting white Americans to think about relations between marginals may be expecting too much. But there are real differences in the contemporary experience of blacks and Jews. A Mark Fuhrman making anti-Semitic remarks in the way he made antiblack ones would register as an anomaly; he would be seen as a pathological person unfit for police duty. But, in a deep and disturbing sense, the frightening antiblack remarks he expressed were business as usual. The louder the protestations of the Los Angeles Police Department to the contrary, the more hollow they ring.

Similarly, Michael Lerner may feel oppressed by having to walk through New York department stores at Christmas time, but this is hardly the oppression of black men physically abused on the street or in their cars by the police on or off duty. Certainly, I resent the commodified Christian (and now Jewish) religiosity imposed upon the public sphere come December, though oppressed by this I am not. (The staff of the school I direct organizes a "holiday" bash before the winter break. Up go the tree and Christmas decorations, legitimated by lonely "Happy Hanukkah" banners and Star of David signs hanging to the side. Hardly an observant Jew, I request each year that the icons of Jewish inclusiveness be removed. If we are to violate the divide between church and state, I would rather have it trashed in the name of the still overwhelmingly dominant culture. At least that makes the drive to dominance easier to resist. Welcome to the country of exquisite contradictions.)

Even in cases regarding the public representation and recognition of suffering, competition seems the dominant mode, reflected in the claim by Farrakhan and his followers that blacks are the "true Jews." When the Holocaust Museum first opened in Washington D.C., I was asked by an African-American philosopher-friend why it was that Jews get to have a museum embodying their (at least geographically) distant experience in the nation's capital while African Americans could not expect to establish a museum concerning slavery at the heart of America. It is considerably easier to establish a Disneyesque exhibition of slavery's history in Virginia, replete with live replicas and reenacted genteel peccadilloes, than it is to create a serious history on the Washington Mall. Sociological explanations were ignored; the internecine political economy of museums was hardly compelling testimony. "The meaning of African-American citizenship," writes Gerald Early (1966, 45), "is central to the very meaning of American citizenship ... in a way that Jewish citizenship is not.... The Jew is an important contributor to America, but the black is the co-creator of this place, central to its reality." My friend's question, no, his provocation and distress, then, were about something else—about recognition, social place, historical acknowledgment—about the public face of pain and suffering. And clearly Jews have managed those strings.

Therein lie the threads of an explanation about differences over racial preferences. Jews have viewed race-configured preferences with suspicion because of their historical experiences concerning the abuse of such preferences. These experiences and their collective memory have prompted American Jews to embrace dominant secular principles of liberal universalism and individual merit coupled with a rejection of group-defined social and economic benefits in the public sphere (legally conceived). This embrace of liberal moral and political universalism, in the name of which Jews saw themselves advancing, oftentimes came at the cost of Jewish self-identification, and hence of identity. Or so the story goes.

Jewish commitment to liberal humanism no doubt contributed substantially to Jews' involvement in the Civil Rights Movement at mid-century. This involvement was not fueled only by the liberal embrace, however. Jewish engagement equally had to do with children of the emergent Jewish bourgeoisie being not so distant from their own sense of dismissal, and so more sensitive to—more caring about—the dismissal of those in positions not too dissimilar from themselves. Beyond that, Jewish engagement had to do with the appeal of contemporary black cultural expression, a spirit of freedom and drive for equality (principles that hardly are limited to liberal humanist expression), and the headiness of being engaged in a truly transformative and so meaningful moment. The general Jewish embrace of liberal humanism accordingly is as much the outcome as the cause of their Civil Rights engagement. For African Americans, by contrast, liberal universalism has been experienced as racially tinged, if not racially immersed, and more times than not as a rationalization of their exclusion, a silent "I told you so" offered as legitimation of their manufactured invisibility, their being ignored or overlooked.

Thus, the distinction in class differences and their attendant representations and rationalizations add an element often overlooked in accounting for acknowledged Jewish antagonism to affirmative action. Affirmative action quickly was experienced by Jews, and in particular middle-class and upper-middle-class Jews, as a competitive disadvantage in increasingly competitive domains. If rational choice theory, for all its shortcomings as a cornerstone of liberal theory, can predict at all, it should tell us that, on the basis of short-term and purely economic inputs, Jewish members of the middle class likely would declare affirmative action unacceptable. And so they did. In this, the perceived self-interests of Jews specifically are little different from those of whites generally. In turn, this reinforces the generalization about Jewish whiteness expressed above.

The identity of blacks and Jews, their need for each other, is usually put down to a common history—of slavery, of otherness, of exclusion—but also in this country to political interaction. No doubt this is partly right, but the disanalogies may run as deep as the similarities. I want to add to this some thoughts about the connections and misunderstandings between the two groups. For one, the sense of Jewish enslavement depends on a more distant, more metaphorical experience (through the

Passover reenactment) than African-American slavery. Jews were not removed from their land into slavery in Egypt. The story goes that they voluntarily moved into Egypt, freely choosing to stay, and there enjoyed a relatively appealing existence before being enslaved in a place they had come to know as, if not quite to call, home. African Americans, by contrast, were displaced, captured, and carried across middle passage (the very name coming later to symbolize cultural passing that deepens the divide) by means not of their choosing nor to a land of their choice. So the slavery connection between blacks and Jews is not as clear as some would have, though not as distant either. It might be more instructive to think of the commonality between blacks and Jews, especially but not only in their modern histories, as concerning their migratory experiences, though differently produced: moved on and moving on by a mix of choice and circumstance, othered by their foreignness in kind and culture, settled and unsettled by their communal conditions, talents, and constraints.

The historical memory of both blacks and Jews is related to their long experiences of migration, of the relocations and difficult dislocations attendant to the diasporic experience. African-American migration has consisted largely of movement to and within the United States (with some further movement in the past century or so to Europe and to Africa). This movement, until the early twentieth century, was ordered largely by the legacy of slavery. As the Egyptian story attests, Jews in turn have always moved and settled, even regarding Israel, and settlement has never been much more in the long duration of Jewish history than temporary. (If, *arguendo*, Jews in America were to find themselves, like South African Jews over the past two decades or so, faced with a choice of leaving the United States, I would not be surprised if they followed the example of their Southern African brethren—namely, continue to send money to Israel while immigrating to any other predominantly white, English-speaking country.)

The charge often leveled against American Jews—that they are Jewish and committed to Israel first, while Americans only secondarily—is reflected in the dominant nomenclature of ethnobelonging. Common usage speaks more readily in terms of "American Jews" than of "Jewish Americans," revealing more like American Indians than African Americans, Italian Americans, Asian Americans, Mexican Americans, and so forth. This suggests that Jewishness transcends Americanness, ethnic belonging subsumes national identity rather than the reverse. For a nation-state so mired in patriotism, the merest hint of more basic commitments is insult indeed. The greater the assumption of Americanness, the more it has come with the cost of hiding—in effect, giving up—one's Jewishness in public.

For African Americans, self-doubts about national identification were mobilized externally, prompted by others. Until recently, and still for more than a few, "the whiter the better" (to use a well-worn phrase of the anti-immigration movement in the 1920s) was a synonym for America the beautiful. Actually, the skepticism and self-doubt that are the products of this racist imposition have fueled the fire of separatist alienation, nationalism, and the double-consciousness that DuBois so trenchantly characterized. The terms African *and* American characterize this consciousness and its attendant difficulties differently than that characteristic of a presumptive Jewishness qualified by a sort of second-order American determination.

These considerations promote for both Jews and blacks a paradox of assimilation and separatism, though it manifests differently for each. Because of Israel, ethnic separation is less concern for Jewish Americans than it has been for African Americans. Assimilation has tended to be ethnoracially easier for Jews, qua whiteness, than it has been for blacks. Yet the more successful

Jewish assimilation is in the United States, the more it becomes problematic, for assimilation promotes ethnic dissolution. By contrast, the more blacks seek separation of their cultural and political institutions from white-dominated institutions, the more isolated blacks become, the less access they have to dominant institutions and power, and so the less independent. Critical multiculturalism has sought a way out of these sticky differentiations, seemingly licensed by America's split past, by re-articulating what it means to be "American" (Goldberg 1994; Biale et al. 1996; Gordon and Newfield 1996).

The relation to their respective nationalisms goes a long way in explaining the range of differences between blacks and Jews considered here. The "birth of a nation," by definition, is predicated upon a mode of exclusion. Given that the conceptual histories of "race" and "nation" are so tightly intertwined, and that race has figured so largely in specific conceptions of nationhood, racialized exclusions (i.e., racisms) have been not just a product of nation building but often integral to their conception and possibility. Blacks were excluded from citizenship at the birth of this nation, as in some ways, too, were Jews (by controlling their immigration rather than their participation), though Jews could pass more easily and so assume whiteness. In the birth of Israel, the Jewish nation-state, Jews assumed the position of those able to promote and execute institutionalized exclusions of their own, and these exclusions were configured precisely in racialized terms.

Edward Said is close to the mark, then, in seeing Zionism historically as an extension of European colonialism with Euroracial undercurrents. Witness Theodore Herzl (1904), principal articulator of the early Zionist vision, writing about the Jewish State:

> Supposing His Majesty the Sultan were to give us Palestine, we could in return pledge ourselves to regulate the whole finances of Turkey. We would there form a portion of the rampart of Europe against

Asia, an outpost of civilization as opposed to barbarism. The sanctuaries of Christendom would be safeguarded by assigning to them extra-territorial status.... We should form a guard of honour about these sanctuaries, answering for the fulfilment of this duty with our existence. (96)

Leaving aside the embarrassing presupposition of Jews as natural money managers and guardians of Christian sanctuaries, Zionism emerged as a secular commitment to self-protection and self-determination. Israel became the realization of the late-nineteenth- and twentieth-century Jewish drive for security, a realization made more readily possible in political and economic terms ironically by the holocaust. Israel was established thus both as an extension of European colonialism (a bastion of civilization in the face of Asian barbarism) and a limit to it, Europe's last colony and first postcolonial state, its first postcolonial "success." Again ironically, the Jewish state bears out the prevailing presumption of Jewish difference, of Jewish exceptionalism, at once a Jewish blessing and burden. A Jewish state thus ends the historical condition of Jews' migration, *aliyah* supposedly the last journey, the return "home" (in retrospect, a totally naive and simplistic presumption). It is Israel's "success" that in a sense made possible also the assimilability of Jews in America, the holocaust that perversely led America finally and (almost) completely (and somewhat misleadingly) to see Jews as European and therefore white. That one could be Jewish in relation to the State of Israel meant that one could be white, one could assimilate, in the United States.

Black nationalism before the 1960s, as expressed most clearly in Garvey's Universal Negro Improvement Association, was about black self-development and collective self-determination in the face of oppression and powerlessness through developing independent and racially based separate organizations and institutions. Garvey's (1926) statement of beliefs for UNIA summarizes this spirit:

The Universal Negro Improvement Association advocates the uniting and blending of all Negroes into one strong, healthy race. It is against miscegenation and race suicide.

It believes that the Negro race is as good as any other, and therefore should be proud of itself as others are.

It believes in the purity of the Negro race and the purity of the white race.

It is against rich blacks marrying poor whites.

It is against rich or poor whites taking advantage of Negro women.

It believes in the Fatherhood of God and the Brotherhood of Man.

It believes in the social and political physical separation of all peoples to the extent that they promote their own ideals and civilization, the privilege of trading and doing business with each other. It believes in the promotion of a strong and powerful Negro nation in Africa.

It believes in the rights of all men. (81)

So, black nationalism was invested in a unity underpinned by racial authenticity (Edward Blyden's "black Zionists" and "racial purity"), which produced a racial solidarity with a view to racial and self-liberation. Garveyites like Tony Martin should note that Garvey nowhere demeans Jews, citing Zionism repeatedly as an example for black nationalists to emulate. Black redemption was sought politically through the pursuit of freedom and equality and spiritually by unshackling the mind through autonomous cultural expression. These were combined in a perfectionist program of moral uplift effecting collective black advancement.

Pre-1960s black nationalism, then, turned on notions of self-protection, self-determination, and self-development in the face of the recognition that blacks by definition were not assimilable into white America. Here black nationalism promotes a separatist embrace in the face of prevailing segregationist sensibilities. It was a separatism that in territorial terms, however, was never to have the mainstream material support directed to Jews in the wake of the Shoah even as it had a long history of white ideological endorsement stretching at least from President Lincoln to Pat Buchanan. In any case, the fact of successful black-Jewish coalitions from the 1930s into the 1960s suggests that, for local intra-American concerns, the respective pulls of nationalisms were not so great that blacks and Jews couldn't be engaged in vigorous mutual political projects motivated by coinciding group interests.

By the late 1960s this had begun to change. After 1967, there were newly emergent forms of black and Jewish nationalisms. Julius Lester (1995, 85–86) suggests that black-consciousness and the expansionist Jewish nationalism in the wake of the Six Day War began to compete as nationalisms. Rather than competing nationalisms, I think it better to see this moment as marking the end of alliance or coalition politics. Black and Jewish interests respectively become self-absorbed, turning inward and so away from each other. Blacks become concerned increasingly with economic, political, and cultural visibility, Jews with land settlement; blacks grow culturally self-assertive, Jews increasingly politically and economically influential.

In the wake of these developments, both nationalisms since the 1980s have been assumed and consumed, shaped and framed, increasingly by religious sentiments: American Islamic, on the one hand, ultraconservative orthodoxy on the other. Both ethnoracialized and religiously based nationalisms protect their Chosen through bloodline, weaving a protective web, whether doctrinaire or material, around the mothers of the nation. These world views destine women to give birth to and bring up the next generation of national subjects. Protecting women from the invasion of otherness is not just a preoccupation with sexual competition, but a defense against national disempowerment. These religious frameworks and overlays, these contrasting ideological commitments, have prompted and promoted the growing sense of current competition, threat, and antagonism between blacks and Jews in urban settings, occasionally with deadly consequences—in education, in cultural style, on the streets as, for example, in Crown Heights and at Freddy's in Harlem.

For blacks and Jews the respective nationalist narratives are both backward and forward looking. The most visible component of the retrospective narrative for each is historical suffering. For Jews it runs from the Biblical accounts of wandering—through medieval migration, inquisition, European exclusion, and partial assimilation—to the holocaust. For blacks, it is a story of colonialism, slavery, Jim Crow, and segregation, to the contemporary confines of retroracism. Prospectively, Jews are committed to the freedom represented by the promise of the Promised Land, "Next year in Jerusalem," as the Passover refrain puts it; black nationalism to autonomy through self-direction, "Liberty or Death" and "Africa for the Africans," rather than the "We Shall Overcome" of the Civil Rights Movement.

The retrospective narrative has been thicker for Jews than the prospective one. Jewish nationalism is now predominantly inward and conservationist. Like all nationalisms, it is "for members only," seeking to conserve the already established and what is taken to be historically given. If there is anything like a pan-Jewish movement it exists in relation to support of, and the right of return to, Israel. For black nationalism, the prospective narrative has tended to be thicker than the retrospective one, outward and globally expansive to include under the pan-Africanist umbrella both the mother continent and the diaspora. (Afrocentrism has sought mythically to extend the backward-looking narrative, especially concerning precolonial history.) Black nationalism, then, has been activist rather than conservationist, and activist not so much in relation to Africa as it has been in relation to the emancipation, especially economically and culturally, of African Americans. Afrocentrism accordingly is a peculiarly American expression of black nationalism, even though it has its proponents elsewhere, shifting nationalist articulation from a political movement to a proactive culturalist expression: ideological, epistemological, philosophical.

Thus, blacks and Jews are alike in their respective drives toward self-protection, survival, self-determination, and self-advancement. Their respective understandings and experience of nationalism have pulled in different directions, however. For the one, the pull of nationalism serves as a critique of power; for the other it has served as an instrument for power's retention in relation to Israel. Jewish nationalism, such as it is in the United States is outward looking, to a state already established. Black nationalism in the United States has tended by contrast to function as an idealized limit, a metaphor for or dream of self-determination (I think here of the likes of Derrick Bell's 1992 metaphor of Afrolantis). While there have been obvious moments of exception, the relation of African Americans to Africa as a *place* now is not as one of return, of settlement, but as a place of origin, of initiation. In that sense, it serves as inspirational source, a place around which solidarity in the United States can be mobilized. Israel for Jews provides a sense of psychological security, and an object of political and economic mobilization. Israel is thus the object of local lobbying and direct support campaigns that black Americans likely see as more appropriately directed to needy brothers and sisters at home. This tension has loomed larger as U.S. economic support for Israel has neither stalled nor diminished as educational funding, job training programs, and welfare support in the United States have been decimated. "Africa" for African Americans, by contrast, strikes me as a necessary object of the imagination, a place of dreams, the making of memory, and the remaking of freedom once lost.

Jewish and African Americans are both considerably more heterogenous than dominant social stereotypes recognize. They share some history even as they sometimes face away from each other, and as tenuous relations in the present are filled with tension. But if the white-power nationalism of the Ku Klux Klan or the militias are to have their way we surely face a common future.

I choose nevertheless to close on a lighter, more hopeful note by facing down fervent fascist fantasies with a social imaginary considerably more appealing. I am reminded of a magical video moment in Reginald Hudlin's social satire, *Reggie's Wide World of Soul* (1985). Hasidic Jews and Rastafari blacks in Brooklyn join to establish a new religion worshiping the imagined hybrid god Moishe X. Members of the group dress in black suits and starched white shirts, black fedoras bedecked in rasta striped ribbons. They celebrate their mutual embrace by dancing the *hora* in common clutch on Brooklyn streets to a reggae version of *hava nagilah*. The deflation of stereotypes, through a form of self-effacing and ironical social humor, cuts to the core of both Jewish and African American cultural sensibilities. To recover the ability to laugh with and at each other as both laugh at themselves, would help in solidifying or renewing coalitions working together on mutually beneficial projects. But to do its work, such humor requires a keen sensitivity to the concerns of the other and a critical disposition to one's own demands.

It is this sensitivity that has been all but drowned out, if not altogether lost, to the bellows of Farrakhan and his followers, and the grunts of Jews about *schwarzes*; to the groans and grumblings over affirmative action; to Johnnie Cochran's Nation of Islam bodyguards and Bob Schwartz's acrimonious accusations of anti-Semitism; to Afrocentric claims about Jewish control of the slave trade and Hollywood; to Pat Robertson's claims about the cabal of Jewish bankers controlling global capital markets; and to Michael Levin's, Richard Herrnstein's, and Linda Gottfredson's insupportable claims about inherent black criminality or intellectual inferiority. Lost beneath the clatter are the quiet alliances between blacks and Jews—in Washington, Atlanta, Boston, Los Angeles, and the like—for purposes of communal and urban betterment. Lost, too, is that, in contrast to a Farrakhan, Robertson, or Kahane, there are Jews and blacks alike in positions to effect urban and national policies in ways much more appealing than these noisy, often self-serving bigots.

American culture is in good part black and Jewish. "What white, gentile American," asks Early provocatively (1996, 45), "is not really part Jewish and part black...?" Blacks and Jews, often in collaboration both artistically and commercially, have dominated public cultural expression in America (*pace* the stereotype that the former produce the art and the latter merely collect on it). Sometimes they produce or reify stereotypes of each other, singularly or collaboratively. Think of "Porgy and Bess," but also of the figure of the Jew in Hudlin's *The Great White Hype*. And sometimes, just sometimes, the stereotypes get subverted by the collaboration. Think again of "Porgy and Bess" as hauntingly played by Miles Davis.

As jazz is to the articulation of blackness in twentieth-century culture, so the culture of Talmudic interpretation is to Jewishness historically: a stylistics and a way of being; an improvisation and a conversation; a dialectic that knows no finality, only contingent resting places, even as it is bound loosely by transforming conventions and rules of engagement created in the making. Each requires a training and discipline, though neither is fixed as an academic discipline nor discrete exercise. Each flourishes in the freedom of expression it promotes; and each is identity individuating and identifying even as it is open to promoting transformativity, to the pursuit of possibility and interactive play, and closed to finality. Each then offers the promise of a communitas that is renewable as it is transformable, free and unfixed rather than reified and restricted.

There are different ways of being black, and different ways of being a Jew. Blacks and Jews need to affirm the ways of being black and Jewish that enable and encourage Jews, black people, non-Jews, and nonblacks to flourish, and to do so in relation to and in interaction with each other. Assertive nationalisms restrict rather than promote others' well-being, thus tending to be self-restrictive also.

The denial of Jewish and black influences on American life by those Americans neither black nor Jewish—a denial that is as much a self-denial as it is historically and contemporarily violent—is a denial of one's Americanness. There may be "no black in the Union Jack," but Old Glory drips with the blood and sweat of black folk, and "Stars and Stripes" and "America the Beautiful" reverberate with the sometimes harmonic, sometimes discordant voices of both blacks and Jews. Between blacks and Jews, then, lies, well, America. But absent blacks and Jews in the land of the free and home of the brave, America wouldn't be, well, America either.

A World of Difference:

O. J.'s Jury and Racial Justice

8

In the *State of California v. O. J. Simpson* there were at least two trials, the legal one and the trial of public opinion. Indeed, it was often difficult to distinguish one from the other. At times, the entire drama—from search to warrant for arrest, from chase and arrest to pretrial hearings and jury selection, from the court proceedings to jury deliberations and verdict—seemed orchestrated by and for the sake of public opinion, debate, conversation, whispers, and rumors. It is hard to imagine that it could have been different. Nobody should be found guilty under such conditions. It is remarkable that so many still think otherwise. Remarkable even more so that Simpson's not being found guilty, that his being found not guilty—not quite the same as innocent, mind you—generated such resentment. Though less remarkable (even as it was more remarked) that it prompted such celebration. What was all this about, then?

The proceedings were racialized from their inception. How could one expect otherwise in the United States where a black man, race-ignoring celebrity or not, was accused of the brutal murder of his blond former wife and her young white friend who just happened by at that awful moment? If anyone failed to notice that little transgression of the American way (even at the projected expense of racial self-effacement and social self-aggrandizement), how could one fail to notice the racial competition over the public face of legal teams and jury membership, of media analysis played out publicly in a television series (the trial ran about the average length of one)? J. R. got replaced in the ratings by O. J. And during the commercial break between courtroom antics and postgame verbal diarrhetics, orange juice displaced De Beers diamonds as white America's favorite commodity. The racial story of color-blind justice we've been lured into recounting for ourselves all those years just got turned on its head, if not quite shattered.

Two people were brutally murdered. Nobody should forget that, for it was horrible and nobody denies this. Yet there has not been too much acknowledgment—actually, there is little call for acknowledgment—that young black people get brutally murdered every day. Homicide is the primary cause of the death of black men under thirty. Black men can count themselves lucky to live past the age of twenty-five. Also little noted is that, in the name of domestic service, African-American women have been subjected to rape since arriving in America as plantation slaves. Domestic abuse is abhorrent and O. J. Simpson was a sometimes violent spouse. A good friend and father perhaps, a terrible husband no doubt, if these things so easily can be distinguished. But domestic aggression is not murder, nor absent some causal connection does it amount to proof. If O. J. wasn't quite black in the white public's mind before the murders, how did he so quickly become racialized in that mediated image after them?

Remember the *Time Magazine* cover! Wealth and fame allow one to choose when and how one is presented. But only sometimes.

Did O. J. do it? Criminal trials are not about who did the act in any straightforward commonsense way. They are about whether a person can be found guilty or not for an act violating the criminal code. The code defines both the act's degree of specificity and the different degrees of guilt. This raises the possibility that different legal acts can be committed (or not) by the same physical movements. It also makes it possible that there are different degrees of legal innocence. Some evidence in the trial pointed to the probability that Simpson committed the killings. But was he guilty of the murders? More than a smattering of evidence raised significant skepticism. And reasonable doubt—there was plenty of it—is all the American legal system requires to establish that an accused is not guilty. The prosecution's time line didn't quite add up. The principal evidence—the blood samples—seemed irrecoverably contaminated. Much if not all of the scientific evidence appeared to have been handled in a sloppy and scientifically questionable way. The police department's longstanding and altogether present racism was exposed once again. And then there was Fuhrman, racist fascist and perjuring braggart to boot, the "h" all too often deleted from his name to distance him from the suggestive title of one whose views he seemed ready and willing to emulate.

For once, the goal posts of racial justice seemed not to move. If there is one thing at which O. J. has been brilliant, it is knowing where the goal line is. Once again, the crowds cheered, only this time it wasn't for the man or for his myth but to acknowledge that the myth of modern law had been made to work for those it so often fails. This time the myth of modern law got turned inside out. The myth? That law's empire is neither white nor black but universally applicable and neutral; that justice is (to be) applied equally to all, irrespective of social position or status, identity, and social inheritance. But is it, and was it?

If most whites seemed to think Simpson should have been found guilty, most black people seemed to think he inevitably would be. Between that *should* and *would* lies a world of difference. The world of the law, the experience of it and the attendant reverence for it, is racially marked. Just as the same physical act may produce two distinct and competing legal acts, so "racial law" may produce two different acts, a "white" one and a "black" one—window shopping, for instance, or loitering—the latter considered a crime in the way the former is not. Of course, when the example concerns maintaining law and order contrasted with police abuse, the force of whiteness likely promotes a different view. Welcome to the world where race rules.

The jury (it is common knowledge, though you couldn't tell this from mediated public reaction to the verdict) was not all black. Indeed, the only significant discernible jury homogeneity was its middle-class constitution. This got effaced behind the veil of racial presumption. Poor people probably couldn't afford to be on the jury, even with the promise of a future payoff by way of television deals or book contracts. People with little other means to support their families couldn't eat the hints of contractual promises for nine months. And the absence from the home for a year of a parent in *any* family, Moynihan, Farrakhan, and poverty of culture proponents notwithstanding, may be the difference between survival and breakup, dissolution or death. In this, poor folk are no different from rich. But the wealthy *can* afford their freedom from (or to) jury obligation or burden (as they see fit), from (or to exercise) their civic duty. If "white America"—as mythically totalizing a concept as "black America"—wants a jury in central Los Angeles to represent the racial composition of America at large, moving the trial to Santa Monica, the Malibu Hills, or Simi Valley is hardly going to produce proportionality. Better to rid Los Angeles of apartheid, to make the city less segregated—residentially, commercially, sociopolitically, educationally, and culturally. It's funny how racial proportionality gets to be cherished here by the very folks so threatened by it in contexts (recently close to the hearts of Californians) like voter apportionment, affirmative action, or immigration policy.

Actually, the jury deliberations, or at least what is public knowledge about them, struck me as eminently reasonable. Think about it. The prevailing view in moral, political, and economic theory is that human agents are rational calculators who set out (or ought to, if rational) to maximize their egoistical and atomized self-interest. There are two interests I would have wanted to maximize as a Simpson juror facing deliberations: to get home as quickly as possible and to reach a fair and reasonable verdict as painlessly as possible. Despite Monday morning quarterbacking to the contrary, these interests were not mutually inconsistent or contrary. Actually, postverdict juror interviews indicate that the jury carefully and thoughtfully balanced these interests. Why deliberate longer when it's clear that the strongest case for the prosecution—the only eyewitness—couldn't identify the accused and that the time of sighting didn't quite fit the prosecutorial time line? To assume legal guilt in the face of legally required, reasonable skepticism presupposes prejudging the case (yes, prejudice), and implies that the jury rushed to judgment. In short, because the jury was presumed to be all black, the mob rushed to believe that the jury was irrational. Again! Having satisfied the constraints of the law and the criteria of rationality and reasonableness, surely it was time to go home. Sorry, folks, the jury might have said, it's a wrap; the soap opera is over, another racial drama has been brought to a close. Time for the talking cure to take over, to placate the hangover, to fill the daytime talk shows and nightly newscasts; Oprah meets Larry, Sally Jesse treads on Ted's turf. Good morning, America.

The morning after gave an indication that the multicultural wars we have read so much about in the academy have invaded the law. The law is supposed to be race neutral. As Republican Representative Bill McCollum put it in another context, "The law is color-blind." But almost every black person knows from painful experience that in a racially marked society the law is abidingly color-coded. Historically, law in America is framed by and reinforces racial consideration. By hiding behind black letter law, the law could appear to dispense justice, to be above the fray of racial and cultural politics, when it serves to codify racial experience. If the political economy of the post–World War II military-industrial complex was founded on controlling inflation through largely black unemployment, then the political economy of the prison-industrial complex that has now replaced it is predicated on the presumption of black criminality. McCollum can insist that mandatory sentencing for crack possession but not for powdered cocaine is race-neutral, but 52 percent of crack users are white and 97 percent of convictions are black. These concerns about race and the law predated the Simpson case, and no doubt would have been raised in the political culture in another way had the case never occurred. Nevertheless, the *State of California v. Simpson* provided the hub around which these concerns could become public precisely because the case was so much about race. In that sense, it is a deep misunderstanding to reduce lawyers' considerations of race merely to "playing the race card." The imposition or invocation of race is not a game, the rules of which can be manipulated at will, but the stuff of lived experience and the effects of discriminatory exclusions and racist imposition.

Black men were being asked to take responsibility for their lives and to do so, ironically, under a widespread popular conception of the black family as pathological. Moynihan must feel vindicated. Talk about squaring the circle. Against this, perhaps the unspoken message the Simpson drama conveys more loudly than anything else is that society should live up to *its* responsibility to all its citizens. This is the age of "revolutionary" budget cuts, antigovernment (read: antiwelfare state) sentiment, and the facade of raceless legal correctness. In this context, the Simpson trial reaffirmed the abiding necessity for equal treatment before the law so that those without capital aren't the only ones to get punished. It calls out for juries that reflect communities and for laws against discrimination, especially by those in positions of power. It demands that citizens' boards, constituted by a cross-section of the community, oversee the police; it calls for protection against domestic abuse in all its expressions; and it urges media reexamination of its stereotypes and racialized projections. By contrast, the sad saga of O. J. Simpson's life, which continues to be mediated by talk shows, tabloids, and current affairs programs, not to mention civil proceedings pressed by the families of the victims insisting on his guilt, pales in insignificance.

CRIME AND PREFERENCE IN THE

MULTICULTURAL CITY

9

In the increasingly paranoid moment that closes not just a century but a millennium, crime and preferences have come to consume the consciousness of postmodernizing (urban) America as much as crime and punishment a century past occupied the mind of modernizing Russia.

Crime and preferences are connected through the common medium of race. The current concern over crime and preferences—the latter racialized by conception, the former by social formation and ideological projection—can be understood only against the background changes in political economy I noted in my introduction. These include shifts from accumulation through fixed production sites to flexible modes of accumulation, from national to transnational (and increasingly mobile) capitals, from intranational to international competition (not only for products but also for production sites), from high-wage employment in the economies of the North and West to desperately low-wage ones in the South and East, from a manufacturing economy to a service economy in the United States, from national cities to global financial centers, and from public welfare states to deregulated trade zones.

Escalating in the United States since Ronald Reagan took office in 1980, these shifts have marked especially the lived environments that are our cities, those pressed and pressured spaces where lives are thrown together—in the subway or on the street, in an elevator or on the bus, at the movies or at a ball game (if you can afford to be there), in the museum or at the mall, at the arcade or on the plaza. Cities are defined by the public spaces they make available, and it is these civic spaces that reveal the character and culture of the people inhabiting them. Such spaces make us visible to each other. Where once the public spaces were libraries, parks, even street corners, now they are increasingly privatized: malls, stadia, theme parks, model housing developments, golf courses, skating rinks, and tourist seaports. Thus, such spaces render visible those who find the means to be present and render invisible those who don't.

Questions of race (as culture and character) have marked this country in and from its founding moment. Nevertheless, such questions have become most visibly pressing in contemporary urban contexts. For cities—as intersecting points of attraction and dispersion—mobilize heterogeneity and hybridity. Indeed, a doctrine of segregation emerged (it was seen as necessary to reinstitute racist hegemony) only after urbanization took off in the wake of abolition and through Reconstruction. Far from being "natural" in either a racial or an urban sense, segregation had to be viciously imposed as the artifact of a drive to establish and to maintain homogeneity in the face of an always historically emergent heterogeneity. Once instituted in the historical cloth of a society, segregation could be left to reproduce spatially and

RACIAL SUBJECTS

institutionally through the informalities of privatized and de-regulated "preferences," choices structured in and by racializing dominance, one so well established as no longer to necessitate its legislation.

Throughout its history, then, the American body politic has split on the question of race. On the one hand, we say that we would like race to go away. We have grown used to thinking of ourselves as color-blind, a society that does not judge people by racial membership but by individual qualities, characteristics, and virtues. On the other hand, we are still, as we always have been, a society deeply divided by the six degrees of racial separation, a society in and to which race matters. As invisible as we may want to insist the color line is (or at least should be), it still marks us indelibly as a society distinguished in black and white. As I demonstrate in my "Taking Stock" chapter, the racial categories in the census may have changed over this past century, but the changes are deeply revealing. At the beginning and for roughly the first half of this century, people were marked as black and white according to the "one-drop rule"; as the century closes, we are asked, consistent with the emergent ideology of regularized and privatized deregulation, to mark ourselves according to how we self-identify. But we are still asked to mark ourselves in colors that color no human being.

Underlying the assumption of social homogeneity (whether the terms of specification purport to be natural, racial, or ethnic) is an image of community that is static. Fixed claims are made to a land, a place, or a space—a country, countryside, city, or neighborhood—and to their political, economic, and cultural expressions. These claims are couched in terms of origination or initiation: "Our origins can be traced to this common point and that's why we're homogeneous; this is what we've created and want to protect because it has value."

Actually, at least for the past century—witness the racializing of the figure of Jack the Ripper in East London in the 1880s (Gilman 1990)—the presumption of a fixed, static, and closed homogenous community has supported moral panics around criminality. Crime has been perceived as an invasion of alien others in which strange (im)migrant habits undermine "natural" communal homogeneity. This ideological insistence on reinventing an imagined homogenous order by reasserting a closed "communal" homogeneity via the administrative intervention of law and order offers a psychologically reassuring but ineffective response to the "crime crisis." Such claims to homogeneity are either completely ahistorical or only a partial representation of the historical record. Claiming a singular genesis always cuts off memory. What preceded it is either wiped away entirely or put aside as the timelessness of the Primitive Other, at best considered the noble savage in a state of nature, at worst its contemporary tropes, the "urban jungle" and "inner city." "America's Most Wanted" meets Disney's "Adventureland."

It is far more accurate to insist that human engagement is promoted by, as it effects, heterogeneity, not insularity; fluidity, not fixity. The conservative thrust of the appeal to community belies this. A perceptive student brought to my notice the way in which "community" has been invoked in public discourse of late to refer homogeneously to othered racialized groups, as in "the black community." So William Bennett in Congressional hearings on welfare reform persistently referred to inner-city black people in a euphemistic, indeed, paternalistic, way as "our communities." (What expertise besides self-proclaimed moral authority gives Bennett, dictator of the virtues, the right to speak about welfare is beyond me.)

It is the denial of heterogeneity, and the insistence on identifiable and excludable difference, which magnifies the fabricated crises concerning racial crime and preferences. I want now to discuss these issues against the background I have just painted.

BLACK CRIME, WHITE JUSTICE

From 1971 to 1994, the number of people in federal and in state prisons rose from just under two hundred thousand to just over one million. From 1978 to the present, the number of local jail inmates rose from roughly 150,000 to almost 500,000. Interestingly, the percentage of federal prisoners characterized as black (33.8 percent) is significantly smaller than state or local jail prisoners so characterized (both roughly 47 percent). For those marked "Hispanic," the federal inmate population rate is just about double that of state and local rates. Since only two-thirds of federal prisoners are U.S. citizens, and noncitizen federal inmates are overwhelmingly not white, the percentage of African-American citizens in federal prisons is likely to be even smaller (and similarly for "Hispanic" citizens). These trends are supported by the types of crimes for which African Americans are most arrested: four are victimless crimes (disorderly conduct, drunkenness, drug abuse violations, driving under the influence), together totalling over 40 percent of the principal arrests of black people. (Over 70 percent of crimes for which African Americans are arrested can be characterized as less serious, Part II offenses according to the Uniform Crime Reports, the standard police-based crime reporting system in the United States.)

The prevailing public profile of the violent black offender is manufactured by collapsing the image of a distinctly small minority of violent black offenders with the presumption that runs deep in racist culture of naturally violent and oversexed black people. Statistics again contradict the image. Regarding the four most violent categories of crime—murder, rape, robbery, and aggravated assault—blacks are arrested principally for the latter two, and those arrests make up less than 7 percent of total black arrests. Murder and rape, so central to the symbolic public profile of black criminal proclivity, constitute less than 1 percent of criminal arrests of African Americans.

The intersection of race and crime is faced by well-known difficulties of measurement, both generally and specifically regarding rape. First, the decennial census repeatedly undercounts poorer black people, especially young black men, and so the reported proportion of black arrests and convictions relative to population size appears magnified. Second, the dominant social image, emphasized especially by misleading media (and social science) reports and portrayals, is of black perpetrators and white victims, indeed, that black assailants seek out white victims, especially for rape. William Wilbanks (1987), the criminologist most persistently pushing this portrayal, reports that 55.2 percent of black offenders choose white victims (whom, I must ask, does the .2 percent represent here?). Nevertheless, it is now well known that the spatial dynamics of urban environments dictate that most crime is committed close to where people live. So, in racially segregated cities the overwhelming objects of black- and white-perpetrated crimes are African Americans and whites respectively. Besides, statistics from seven large urban areas show that, demographically, a black person is nearly three times as likely to interact with a white person as a white person is to interact with a black person (19 to 1 as compared to just over 7 to 1) (Mann 1993, 32–41). Given these figures, the occurrence of black-on-white crime turns out to be smaller than demographics would lead one to expect.

More specifically, many criminologists argue that data on the rape of white women by black men are inflated, partly because of false or mistaken reports. (The legacy of Emmett Till looms large here, for he was murdered because his whistle to self-control a stutter, as Lucius Outlaw has recounted to me, was misread as an "illicit" pass at a white woman in the Mississippi of the 1950s.) What this points to is the way in which blacks are stereotypically framed criminologically (the ambiguity of which was pursued with occasional brilliance by O. J. Simpson's criminal trial defense team).

Stereotypes frame the perception of criminality both at the "street" level of accusation and at the more formal levels of arrest, processing, and conviction. In Portland, Oregon, for example, Anne Schneider (1981) reveals that victim reports of offenders' racial characteristics jibed with police report characterizations in only a third of the cases, with victims' reports dramatically overestimating the involvement of black suspects. This disposition to frame perception in terms of racial stereotypes is borne out by social psychological testing. Tests show that whites often "see" those engaging in criminal acts as black when the perpetrators are white. Similarly, little is made of the fact that serial murders in the United States tend to be committed by white men, or that the primary perpetrators of the Iran-Contra affair (as of *white*-collar crime more generally) were exclusively white. Meanwhile, the mere accusation by white people of a black person tends to be widely believed, both by the public and by the police (witness Charles Stuart; Jim Anderson who, having murdered his wife, in turn was murdered alongside Jeffrey Dahmer in a Wisconsin prison; and Susan Smith). Indeed, the police disposition to stereotype may go beyond informalities, as illustrated by the fabrication of the "symbolic assailant" or of "drug pusher profiles," both of which are presumed black. This stereotypical framing would account for the differential rates of black incarceration at the federal and local levels, for the stereotypes loom larger and more direct at the local than at the federal levels.

PREFERENCE, PRIVILEGE, AND POLITICS

Racialized stereotypes also cloud judgment in what passes for public debate concerning preferences. The U.S. Census Bureau reports that, between 1979 and 1993, the disparity between blacks' and whites' median income has reduced only slightly;

indeed, median family wealth of African Americans remains substantially what it was in 1969 ($21,550) while white family income ($39,310) has increased by 9 percent in the past twenty-five years. Black men continue to earn but three-quarters of white men, and black women's earnings, 92 percent of white women's in 1979, had actually diminished by 1993. Yet job prospects for college-educated black men improved almost to match those for white men (28 percent of college-educated black men, 30 percent of the latter held full-time executive, administrative, or managerial jobs). Despite these encouraging figures, however, African-American professionals earn only 86 percent of "comparable non-Hispanic white men" ($46,980 to $54,680). Public administration and corporations may have improved their race-related hiring practices, but at least part of the motivation must be that they can get black male professionals on the cheap. Most notably, white men, while only 43 percent of the work force, continue to hold 95 percent of senior management positions.

Moreover, contrary to widespread perceptions, the high school dropout rate among blacks is now only 5 percent (it's 4 percent for whites). Ninety percent of black girls between fifteen and seventeen are childless, as are 76 percent between seventeen and nineteen, and the rate of babies born to unwed black teenagers (80 per 1000) remained virtually unchanged from 1970 through 1990. Across the same period it is the rate of white teenage pregnancy that has increased dramatically (from 7 to 20 per thousand). The claim that there has been a sharp rise in out-of-wedlock African-American births is a function less of increased teenage pregnancies as of a (norm-consistent) declining birthrate among black married couples. Similarly, more than three-quarters of single black mothers hold jobs. Nevertheless, 47 percent of black children in America now live in poverty (compared to 17 percent of white children). The crisis, it seems, is one of moral imagination, the panic one that serves to rationalize, as it prompts, policing the crisis that the political imaginary is invested in reproducing. The actual crisis concerns children in poverty, who are overwhelmingly black.

More directly pertinent to the question of affirmative action is that from 1979 to 1993 the median income for men dropped while that for women rose. Median income for white men dropped 10 percent, for black men 8 percent, while it rose by the same percentage for white and black women (10 and 8 percent). In 1994, the annual income of black men working full time remained at 72 percent of non-Hispanic white men's, while black women's full-time annual income remained at 85 percent of non-Hispanic white women's. The cost of university education in the past fifteen years has doubled, even at public universities, while median family income has grown but 5 percent. A household headed by a high school dropout can expect to earn about $28,000 annually, $14,000 less than that of a high school graduate. Family income for college graduates is roughly $73,000, and for professionals $122,000. All this bears directly on a line of argument I now wish to pursue concerning preferential treatment programs.

Affirmative action represents the ambivalence, the two-mindedness, over race I referred to earlier. It does so as well as any contemporary social issue could. Designed to delete the color line by insisting on institutional integration, it presupposes color-consciousness as the means necessary for undoing the social arrangements prompting the necessity for affirmative action in the first place. The dilemma is general. In a race-conscious society, it may be necessary to undo the deleterious effects of race-consciousness by invoking the very racial terms instrumental in producing those effects, thus risking further reification of the problematic terms.

Designed to overcome the deep-seated institutional consequences of two hundred years of racist practice and with a view to promoting heterogeneity, affirmative action is charged now with reinvoking the old terms of exclusion, licensing new racisms and homogeneity, and further dividing the body politic along racial lines. Affirmative action is supposed by its critics to furnish those socially identified as "minorities" with unfair opportunities that whites, particularly white men, are denied, and all because of racial membership. Interest groups in California introduced a ballot proposition to end state-mandated affirmative action. Though two-thirds of Californian voters are thought to support the initiative at least when asked whether they support preferences, the measure passed by a slimmer margin on the 1996 ballot.[1] And where California goes, can the nation be slow to follow? If President Clinton's waffling response is anything to go by, the nation has already followed. Once again, the courts seem intent on leading the charge, only this time in promoting a dehistoricized annulment of affirmative action programs. So the Fifth Circuit recently ruled in *Hopwood v. Texas* that it is unconstitutional for colleges to refer to race at all as a criterion in their admissions programs if race is not demonstrably the cause of ongoing discriminatory exclusions from the institution.

The current slew of reverse discrimination suits proceeds on the assumption that institutional racism is largely a thing of the past, and that institutionally mandated programs of affirmative action extending preferences to classes of minorities are inappropriate responses to the remnants of personal racism. Why, asks Robert Peck—the construction company owner in Colorado who recently sued the federal government in *Adarand v. Pena* over its minority set aside programs—should he have to pay for remedying past discrimination that he purportedly has had no part in perpetuating? Peck's question echoes a sentiment currently being expressed by increasing numbers of white men. But reverse discrimination suits intended to undo, or at least to restrict, affirmative action programs are not the only ones working their way through the courts. There are cases that allege deep-seated, ongoing (though informal) employment discrimination, and provide lots of evidence to support the allegations. In urban centers throughout the country, African Americans as well qualified as their white competitors continue to face three times the latter's difficulty in landing interviews, let alone securing job offers. Similar prospects confront minority subcontractors in the absence of affirmative action programs.

This suggests that (but for the exceptional excesses all social programs suffer: think of procurements by the Pentagon, abusive behavior by IRS agents, the excessive use of chokeholds by police, or farm subsidy abuses by wealthy *non*farming landowners) preferential treatment programs are neither about remedying past discrimination nor about advantaging less well-qualified candidates.[2] Rather, they are about leveling the competitive playing field. After all, preferences are invoked as the principles for offsetting past (dis)advantages of monopolistic corporate practices, as in a recent court ruling against Microsoft; quotas are employed without fuss in trade agreements with Japan; and according to recent survey data the public appears considerably less exercised about gender-relevant preferences (roughly 55 percent support) than about race-related ones (only 35 percent).

Actually, white women have been the overwhelming beneficiaries of affirmative action programs. Between 1970 and 1990, the percentage of white male physicians dropped from roughly 88 percent to 65 percent while white women increased from 9 percent to 15 percent, and black Americans, both men and women, increased from 2.2 to 3.5 percent. White male lawyers decreased from 93 to 71 percent while white women lawyers increased from 4.5 to 21 percent, and black men and women from 1.3 to 3.4 percent. White male college faculty dropped 19 percent down to 50 percent of faculty while white women increased by nearly 8 percent to 34 percent of faculty, and blacks by a meager 1.3 percent to 4.8 percent of faculty. White male engineers dropped from 96 to 79 percent of their field while white women increasing from 1.6 to 7 percent and blacks from 1.2 to 3.5 percent. White women now outnumber men in journalism (45 to 44 percent), with black journalists rising from 1 to 5 percent. Interestingly, given prevailing stereotypes around science and technology, white male computer analysts dropped to 59 percent of their field from 82 percent, white women almost doubled to 25 percent, and blacks almost quadrupled to nearly 10 percent. In all cases but in the field of engineering, black women's increases outstripped those of black men's.[3] No doubt part of these changes would have occurred without affirmative action, and the increases are clustered at the lower end of job ranks. Nevertheless, the introduction of preference programs cracked the cycle of white male privilege. This said, these numbers suggest that white men are more determined to keep the workplace white than male.

Lacking affirmative action programs, consider that where the average African-American man has at most three serious job opportunities throughout his full-time working career; a white man potentially has nine. Preferential treatment programs are supposed to increase the potential opportunities of the African American to six or so, while decreasing the white person's to roughly the same number. Whites, and white men in particular, cannot justifiably call foul, for their initial plethora of opportunities has been available because of the unfair advantage (or disadvantage, as the case may be) of employment discrimination. This argument can be summarized thus: in a society where there continues to be a studied absence of "racial (and gender) justice," the lack of preferential treatment programs amounts to a preferential treatment program of sorts—for white men. The figures I cited a moment ago suggest that if affirmative action programs were summarily rendered illegal, the tenuous gains of most middle-class African Americans are likely to disappear, or at least the opportunities licensed by affirmative action will be unavailable to present and future generations.

Now those who, like William Bennett, have libertarian leanings on economic issues, though they are decidedly antilibertarian on social issues, may deny the moral force of "opportunities" here. Opportunities, for them, carry no moral imperative; they are just something you have or don't, the cards the world happens to deal you. If the cards are bad, even the product of a deck that in some former time was doctored, no moral responsibility is incumbent upon present beneficiaries of that doctored deck to introduce a full pack. The only recourse for those with bad cards is to get better at manipulating the existing cards. Hence the attack over the past decade or so on the principle of equal opportunity. Of course, remove the commitment to equal opportunity and contemporary discrimination will pile rapidly upon historical discrimination. Libertarian largesse is simply a smoke screen for a status quo dominated by white men.

White men, nevertheless, are crying foul, and in large numbers. Affirmative action is being cast by them as the culprit. Are there any ways to proceed that neither presume the endless justifiability of affirmative action programs nor the self-righteous indignation of their projected curse? Can a compromise of sorts be struck?

Perhaps. Proponents of affirmative action may propose clear, reasonable, and foreseeable limits on the program's applicability and justifiability. Accordingly, they may accept the dissolution of such programs, on a case by case basis, once it can be demonstrated reasonably and to widespread and mutual satisfaction that the potential beneficiaries in the particular case at hand (an industry, government agency, school district) no longer do or will suffer discrimination in education admissions and competition, hiring, promotions, and contract procurement. Here, critics of affirmative action would have to

demonstrate beyond a reasonable doubt that potential beneficiaries of the programs face no more egregious discrimination—in
schooling, in getting jobs or government contracts, in getting
ahead, and so on. Sometimes this may be demonstrable, but as a
general social phenomenon, widespread indicators continue to
suggest widespread discrimination. Public schools remain largely
segregated, with schools attended by blacks savagely under-
funded in comparison with those attended by whites (Kozol
1991);[4] the rate of black unemployment remains double that of
the general rate of unemployment; institutions like the Alabama
State Police and Fire Department (not to mention many colleges
and universities) still have few black employees in executive
positions. The figures I cited above indicate that the gains
achieved in some quarters (with the assistance of affirmative
action programs, it must be insisted) remain tenuous and are
likely to evaporate if those programs are now outlawed without
de facto and institutionalized guarantees of discrimination's
demise.

Until there is a reversal concerning these sorts of indicators,
criticism may be directed more effectively at the sources of
discrimination than at affirmative action. The misrepresentations
of *The Bell Curve* notwithstanding, it is not the lack of a potential
pool of well-qualified and competitive African-American candidates that is the issue. A presumptive indicator that affirmative
action programs are increasingly unnecessary would lie in finding African Americans (and other groups historically discriminated against) securing educational and professional positions
within a standard deviation of their numbers in the population.

Thus, for those proponents who refuse to accept the challenge—if affirmative action is fairly and clearly stated, if the
criteria of proof are generally agreeable, and if there is a sliding-
class component to the program—affirmative action seems to
function as a form of political pork. And political pork, these days,

quite rightly, is no longer politically kosher. But the failure of critics to accept the challenge indicates that affirmative action is to economic considerations what Willie Horton was to crime—namely, a commitment to playing the race card only in a cynical political game (as though that card is not already in play). Giving up on affirmative action may not be giving up on discrimination, as its critics proclaim; rather it may be giving *in* once more to the silent forms of racism that have marked us far too long.

CRIME AND PREFERENCE

To conclude, a little noticed justification for (and the perceived threat of) affirmative action is its part in generating or facilitating the development of multicultural institutional heterogeneity. By contrast, the moral panics over crime (in just the sense that Stuart Hall and his coauthors mention in their wonderful book [1978]) serve to institutionalize (by assuming) homogeneity, to reify racial divides (by presupposing them), and to oversee the transformation of the military–industrial complex into a policed society, the urban space of America into law and order grids rather than into the vibrant interactive heterogenous publics that our cities hold out as possibilities for us.

In the face of the common observation that for every white and male racist and sexist there is a black and female one, it should be stressed that white, (especially upper) middle-class, middle-aged, nondisabled, and heterosexual men continue to be better placed to assume authority in the city. Because of the legacy of privileges and power they and their forebears have enjoyed, they can assume authority more readily than anyone else can. Look at most urban, university, institutional, or large corporate administrations nationwide, though it is not quite so stark now as it once was. Men, and white men in particular, are brought up to be at ease with such positions of authority, socialized and eased into them, acquiring and assuming authority's institutional positionality, voice, and tone. They are more practiced at social expression and persuasion, tend materially to be more privileged and more confident, and they have a history of institutional backing.

It is because the multicultural movement at its best has sought to challenge this collusive, all but monopolistic hold on the reins of power that it has been subjected to such a vicious counter-reformation. (This is not to deny that there are reasonable criticisms that may be directed against some of what flies under the title of the multicultural, see Goldberg [1994].) Multicultural heterogeneity is committed to making opportunities more amenable and accessible to all. It undertakes to promote procedural fairness, but it is concerned to problematize the univocal by multiplying both quantities and kinds of inputs. So multicultural heterogeneity is committed to airing the needs and interests of all the city's constituents related to administrative governance and service provisions, including those concerning security, the structure of opportunities, and investment. Thus, it politicizes explicitly what is otherwise silent and without acknowledgment (that is, what gets denied as political in the name of universal value). It renders explicit the contestation over values and entitlements. Making overtly political what is implicitly so reduces the possibility of manipulation and control as well as the maintenance of the status quo, though it obviously unsettles the (relatively) privileged and powerful (Goldberg 1994, 32; Young 1990, 184–86).

Concerning the practical issues at hand, then, economic restructuring seems to render cities and states readier these days to raise local taxes to fund stadia and prisons than schools. It was once popularly thought that a town grew into a city only upon completion of a cathedral; now "city-dom" is conferred in the public image only upon completion of a major stadium/arena, the imagined return of Rome. The political economy of stadia is not straightforward, however. The argument most often invoked in their behalf is that long-term benefits trickle down through the economy to benefit stadium consumers and nonconsumers alike. But the results are actually mixed, and stadium-related employment tends to be seasonal, service-related, low-wage, and requiring little education.

By contrast, the political economies of prisons entail that, however many and large, they necessarily fill. And so they do. Indeed, prisons in the post military–industrial complexion of social life have replaced military bases of the modern(ist) complex. Again, no need for education.[5] Of course, equal access to quality education is no absolute guarantee that crime will recede. After all, if we follow the curved logic of those for whom *The Bell Curve* tolls, it should either substitute white-collar crime for the violent variety or, more "predictably," render white-collar crime more violent and, supposedly, black.

While I am not much one for wagers, especially of the Pascalian kind, this is one I'll bet on: a vigorous social commitment to more equal educational environment, resource distribution, and access will foreclose the need for both affirmative action and more prisons. Most crime is committed by (or at least most convictions are of) high school graduates or those who failed to complete their schooling. (Criminal intentions perhaps do not occur quite so readily to those with less than an eighth-grade education; and the college-educated seem too self-conscious to commit crime or too well connected to get caught or convicted when they do.) Crime and preferences are linked together as common technologies of racial administration, bureaucracies of racialized state control, at each end of the spectrum of opportunity and access to an American dream, the racial standards for which have been defined always by white power.

Affirmative action programs emerged to redress the institutionalization of differences in educational resources. In a crucial sense, however, preferential treatment programs were established due to a deep lack of resolve in implementing *Brown v. Board*'s "with all deliberate speed" (it is more accurate to say that *the lack of speed was deliberate*). This lack of resolve has a long legacy. Writing in *My Southern Home* in 1880, William Wells Brown noted the pitiful state of public schooling for blacks. It follows, then, that there is a sense in which affirmative action serves as a substitute for—a rationalization of—the absence of a sociopolitical commitment to equal education resources. Against this background, it is unsurprising that affirmative action has had the partial effect, in some ways inadvertent and in other ways careless, of extending informally the modes of segregation previously formalized. Affirmative action is a bridge over which black people are forced to pass (and I invoke "passing" here with all the loaded connotations the concept historically carries). The value of preferential treatment programs accordingly is that they create opportunities otherwise unavailable; their disvalue is that they squeeze African Americans into the scales and standards of whiteness. By extension, affirmative action is linked perversely in the (white-washed) public mind as inversely correlated with the racialized image of crime: "If you can't make it with the help of affirmative action, there's nothing more to be done to help—so prison time is likely all you'll get." The not so silently racialized "you" here—a more cynical substitute for "our communities"—refers straightforwardly to those for whom affirmative action is irrelevant. If it's true that the poorly educated commit fewer crimes, Republicans may be looking to resolve the "crime crisis" by de-educating the population. Democrats are, similarly, none too bothered. Or so it seems. By contrast, if we are to fashion just and vigorously heterogenous multicultural urban ecologies, the wager on equalizing educational environments and resources is one we cannot afford to pass up—or to lose.

WEDDED TO DIXIE: DINESH D'SOUZA

AND THE NEW SEGREGATIONISM *

When asked to review *The End of Racism* (1995), I jumped at the opportunity. I'd read excerpts from the book, disembodied quotes in the popular press, and chapters published by D'Souza as articles in semi-serious fora; I'd read with curiosity the outrage expressed at D'Souza's claims by the same black neoconservatives he cites approvingly in the book; and I'd read reviews by the liberal reviewers attacked by the author who seemed to be treating the book gingerly. From all of this I gained the sense that *The End of Racism* was an extreme and contorted work that was extended too much license by those who should know better. The question I felt compelled to address was why. Why was it that a book purporting to be scholarly but that

---

* All responsibility for the force of opinion expressed in this essay should be directed to Dinesh D'Souza. All parenthetical page numbers in the text are references to D'Souza (1995).

flouted the most basic tenets of serious scholarship was granted so much credit by serious scholars and policy analysts? It was this question, rather than another book by D'Souza being provocative for its own sake, that called for critical engagement.

D'Souza's written work is almost invariably extreme. He nevertheless drapes himself in the mantle of reason and moderation because he articulates a line on race—on blacks and whites—that prevails widely in the United States among politicians, throughout the media, and in daily life. His view reflects the prevailing and the dominant view. Yet it is a view that must trade necessarily on twisting truth, stereotyping, and gross generalization. It mystifies by imagining a demonizing and demonized Other that needs accordingly to be set apart, isolated, circumscribed and constantly surveilled. In his renewed clarion call to assimilationist commitments, D'Souza thus explicates the widespread social articulation of a "new segregationism," one no longer purely and unambiguously racial but the product of intersecting dynamics of race, class, and (even more silently) gender. Unlike the unambiguous and more or less formalized segregationism of the post-Plessy moment, this mode of checkered segregationism reflects and represents the anxious, ambiguous, and privatizing legacy of the post-Fordist and postindustrial period. Where the "old segregation" was prompted by urbanization, the "new segregation" has been brought on by suburbanization and subdivisional self-enclosures.[1] If Reagan was the new form's political articulation, D'Souza is its racial ideologue (as were Thatcher, Powell, and *The Salisbury Review* in Britain).

In *The End of Racism,* Dinesh D'Souza has written a dangerous book. Its appeal in the marketplace of demand has been in spite of its danger. It is interesting to compare its market experience with that of *The Bell Curve.* Murray and Herrnstein's book achieved best-seller status by surfacing assumptions in American public culture about inherent black inferiority, by making possible—in purporting to legitimate—expression of genetically based racial hierarchies. Having licensed the explication of bigotry, *The Bell Curve* demanded resistance to both its insidious assumptions and its demeaning deterministic implications. This resistance occurred not just in popular and scholarly reviews, though there were plenty, but in two volumes of collective scholarly responses. At least the debate was joined. Not quite so with *The End of Racism*, despite D'Souza seeing himself as appealing to the same market, which represents intellectually a widely held set of political anxieties and commitments. (The books, after all, share the same publisher.) If there is any virtue to *The End of Racism,* it is that it represents the sentiments on race that have done so much over the past decade to sharpen racial polarization, and intensify racial marginalization. D'Souza has laid out, in a partly idiosyncratic way, the assumptions and implications of that arrogant world view. D'Souza offers a Disney history of racism and a Republican representation of its contemporary realities. That is to say, he denies them both. Or better, he rewrites the history of racism so he can erase reality.

D'Souza's book would be a great deal more dangerous if it weren't so boring. This, perhaps, is the reason it has not fared nearly so well in the marketplace as *The Bell Curve* did. No countervolumes planned here, no broad response. Indeed, my sense is that few, whether supporters or detractors, seemed compelled to read *The End of Racism*. (Even reviewers don't have to read the book, for review copies arrive with a seven-page interview—which appears to be self-executed—in which D'Souza "responds" to the key questions inspired by the book.) The media focused more on the outrageousness of some of D'Souza's claims than on his evidence. Where *The Bell Curve*'s biological determinism offered a fixed target, the very inconsistency of D'Souza's central claims—his elasticity—seemed to offer only a moving one. All the more reason why liberal reviews of his work are so weak.

At 550 pages of text and another 150 pages of footnotes, *The End of Racism* claims to be exhaustive, objective and reasonable, more comprehensive than any competing text.

D'Souza apparently wants to offer a counterreference book to the classic liberal reference books on race (Gosset 1965; Jordan 1968). But unlike the classics, nearly every historical claim by D'Souza is contestable or markedly superficial. There are long pages that inspire only yawns (in contrast to Andrew Hacker whose endorsement adorns the back cover, I had no trouble putting the book down, it was picking it up that I found so insufferable). D'Souza's objectivity is questionable in light of the very political aims he denies he has, and his scholarship is a paradigm of shoddiness. For example, in talking about the emergence of polygenic influence in the early nineteenth century, D'Souza mentions together and without qualification Voltaire, Saint-Simon, and Giordano Bruno (1995). The first is the mid-eighteenth-century philosophical encyclopedist and early polygenist; the latter is the sixteenth-century philosopher-scientist burned at the stake. This not only collapses four centuries into one, but it misconceives the emergence of polygenism.

Further, D'Souza writes that, "In 1920, for the first time, the U.S. Census stopped counting mulattoes, separating American citizens into the stark categories of white and black" (181). As I have shown in chapter three, this is nonsense. From 1790 to 1840, the census counted "whites" and "colored persons," while "mulatto" was introduced first in the 1850 count, disappearing again in 1900 in the wake of the "one-drop rule." In another example, this time of inconsistency rather than one of factual inaccuracy, D'Souza speaks of Edward Long as "a traveler in Jamaica" (62) and later as "of Jamaica" (581). Edward Long, however, was the son of a landowner in Jamaica who had migrated from Scotland, served as a judge on the island, and published the racist apologetic for slavery, *History of Jamaica*. Sloppily the words "of

Jamaica" are lifted without attribution from Winthrop Jordan. While these few examples may be trivial,[2] D'Souza's easy and repeated invocation of such myriad and minute details seems to establish his expertise, his all-knowingness—a "thorough" and "well-informed" researcher, as George Fredrickson (1995, 10) puts it. Appearances notwithstanding, D'Souza is neither. D'Souza may have wanted to write a reference book, but it is unreliable to its roots, unreliable because its real ends are crassly political.

D'Souza projects himself as reasonable, the arbiter of reasonableness: the "nonwhite" immigrant who has examined all the evidence in an unbiased and neutral way to arrive at the most reasonable of conclusions, (a black person when it suits him) so that he "can say things no white boy could." As the only "nonwhite" participant at the "White Preservation" conference organized by the likes of Jared Taylor in Atlanta in 1994, for instance, he "attempted to argue with some of the participants there" (1995, 391), thus establishing his position, quite self-consciously in contrast to extremists, as moderate. His particular views—many insidious and incredible—are projected as representing reasonableness and moderation. Behind this facade, history is rewritten, stereotypical generalizations are established as inescapable truth, and partial representations are imparted as impartial knowledge.

D'Souza's unreasonableness is exemplified in the range of repeated fallacies and logical failures he commits. Examples litter almost every page. I will refer to some throughout my review as evidence of the fraud perpetrated in the name of objectivity and, to demonstrate the skewed and skewered framing of his misrepresentations. But what else might one expect from the editor of the *Dartmouth Review* during its most notoriously inflammatory instantiation in the early 1980s? Or a domestic policy analyst in Reagan's White House whose book was published and advertised through subsidies from the Olin Foundation and the American

Enterprise Institute? I guess the Free Press, in the vanity tradition, is simply living up to its name.

It may help to describe briefly the content of the book's central arguments. D'Souza's driving "vision" is that "liberal antiracism" is "intellectually bankrupt." While he occasionally acknowledges its historical value (demonstrating D'Souza's self-serving resolve to *seem* reasonable), the explicit thrust of his line of argumentation is that "Virtually all the contemporary liberal assumptions about the origin of racism, its historical significance, its contemporary effects, and what to do about them are wrong" (22). Racism was neither the worst thing to happen to people nor now the most urgent problem to be overcome. D'Souza admits racism is a Western idea, but insists that it is a modern and "enlightened" one, rooted in the rational and scientific urge to account for "large differences in civilizational development" (22). Moreover, not only is slavery not an inherently racist or Western institution, but its abolishment can be credited to the Western commitment to end it. Unfortunately, D'Souza continues, liberal antiracist forces in the first half of this century embraced the principle of cultural relativism (by which he means the equality of all cultures) upon which the Civil Rights Movement predicated itself. This "serious problem" disabled Civil Rights leaders like King from seeing that black inequality was due not only to "racial discrimination" but also to "cultural deficiencies" that "inhibited black competitiveness" (22-23). The Civil Rights Movement became a professional class of self-serving bureaucrats and activists elevating only themselves on (largely false) charges of racism against any who would deny them advancement. D'Souza emphasizes that the emergence of "black racism" against those not black has become a problem more serious than white racism. He admits that "rational discrimination" against blacks—discrimination based on group-defined statistical aggregates—still exists, but because it is "rational," he considers such discrimination justifiable. Black racism, by contrast, D'Souza explains as "a rationalization for black failure" (23). He concludes that the basic problem currently facing blacks is not white racism or black genetic deficiency but black cultural pathology. Blacks should cease relying on government, Civil Rights laws should be restricted to the public sphere and should not apply in the private sphere at all, and blacks should acquire the cultural values and habits—the culture—capable of making them "civilized" (22-24).

This summary will serve to frame a series of questions I want to raise about D'Souza's formulation and prevailing "understandings" about race in the United States. These questions concern both conceptual and historical considerations. Conceptually, I focus my discussion on the poverty of D'Souza's understanding and his misconceptions of "race," "racism," and "cultural relativism." Historically, I want to raise questions concerning D'Souza's discussions of slavery, liberalism, the Civil Rights movement, and what he calls "black cultural pathology." I close with a critical discussion of his policy proposals. The key elements of D'Souza's argument accordingly form the ideological and rhetorical components of what I call "the new segregationism." These features include a shrunken understanding of racism and its effects, a fixed understanding of biologically given races, a diminished representation of the effects of American slavery, a commitment to a viciously anti-Civil Rights and antiaffirmative action politics of anxiety and resentment, and a reductionist and simplistic antirelativism.

CONCEPTUAL DEFLATION

On the basis of shrunken understandings of both race and racism, D'Souza narrows the effects of racism, delimiting its nastiness both in historical duration and in depth of experience. He presumes a singular, unchanging form of racism emerging out of the project of scientific racism in the eighteenth and nineteenth centuries and predicated on an unproblematized acceptance of given, biologically conceived races and racial distinction. If racism is no longer as widespread or as strident as it once was, then the new segregation, the outcome of "neutral" and "nonracist" market forces, doesn't face the condemnation the old segregation did.

Running throughout D'Souza's account is the presumption, sometimes explicit, of a fixed conception of race as biological. He writes as though there are unquestionably biological races. "All the members of the various castes [in India] belong to the same race" (31). Races are fixed "gene pools," black and white, and whatever else (478). Though D'Souza argues that the verdict is out on whether biology reproduces the tested differentials in white and black IQ scores, the title of his chapter discussing the subject leaves little doubt that he thinks the obvious argumentative edge is with those who reduce the differences to "The Content of Our Chromosomes" (431–76). So, D'Souza insists, "America can become a multiracial society but not a multicultural society [for] race is not the same as culture" (549). Race may not be reducible to culture, but culture in his view seems racially conceived, if not altogether racially driven.

Where race is reduced to biology, racism is similarly deflated by being tied narrowly to biologically predicated claims of racial distinction: "Racism typically entails a willingness to discriminate based upon a received hierarchy of superior and inferior races." (27) "Racism," accordingly, "requires biological inferiorization" (419). D'Souza identifies four main features of racism: a belief in biologically distinguishable groups or races; the ranking of these races in terms of superiority and inferiority; holding these rankings to be intrinsic or innate; and using these rankings as a basis for discrimination, segregation, or denial of rights to others (28).

I have criticized this conceptualization elsewhere and won't rehearse those arguments here (Goldberg 1993a, 93–96). I should point out only that this conceptualization blinds D'Souza to seeing how "races" are fabricated in the imaginary, how immigrant groups like the Irish or Jews can arrive, and be conceived and treated, as not white or European, and over time acquire the status of whiteness through a combination of class elevation with sociostructural and cultural contrast against blackness. D'Souza's conceptual understanding of "race" is inconsistent. He wants to claim that members of different "tribes" (he lists Protestant and Catholic, English and Irish, Sikh and Hindu, Turk and Armenian) may belong to the same "race" (because they are "of the same skin color"). He concludes from this that, though conceptually distinct, "racism is a subset of tribalism" (34). Presumably racism is a subset of tribalism because "races" supposedly are a subspecies of "tribes." But he has insisted explicitly that "tribes" are subspecies of "races." Clearly it makes little sense to say that they are subspecies of each other (unless they are identical, and then it is redundant).

D'Souza's malicious ignorance here extends to textual interpretation. Thus he repeatedly interprets Darwin's use of "races" as referring to human groups (see, for example, 129) when Darwin's primary reference was to animal subspecies.[3] Indeed, more generally, D'Souza self-consciously reduces Darwin's work to Social Darwinism (128 ff.), blaming Darwin for the inaccuracies and embarrassments of the latter (124). In contrast to Social Darwinians, Darwin himself was always ambivalent in using "race" in reference to humans. Indeed, the supporting line D'Souza quotes from George Stocking's terrific account, *Victorian Anthropology* (1987), proves the point. Here Stocking's discussion is about the Darwinism of the late Victorian anthropologists, the last reference in his book to Darwin's own work being at least thirty pages earlier. For Darwin, human races or subspecies are derived by generalizing from morphological traits. Evolution, and by extension natural selection, is not in its implementation group predicated but an individualized process: one does not inherit genes from one's race, but from one's mother and father. In this sense, there is no racial gene pool, black or white, only a human one. D'Souza's deep misconception is exemplified in the implication he wishes to elicit concerning the Darwinian lesson: The central scientific discovery of Darwin's theory of evolution, he writes, "had social implications, because it appeared to suggest that racial groups which did not show the highest traits of civilization could not be expected to acquire and transmit them to their children" (129). This is not the implication Darwin wants drawn, but the Social Darwinian manipulation of his points. For Darwin, the implication is only that those individuals not able to adapt to their environments cannot survive; if all members of the species fail to adapt, the species (or the subspecies where relevant) disappears.

Similarly, D'Souza cites George Stocking to support his claim of the "civilizational superiority" of Europeans. He insists, on the basis of Stocking's supposed authority, that Tasmanian aboriginals (among others) were still caught in the "paleolithic stage" of (un)development at the moment of their European "discovery" (570, fn. 126). Familiar with Stocking's work, I found myself unconvinced and checked the source (1987, 274-83). Even a quick perusal of the (short) chapter, "Epilogue: The Extinction of Paleolithic Man," reveals that Stocking's reference to "the extinction of paleolithic man" is designed to characterize the claim of the Victorian anthropologists—and accordingly their implication in producing the outcome—and so is intended as ironic. As Stocking concludes the chapter, "Not only did the paleolithic equation help to distance the horror of the Tasmanians' extinction; it seemed even to set the seal of anthropological distance upon their fate" (283). Had Dinesh only read beyond the first three pages? I am tempted to paraphrase a line Castro apparently used about Reagan: He was a nineteenth century man, if that's not being unkind to the nineteenth century.

D'Souza's definition of racism fails, by extension, to comprehend the nuances in racism(s), the new forms racism assumes. Thus he fails to distinguish between the individual harms anyone can suffer at the hands of a racist (namely, a person who is racially motivated to commit a harm), whether black or white, and structural or institutional positions people occupy by virtue of ethnoracial belonging. This is the distinction roughly between personal and social power. We need to keep in mind, then—in a way that D'Souza's claims of biology, superiority, and inferiority sometimes openly denies—distinctions between different kinds and levels of racism. Defining racisms in terms rather of racially predicated exclusions, whether intended or ultimately patterned, captures the sorts of nuances and distinctions D'Souza's restrictions elide. Racist institutions, by extension, are those whose formative principles incorporate and whose social functions serve to institute and perpetuate the racist beliefs and acts in question.

D'Souza's (mis)understanding of "institutional racism" actually rests on a formal logical fallacy: "Instead of being guilty of racial discrimination, companies *could simply be* guilty of statistical variance. The charge of institutional racism, in this analysis, *is nothing more* than a mathematical fallacy: blacks are being oppressed by the law of averages" (298, my emphasis). Here, as the emphasized terms indicate, D'Souza is moving from the hypothetical premise ("could be") to actualized conclusion ("is," indeed emphasized by the qualification "nothing more"). As Hume might have put it, one cannot derive an "is" from a "could be," fact from possibility. That a person could be white doesn't make it so! To think otherwise is to commit a fallacy, is to be confused. I am accusing D'Souza of a category mistake, not engaging here in an ad hominem, though he repeatedly attacks character as a way of dismissing arguments.

From his narrowed definition of racism D'Souza argues that "assimilation even of the forced march variety, can hardly be construed as racist, especially when their [*sic*] manifest purpose was inclusion rather than exclusion, and when many of their objectives were shared by the new immigrants themselves" (139). For one, this erases the forced assimilation of American Indians, which after all was U.S. governmental policy from the 1880s to the 1930s, and the presumptive unassimilability throughout much of American history of black people, who after all were not immigrants. Nevertheless, even with regard to immigrants, D'Souza's lack of historical knowledge and insight is both staggering and yet completely consonant with prevailing social sentiment. Despite the official line, not all immigrants were always welcomed. Indeed, their acceptability and assimilability were directly related to their ascribed group status in the hierarchical chain of racial being. Whether "the great experiment in democracy called America," as Cornel West has put it, inclusively assimilated an immigrant group's members depended directly (and implicitly still does) upon the understanding of their (changing) racial belonging (witness the different treatment Haitian and Russian immigrants have received recently). D'Souza seems unaware that in the nineteenth and early twentieth centuries American governmentality viewed poor immigrants from Eastern and Southern Europe, those who were Jews and Japanese, Chicanos and Chinese, as racially "nonwhite," thus nonassimilable, and at the extreme legally excludable: recall the 1924 Immigration Restriction Act. In any case, coerced inclusion of racially defined Others into a fixed set of constraints and values closed to negotiated transformation hardly fails to be racist even if the racial group is culturally rather than biologically conceived, and especially where racial superiority or inferiority is presupposed.

As we'll see, D'Souza's own views concerning "black cultural pathology" and "civilizational inferiority" thus cannot escape the charge of racism by definitional sleight of design. To end racism, D'Souza would have us reaffirm the existence of biologically differentiated races even as he calls for color blindness when it suits him, a paradox indeed.

FABRICATING HISTORY

The appeal of the new segregation lies in the rhetoric of "new segregationism," the central component of which is a rewriting of the history of racism, and in particular of African Americans, in the United States. D'Souza projects a comprehensive but unconvincing historical reframing in this regard.

Racism's Origins

One might live begrudgingly with D'Souza's brief history of premodern peoples. The account he offers is dull, neither particularly insightful nor particularly knowledgeable. His tone of studious neutrality, however, shifts dramatically once he turns to modernity and European domination. From page 47 on, the West—and Europeans in particular—is elevated as civilized and technologically advanced (48); everybody else is debased. Africa in particular is taken to have no history of art or culture worthy of mention. (Over)generalizations hide counterinstances. Fanon (1968, 92) writes cuttingly that "The white man was wrong. I was not a primitive, not even a half-man, I belonged to a race that had already been working in gold and silver two thousand years ago." By contrast, D'Souza takes European advancement to have "generated rising standards of living" (D'Souza 1995, 49), without giving any indication that it also led to the emiseration both of other Europeans and of people "discovered."

Far from being a product of irrationality, fear, and hatred, racism on D'Souza's view "developed in Europe as a product of Enlightenment, part of a rational and scientific project to understand the world. Racism emerged as a theory of Western civilizational superiority" (27). The "Enlightenment would help to produce Western success, and also Western racism" (51). Thus D'Souza elevates racism from an ideology seeking to legitimate arrogant European expansion(ism) to a justified world view. A product of the Enlightenment, of European civilization, racism is projected as justification of and justified as worldwide European dominance. Racism is borne out as and in the racial superiority of Europe. And it is precisely here that D'Souza's apparent boredom and disengagement give way to disdain and arrogance. The rest, it might be said, is the fabrication of history according to Dinesh—the History of the World, Part III.

In narrowing the notion of racism, D'Souza insists that racism and anti-Semitism are quite distinct (34). This fails to acknowledge that after 1500—that is, after the generic emergence of the concept of race—Jews are often called a race, and a race apart, a fact D'Souza explicitly admits just a few pages later (48). This acknowledgment is especially damning, given his conceptual commitment to biological races, for it concedes the discursive emergence and disappearance of races. Jews are conceived sometimes as a race, sometimes as an ethnic group or religion; and when racially conceived it is unlikely to be on biological grounds (unless those making the claim are self-evidently confused).

Benzion Netanyahu (1995) has argued recently and, I think, convincingly, that racism has its initiating expression historically among Old Catholics in Spain in the 1440s who dismissed the new Catholic *conversos* or *Marranos* as not really Catholic because they were by conception "of Jewish blood." D'Souza cites the case of the Marranos as evidence of the uniqueness of anti-Semitism by insisting that "the Jews ... belonged to the same white race as their oppressors" (1995, 35). This example reveals that he thinks not only that there is such a thing as a "white race," biologically conceived (in all his "thoroughness," he fails to address the now voluminous literature to the contrary), that Jews are "racially" homogeneous (which is as questionable on biological grounds now as it was in the fifteenth century), but also that those who refer to culturally defined groups as races somehow must be mistaken. Consequently, D'Souza must insist that there is a crucial fact about racial definition, that the very concept is not invested at its core with normative imputation. Such a commitment is as deeply misleading as claiming that slavery was not inherently racist, which (as I will turn now to discuss) D'Souza does assert. The Gordian knot tightens.

Slavery

Those who insist that racism's effects are now less widespread and deleterious than antiracists generally claim, begin by denying the depth of slavery's harms, in much the way that contemporary critical attacks on Jews often are supported by holocaust denials. Somehow contemporary dismissals of racially defined Others are licensed by diminishing the seriousness of past wrongs perpetrated against them. Restrict or remove the seriousness of past harm and a politics of redress is delegitimized, while a renewed segregation is rendered easier. Consistent with this logic, D'Souza takes it upon himself to deny that American slavery was primarily a racist institution, an equation he calls "facile" (75).

D'Souza offers three principal arguments to support this denial. First, he insists that there is a long history of enslaving nonblacks. This, of course, is true. Even in America before the late seventeenth century, whites served as indentured servants and slaves. But this point is irrelevant to the claim that post-seventeenth-century slavery in the colonies and states, as elsewhere, was racially predicated and enforced. Second, D'Souza insists that slavery preexisted racism. Again, this is true: slavery dates back more than twenty-five hundred years, while racism is a peculiarly modern phenomenon. Once more, this says nothing about how racism fashioned American slavery. Third, D'Souza argues that blacks and Indians also held slaves. True yet again, and now well known, but it still says nothing about slavery's racisms and the slavery in America that racism helped in large part to produce and shape. Why, if racism was not a centrally determining factor, were there only black slaves in America from the late seventeenth century until abolition?

Changing the terms of D'Souza's argument illustrates how deeply misguided it is, and in revealing ways. The holocaust (or Jewish genocide) was not anti-Semitic (read: racist) because, first, there were genocides of non-Jews before the holocaust (Armenians by Turks, Australian aboriginals by British settlers); second, Jews were not the only ones targeted for death and harm in the holocaust; and third, Jews too were implicated in implementing the holocaust. Only the ignorant and absurdly anti-Semitic would embrace such a line of argument. What this *reductio* reveals, besides D'Souza's ignorance, or manipulative and self-righteous arrogance, is that slavery, like genocides (see Rosenbaum 1996; Thomas 1993), has different, context-specific historical causes. Racism was a defining condition of American slavery. He admits that the holocaust was anti-Semitic, though he denies it was racist (34–35). Denial it is. This denial is bizarre in light, for instance, of *Mein Kampf,* or the work of Alfred Rosenberg (1970), or the language of Third Reich laws, as a visit to the Holocaust Memorial Museum in D'Souza's adopted hometown quickly would reveal.

Now it is true that slavery "is not intrinsically racist" (86). However, D'Souza wants to argue something stronger, namely, that American slavery was not intrinsically racist. While perhaps literally true (there were white slaves, as we've seen, in the early colonies), it is historically misleading, for it denies—as D'Souza seems to want to insinuate for political purposes later—that racism had any part in forming and fashioning American slavery after 1619. Indeed, D'Souza wants to claim that American slavery treated its black slaves relatively benignly: "the American slave *was* treated like property, which is to say, pretty well" (91,

RACIAL SUBJECTS

emphasis in original). Now tell that to Frederick Douglass as foreman Covey's whip struck his back. It is self-evident that not all property is treated "relatively well": punching bags or soccer balls are, well, punched and kicked; mules are made to bear heavy loads; cars, expensive property at that, are often driven into the ground; and more directly and disturbingly analogous, men sometimes beat and rape the women and parents the children they take to be their property.

D'Souza wants to insist that slavery was not racist precisely because he is committed to claiming that slavery was less severe for blacks than commonly acknowledged. Accordingly, he misrepresents Derrick Bell's claim (1992, 12) that "slavery is ... a constant reminder of what white America might do." For D'Souza, Bell here "contends that for blacks, the restoration of slavery is a real possibility" (68). This is not what Bell contends, as evidenced by what D'Souza omits from the sentence he quotes. Here's the full sentence: "Slavery is, *as an example of what white America has done*, a constant reminder of what white America might do" (my emphasis). What Bell means, then, is that the extremities of slavery serve as a constant reminder for blacks that other extreme forms of treatment (lynching, cross-burnings on front lawns, random shootings, police brutality) at the hands of whites are constantly possible, a claim that is hardly contentious. D'Souza's elliptical omission suggests he intentionally misrepresents Bell to suit his own ends, a practice he repeats frequently.

D'Souza is committed to this diminished severity claim because he ultimately wants to link slavery to the recent emergence of what he characterizes as "black cultural pathology." Out of slavery, D'Souza proclaims, with great self-confidence but no evidence, developed a black "culture of irresponsibility": "Slavery as a system can legitimately be blamed for a culture of self-defeating and irresponsible attitudes and behavior among black Americans" (97). He concludes that late-nineteenth and early-twentieth-century white stereotypes of blacks were "partly accurate." D'Souza cites three aspects of the culture of slave resistance that reified into a culture of irresponsibility: first, avoiding, postponing, and minimizing work; second, theft; and third, the valorizing of the character of the "bad nigger" (97–99). Radically overblown stereotypes are not only invoked again, they are reified now as truth via historicist rationalization. Out of this (fabricated) slave character, he continues, there developed a distinctively black culture that internalized and reproduced classic stereotype. D'Souza transforms the stereotypes into cultural rather than biological characteristics, features of "black identity" that therefore are "ethnic" and not "racial."

D'Souza thinks he has magically avoided the charge of racism, for he denies making any biological claim. He admits thus to being ethnocentric; that is to say, he favors his "own" group,[4] which he thinks a universal disposition and so hardly condemnable (100). Nevertheless, D'Souza's evasion is consonant with the contemporary racist who denies the appeal to biological claims about blacks, rationalizing the desire for segregated social experience by appealing to the "reasonable" desire to mix with one's own (ethnic) group, to "protect or promote one's culture," no matter that members of racial or ethnic groups are strangers to each other also.[5] Bigots hiding behind partial historical narratives are still bigots. Even—especially—as they mug you with a charming smile.

D'Souza mobilizes this questionable historical revisionism to ask rhetorically "Who Killed Slavery?" He persists in his skewed rewriting of the record. Most societies have practiced slavery, he declares almost gleefully, but "Western" societies alone sought to abolish it. The "campaign to end slavery" was a peculiarly "Western" one, he says. Thus, if the United States owes black people reparations for slavery, D'Souza's quid pro quo logic would have blacks "owe America for the abolition of slavery" (100).

Whatever he means by "Western," few slave owners, Western or otherwise, freely chose to liberate slaves, though there are some ancient Judaic injunctions for slave sabbaticals and liberation for long service (the fifty-year Jubilee). Abolition was prompted usually by two considerations: economic cost tied to falling productivity in contest with technological innovation; and slave resistance and revolt, aided by some well-meaning and courageous free folk, white and black. Economic incentives were used by the British government, for example, to lessen the blow of abolition for slave owners. British colonial slave owners were paid £20,000,000 at abolition in 1833 while slaves over six were required to serve a four-year period of apprenticeship with their former masters, after which the apprenticeships were to be phased out. The U.S. Civil War was fought first on economic imperatives, and only secondarily on moral ones. Lincoln, for all his moral fiber, wanted to repatriate freed slaves to their African homelands. Here D'Souza commits the sort of overgeneralizing fallacy characteristic throughout his book, and of thinking around race more generally. He projects to an entire continent (Europe) or "race" (whites) or geopolitical region (the West) and their sphere of colonized influence, the often courageous and exceptional commitments (beliefs and practices) of a small number of abolitionists (or antiracists) some of whose views in broader terms anyway were quite often racist (I can think of many figures, ranging from Bartolomeo Las Casas through Abraham Lincoln).

Consistent with these stereotypical sentiments, and though he expresses himself committed to nonracism, D'Souza defends Jefferson's and others' pandering to popular racial stereotypes on the basis of the importance of people's consent to democracy: "To outlaw slavery without the consent of the majority of whites would be to destroy democracy, and thus to destroy the very basis for outlawing slavery" (109). Having earlier insisted that free black slave owners in the South had held up to 10,000 slaves,[6] and on liberalism's insistence that whites and blacks are morally equal, it is curious that D'Souza restricts the parameters of democracy here to *white* consent only. The reason is soon obvious. Like so many others, D'Souza believes the Constitution to be founded on a commitment to a principle of color blindness: "the framers produced a Constitution that nowhere acknowledges the existence of racial distinctions" (109). Nowhere? If the three-fifths clause had no explicit racial reference, that's because it was taken for granted. If everyone at the moment of constitutional founding understood that only blacks were slaves, there was no need to mandate it. A century earlier, in the Constitution of the Carolinas and again in the Instructions to Governor Nicholson of Virginia, in the drafting of which his hand was heavy, John Locke draws the equation explicitly. Besides, in 1787 the Constitution mandated that whites, blacks, Indians, and slaves be counted. And if the reach of the Constitution was originally so color-blind, why was the Fourteenth Amendment deemed necessary? Those blindly committed to color blindness ignore the history of color-consciousness that runs to America's finding and founding moments. Here D'Souza quotes Eugene Genovese approvingly: "If the Constitution had not recognized slavery, the Southern states would never have entered the Union" (109). He thus inadvertently admits what—like so many others for whom he purports to speak—he would deny, namely, that the Union was founded on the backs of black slaves.

The populist dismissal of slavery's destructive effects is tied up with an underlying investment in Lockean libertarianism: property rights in one's body and in the products of one's labor. D'Souza is no exception. He writes: "Despite his own allowances for slavery ... Locke articulated a theory of property rights—'Every

RACIAL SUBJECTS

man has a property in his own person; nobody has any right but to himself; the labor of his body, and the works of his hands are properly his'—that was *flatly inconsistent* with forced servitude" (104, my emphasis). Well, not quite. Slavery cannot be rendered anomalous to Lockean libertarianism by a wave of the historical wand. It is true that in his *First Treatise of Government* Locke denies any grounds for natural slavery. Contrary to Aristotle or the Stoics, slaves are not slaves by nature. But that's not the only available legitimation of slavery. In his *Second Treatise of Government,* Locke begins a line of argument, taken up in a novel way again by Hegel in the master-slave dialectic, in terms of which persons facing death from a victor in a just war may resign themselves freely, and so justifiably, to servitude. One may literally trade death for enslavement, contracting oneself—in a fashion later resisted by Kant—into servitude. Voluntary contracts, even under threat of death, are the very grounds of Locke's and the libertarian's most basic commitments. (Locke thought the slave expeditions of the English Africa Company satisfied the "just war" condition; he also thought it altogether reasonable for the English to exclude blacks from their understanding of humanity.) Hardly at odds with Lockean natural rights theory, modern slavery was rationalized in its terms!

As D'Souza would have it, slavery wasn't so bad, and it certainly wasn't by nature racist; rather than the terrible product of "white culture" and the "sacred" doctrine of natural rights, slavery supposedly produced black cultural pathology. Slavery was ended not by the courageous resistance of those directly subjected to it, who often paid with their lives, but by some abstract and whitewashed entity called "the West." D'Souza finds the "ideology" of cultural relativism underlying what he takes to be liberalism's inflation of racism's wrongs and slavery's racialized effects, viewing such relativism as a putative misrepresentation of moral value that was historically explicated under the influence of Franz Boas.

Cultural Relativism

The cheap dismissal of cultural relativism offers a second constitutive consideration in the rationalizing of the new segregation, informally linking the new segregationism conceptually and historically to the old. D'Souza sees the doctrine of cultural relativism emerging in the post-Reconstruction moment, taking hold of the American intellectual imagination early this century. Cultural relativism, then, is attributed with sustaining the development of black cultural pathology in the figure of the "bad nigger," against work and for theft. D'Souza thus takes the pathological figure of the black criminal, drug addict, abandoning fatherhood, and welfare motherhood to be the internalization by blacks of their slave stereotypes, the public rationalization of the new segregation thus rooted clearly in the old. Cultural relativism is supposed to make possible, by licensing rather than censuring, black pathological culture. Black economic woes, such as they are, then, lie not in the political economy of slavery's legacy and post-Reconstruction racist backlash but in the apparent failure of cultural relativism "just to say no." Social structure is reduced to rabid individualism, the poverty inevitably produced by racialized capitalist political economy to the race-coded pathology of cultural poverty.

For D'Souza, the doctrine of cultural relativism holds that all cultures are equal, no group may be considered inferior or superior, group differences are largely the product of the environment and specifically of unjust discrimination, and all attempts to attribute intrinsic qualities to groups reflect ignorance and hatred. He concludes that the policy commitments flowing necessarily from cultural relativism are "not to civilize the barbarians but to fight racism and discrimination" (117). Later in the book, when blaming cultural relativism for the pitfalls of what he takes to be "black cultural pathology" and liberalism's blindness to it, D'Souza repeatedly summarizes cultural relativism as the assumption that "all cultures are equal" (420, 458, 525). The mantra of cultural relativism is for D'Souza what secular humanism is for the Christian conservative: if only black folk would take into their lives the white man's God and Lockean libertarianism, all would be well in the Republic of Virtue.

D'Souza misconceives the usual sense of "cultural relativism," namely (as the name suggests), that value is relative to culture. To judge that all cultures are equal is to presume a point of view independent of all cultures—the bird's-eye or God's-eye view—from which to make the judgment. Relativism supposes there is no such view—God is dead, Nietzsche declared provocatively over a century ago, and all is thus permissible. Accordingly, there is no transcendental reference point from which the judgment can be made that all cultures are equal. So D'Souza miscomprehends the nature of relativism.

Obviously there are differences between groups. That, after all, is what distinguishes them as groups. For human beings, it is not that the groups somehow are naturally different but that the differences, natural or cultural, have been imputed significance, historically invested with value. So to say that some culture is "functionally superior to others" (538) is to choose a set of values to which significance is imparted and by virtue of which superiority is established.

D'Souza attributes the hold of relativism concerning matters racial to the intellectual influence of Franz Boas and his school.[7] He characterizes the cultural relativist frame of the Boasian school thus: "Cultures that seem on the surface to be hopelessly primitive are in fact enormously sophisticated and complex, no less worthy of admiration than Western culture.... so whites have no cause for civilizational arrogance ... they should accept other cultures and peoples on a plane of equality" (151). D'Souza interprets equality here to mean that those deemed equal operate at the same level of sophistication or productive power according to criteria or measures assumed strictly according to Western norms. But transport D'Souza to the forests of Central Africa or the ice caps of North America and see how well his Dartmouth education serves him.

D'Souza too readily reduces all the theoretical objections he raises against liberalism to cultural relativism. Indeed, he misidentifies multiculturalism as nothing more than the contemporary expression of liberalism, and therefore of cultural relativism, which in turn he reduces simplistically to Afrocentrism (422). While I am not interested in defending liberalism against D'Souza's misguided attack, classical liberalism is resistant (in at least one of its two dominant strains) to relativism. It was Immanuel Kant who first dismissed contingent categories of identity like race as morally irrelevant, thus initiating the theoretical grounds of color blindness. D'Souza rejects as liberal relativist the views of those criticizing white rights groups bent on asserting "the right to defend their own cultural norms" (531). However, this liberal critique of "white rights" rests on the Kantian principle of treating moral equals equally, not on the view that people are physically or intellectually equal. Thus, D'Souza's oversimplifying misreading of cultural relativism is exacerbated by his misrepresentation of liberalism and its political expression in the Civil Rights Movement.

Liberalism and Civil Rights

D'Souza and like-minded conservative critics impute to liberalism the dominant rhetorical meaning of licentiousness, and to cultural relativism the anarchistic (anti)commitment that "anything goes." New segregationists accordingly dismiss the Civil Rights legacy as relativistic liberal promiscuity, encouraging the emergence of race-conscious rather than race-neutral social policies and resulting in the contemporary demise of black America (167). "History shows that the principles of the civil rights movement developed as a direct outgrowth of cultural relativism" (169). If "history shows" anything here, it's certainly not what D'Souza projects: the Civil Rights Movement had many influences and determinants. To dwell purely on its intellectual legacy, the appeal of Civil Rights principles had little to do with relativism but rested on Kantian moral foundations—transcendental, deontological, even religiously justified. SNCC and SCLC were organizations hardly committed to cultural relativism; and I cannot imagine Martin Luther King musing, "Well, in public I'll insist on nonviolence, but while nobody's watching we'll just kick some ass" (to invoke a phrase Ronald Reagan's vice-president did so much to make politically correct).

D'Souza suggests that until the Civil Rights Movement emerged, racists were divided between radicals like the Ku Klux Klan, committed to ridding the United States of blacks, and segregationists committed to *protecting* (179) blacks from radicals' attacks like lynching. D'Souza's historical revisionism reduces the worst of racism, all that calls for resisting, to occurring for thirty years or less, an anomaly of American history. "The heyday of racism, symbolized by the Ku Klux Klan, only began at the end of the nineteenth century ... and was over by the 1920s. Segregation developed not as an expression of this radical racism but in response to it: it represented a compromise on the part of the Southern ruling elite seeking, in part, to *protect* blacks" (170, D'Souza's emphasis).

Think of it, moral-minded segregationists looking out for the interests of blacks: "We've got these crazy Klanners out to do you in, from whom we're going to protect you by setting you apart." D'Souza sees segregationists as moral men trying to assure conditions ("equality") that would enable blacks to reach the natural limits of their arrested development (179). This view suggests D'Souza's longing for a pre-Civil Rights segregated age, where the black poor—along with just about all other blacks—were hidden from view for those not black. So he writes, with more than a hint of nostalgia, "In a sense, segregation subsidized the ghetto, because it kept black doctors, lawyers, teachers, and businessmen in the same community as black criminals, alcoholics, and delinquents" (240). What a golden age!

The experience of lynching is grossly devalued also in this scheme of things: "Until the 1890s lynching had no specific racial application, the majority of people lynched were white." (173). The numbers D'Souza cites, however, don't quite bear this out. Blacks, it is true, became the principal target of the lynch mob *after* 1890; the numbers of blacks and whites lynched in the 1880s were roughly equal. After 1890, the lynching of blacks outstripped that of whites at least fourfold. Nevertheless, where white people were lynched, the object of the violence was always individualized; with blacks, not only was it the individual who was violated, but the act of aggression, of terror, was directed by the projection of its spectacle, its publicness, at all blacks—at blacks as a group through the body of the black person. Whites were lynched as retributive punishment and perhaps as deterrent; blacks were lynched as a perverse projection of (sexual) threat and as an expression of white power. Lynching accordingly *is* linked across time to the Civil Rights Movement, not as its false fuel but as the most extreme reminder—the salient symbol—of racial terror.

The (il)logic of D'Souza's position entails that the Civil Rights Movement literally was an overreaction. If racism and its effects weren't all that bad, if segregation was a form of protection not disadvantage, if blacks largely have themselves rather than racism to blame for their noncompetitiveness, then the Civil Rights Movement went too far. The policy and legal changes it effected exacerbated rather than addressed or resolved the plight of black Americans, dividing the nation still further by elevating some over others on racial grounds rather than protecting and extending the rights of all.

Indeed, D'Souza chides the Civil Rights Movement for elevating the purportedly relativistic philosophical assumptions of W. E. B. DuBois over the nonrelativistic ones of Booker T. Washington (184). "For DuBois, blacks confronted a single and obvious enemy: white racism." For Washington, by contrast, blacks faced two mutually reinforcing ills: "White racism which inferiorized blacks; and black civilizational backwardness, which strengthened white racism, and prevented blacks from making advances even in the restricted orbit of segregation" (186). DuBois supposedly offered a color-conscious response to the ills of black America he was thought to find overwhelming, while Booker T.'s black self-help exhortations were supposedly color-blind: "DuBois rejected Washington's color-blind vision, both as a strategy and as an ideal. Indeed DuBois was an enemy of racism but a believer in race, as both a crucial biological and cultural category" (187, compare with 199).

D'Souza's misreading of DuBois and Washington, as well as his misstatement of the underlying principles motivating the Civil Rights Movement are deeply revealing not just of his biases but of the limits of his range of reference. Thus, he is ignorant of the complexity of DuBois's thinking on race; of the subtleties of DuBois's insights concerning "double-consciousness," which have to do exactly with the tensions at play between race neutrality and color-consciousness; and of DuBois's related critique of capitalist political economy. Moreover, as Farrakhan has made abundantly evident in the Booker T. tradition, self-help necessitates picking out those like oneself in order to help, and so it is anything but color-blind. Washington, after all, agreed to take his meal in the kitchen upon visiting Theodore Roosevelt in the White House.

Having sold their souls to race-consciousness, D'Souza argues that black leaders who emerged in the wake of the Civil Rights Movement established a professional class—a civil rights *establishment* rather than movement (206)—committed less to black advancement than to self-aggrandizement. "Civil rights activists found the color-conscious approach far more profitable for themselves" (233). Committed to promoting equal results for groups rather than equal opportunity for individuals, their key strategy apparently has been to insist on black solidarity. This insistence, D'Souza supposes, is a direct implication of the Civil Rights marriage to cultural relativism (206). Faced by growing black class division between middle-class and "underclass" blacks, what D'Souza identifies as the civil rights establishment (including the NAACP, Urban League, Leadership Conference on Civil Rights, etc.) has resorted to the very principle racists had used to segregate them, namely, the one-drop rule (204-05). D'Souza quotes Julian Bond: "I very much oppose diluting the power and strength of numbers as they affect legal decisions about race in this country" (205).

Here D'Souza's interpretation is perverse. Those like Bond are responding to an understanding of the peculiar and troubling dilemma foisted on blacks by a political status quo that continues to exclude them. They are not endorsing the one-drop rule, implicitly or explicitly. The dilemma is this: at the very moment blacks acquire some economic and political power and status in society, ways are devised to dilute their numbers, to reduce the weight of their lobby. (The movement to introduce a mixed-race category into the next census count can be read in this light.) Color blindness is an invisibilizing strategy in a society that continues, at the very least informally, to be altogether color coded and color conscious.

Citing no evidence, and acknowledging no difficulties facing blacks, D'Souza brazenly insists that "it is not a polemical claim, merely a fact, that there are two standards of civil rights today: one for white males, another for women, blacks and other minorities" (223). The civil rights establishment, he claims, has

RACIAL SUBJECTS

mobilized a whole range of "affirmative action groups ... to act as pressure groups within the private and public spheres. They are formed under the aegis of racial preferences" (231). As examples, D'Souza cites every national black professional association.

D'Souza cannot have it both ways. On the one hand, he wants blacks—especially black leaders—to engage in "the American way." On the other, when blacks do play politics as usual, he picks them out for special chastisement. I am reminded of a recent photograph in the *New York Times* of President Clinton meeting with the heads of the national television networks and cable channels. Among the ten or so men in the photograph (including Michael Ovitz of Disney, Ted Turner of Turner Broadcast Station, Rupert Murdoch of Fox, and so on), all but one (Ben Johnson of Black Entertainment Television) are white. The racialized representation of power in America, and the power to represent, could not be more evident. Now politics in the United States is all about lobbying. What about Jewish organizations like the Anti-Defamation League? Or the Christian Coalition? Or the Moral Majority? Or, for that matter GOPAC; the Heritage Foundation; D'Souza's employer, the American Enterprise Institute; and his patron, the Olin Foundation? Why dump exclusively on African-American organizations for engaging in exactly the sorts of self-help exercises D'Souza identifies as necessary for individual and group self-advancement?

D'Souza resorts all too readily to psychological explanations for the motives of civil rights leaders when social imagination fails him: "civil rights has [*sic*] gone from a specific crusade to a way of life. Many black activists who once came from poor and rural backgrounds have found, upon winning their battles for legal equality, that they do not wish to return to obscurity" (234). D'Souza offers as evidence only the case of William Gibson, former NAACP chair. He notes Gibson's personal excesses at the organization's expense without indicating that both he and Ben

Chavis were consequently ousted from the organization (why is this case any different from that of William Aramony, of United Way infamy?) (235). Lacking any other examples, D'Souza is driven to making up imagined quotes "capturing" what he considers the spirit of the contemporary "civil rights establishment" (235). He resorts to psychologistic reductionism in his reading of a range of texts that seeks to understand complex social, cultural, philosophical, and political arguments in a nuanced, sometimes metaphorical way.[8]

Similarly, D'Souza asserts that the desegregation decision in *Brown v. Board of Education, Topeka, Kansas* was not about integrating schools but simply about removing the legal dictates of segregation. D'Souza mobilizes the rhetoric of reverse discrimination to argue that the post-*Brown* insistence on integration by the civil rights establishment was tantamount to a new form of racial discrimination—against whites (224). He writes: "Desegregation permits racial separation as long as it is *not compelled* by government. Integration, by contrast, is a state-mandated result" (225, my emphasis). Actually, the decision in *Brown* may be read racially. Whites generally seem to have interpreted *Brown* as D'Souza does, namely, as the narrow commitment no longer to mandate segregation by formal legal means. Blacks, by contrast, interpret *Brown* as holding out the reasonable hope of a more formalized commitment to equal treatment and access to equal resources, at least educationally. Unfortunately, shortsighted "white" interests have prevailed, "black" hopes have been dashed. Public schools today face de facto segregation something like the status quo ante. Formalized segregation has been replaced by the informalized, privatized variety extended recently by the charter school, school voucher, and home schooling lobbies.

D'Souza seeks to legitimate these exclusionary trends not just by narrowly drawing the conceptual confines around racism—thus by definition restricting racisms' unjustifiable effects—but by distinguishing between the unacceptability of racism and the acceptability of what he calls "rational discrimination." It is in his discussion of rational discrimination, then, that the grounds of D'Souza's segregationism are most clearly evident.

RATIONAL(IZING) RACISM

D'Souza, recall, defines racism as an ideology of inferiority based on biology. He conceives of racial *discrimination* by contrast as a practice of race-based differentiation. Discrimination can be rational, he thinks, when based on group conduct determined by culture and not on biology (286). "Whites view racial discrimination today as a rational response to black group traits" (246). For evidence of this observation, D'Souza rests heavily on studies claiming that Americans are no longer racist (the studies are ten to twenty years old). He concludes that not only do Americans decline to endorse openly racist views but they "espouse a moral code that is explicitly antiracist" (255). This conclusion hardly follows. Taking care not to say something racist may be a sign of self-protection not a commitment to nonracism. Being antiracist seems to me to require considerably more. D'Souza fails, moreover, to understand the volatility of racisms, the fact that new forms may emerge, and old ones may reemerge, (long) after they may seem to have passed on.

If, explicitly on D'Souza's argument, whites are rational for avoiding all young black men because of the high incidence among them of mugging (259 ff.), it must be that blacks are rational in avoiding all whites because whites assault blacks verbally and physically. The outcome, it seems, is the very segregation D'Souza thinks it would be acceptable to achieve in the private sphere. He expresses commitment, however, to color blindness, that is, to a standard of justice protective of individual rights and not of group results. D'Souza accordingly appears ready to jettison the rights of innocent black individuals to the "rational discrimination" of whites who invoke legitimation of their avoidance of black folk by appealing to statistical generalizations about groups.

D'Souza wishes to deny that the sorts of prejudicial stereotypes people commonly regard as racist ("Black people play basketball, they are good dancers or singers") are indeed so. He thinks such stereotypes are regarded as racist only because of the cultural relativist assumption that all groups are equal (268). Actually, they fail to satisfy D'Souza's criterion for racism, namely, that such claims *necessarily* impute biological determination to group attributes. But, *pace* D'Souza, these sorts of claim made in the usual contexts are racist because they project a stereotypical view that has been and likely is being used to denigrate black people explicitly or implicitly, and by extension to exclude them from other realms of socially legitimate and desirable activity. D'Souza lays heavy emphasis on the assumption that there is some central truth to a stereotype, and that this truth warrants rational discrimination.

D'Souza repeatedly invokes *totalizing* and *stereotyping* categories especially about blacks and by extension about whites.[9] In some "inner city neighborhoods," he writes, "the streets are irrigated with alcohol, urine, and blood" (16). There is now "nothing less than a breakdown of civilization within the African American community.... black culture also has a vicious, self-defeating, and repellent underside.... African Americans seem woefully lacking in the skills needed to compete effectively in a multiracial society" (477, 486, 499; see also, for example, 5, 15–16, 18, 96, 97).

D'Souza thinks that stereotypes somehow express a truth (97), that they are at heart accurate. Stereotypes, he insists, offer the "possibility of accurate generalizations about blacks" (271). Like Hume, he thinks most group traits are "cultural, the distilled products of many years of shared experience" (273–74). Prejudices and stereotypes, far from being explanations of the origins of group traits, "only take into account their undisputed existence." Undisputed? Isn't that the point at issue? The examples he cites are all projections: Jewish avarice or entrepreneurship, Roman machismo, Spanish piety, English severity or self-control (274–75). If stereotypes represent a truth, then one ought to be able to invoke a stereotype and read off from it—even imaginary—individual characteristics.

Actually, when D'Souza visited my campus in the early 1990s to promote his first book, *Illiberal Education* (1991), I took the opportunity to charge him publicly with fabricating the central example in that book, contrasting the black middle-class woman student at the University of California, Berkeley, who was a daughter of working professionals, and the desperately poor, orphaned, Vietnamese boat woman student who, despite slightly better grades, was only admitted to University of California, Davis. D'Souza's response to me was stunning in its (dis)honesty: the examples "were indeed stereotypes." Trading on the ambiguity, D'Souza acknowledged implicitly that he had never met such figures wandering around the Berkeley campus, as he claimed he did in the book, and yet that the characterizations somehow capture a kernel of truth in their stereotypical representativeness of the affirmative action experience. Poetic license becomes a legitimate weapon in the war against what he projects as political correctness.[10]

Here D'Souza conflates a projection of group characteristics abstracted from a convenient mythical aggregate of individual members' markings, with the ontological existence of group traits. This amounts to a reification of projected and abstracted parts for the whole (274). In claiming to establish that group generalizations may be accurate, the examples D'Souza cites engage in a telling reversal. He admits that the medieval stereotype that Jews have horns is false, but then adds that the generalizations that many Nobel laureates are Jewish or that the Mafia is made up of Italians are true. Nobody denies that some group generalizations are (qualifiedly) true. But his group generalization examples are about Nobel laureates and the Mafia, not about Jews and Italians. The fallacy in D'Souza's reasoning is easily observed once we reverse the generalizations: most Jews are laureates, and most Italians are mafiosi. Confusion is D'Souza's epitaph.

By rational discrimination, D'Souza seems to mean discrimination that is instrumentally valuable: "It is efficient, it makes economic sense" (277). With this in mind, he assesses discrimination in hiring, mortgage leasing, and criminal justice to show that considerable discrimination is rational in these areas, and so not racist.[11]

In discussing hiring discrimination, D'Souza expresses some skepticism about the well-publicized Urban Institute study demonstrating serious ongoing discrimination in employment opportunities. He chides the institute's report for being politically invested in the outcome, claiming it unlikely that the report would have been released had no discrimination been found. More strongly, D'Souza charges the institute with bias in the selection of firms studied because public sector agencies and firms with affirmative action programs were omitted (277).

The charge about the report's release is speculation on D'Souza's part (he cites no evidence), and the selection of firms had nothing to do with bias and everything to do with achieving a clear assessment of private sector discrimination in the absence of affirmative action programs. The existence of affirmative action programs in the private sector is associated largely with the pursuit of federal contracts. D'Souza thus reveals his profound ignorance of the most basic of social science methodology, if not his own acute bias. Where any political stake is expressed in all of this, that charge fits D'Souza's profile. He seeks to "justify" the discrimination found by the study as "rational," as

RACIAL SUBJECTS

economically efficient. Accordingly, we should be for Martin Luther King's call to judge individuals on the content of their character, but if profits can be increased by reducing costs (that is, avoid hiring any black candidate who might be a closet gangsta), well, that's just fine (278). The values of efficiency and economy get paraded as empirically established truth, the force of which are unquestionable and so incontestable. Racist discrimination doesn't count.

D'Souza argues that race is not the dominant factor at work because black employers equally discriminate against black potential employees. Here he conveniently ignores the long arm of institutional racism. Consider an analogy. At the age of thirty-six, I bought my first car in the United States. Although I had a demonstrably clean record from nearly twenty years of driving worldwide, because I lacked an auto insurance record, I was entered into the high-risk pool of entry-level drivers—those reckless young men who had just received their licenses. In central Philadelphia where I lived that meant doubling my auto insurance costs for at least three years. After the first year I had the opportunity to transfer my insurance, surreptitiously, to New York, saving nearly $1,000. Of course, nobody was discriminating against me; rules are rules. Rules, I am obviously arguing, place people in positions of disadvantage, in conditions over which they have no control (generally blacks more so than most), driving people, accordingly, sometimes quite "rationally," to transgress them.

D'Souza offers a similar argument to support his claim that banks are rational to use statistical aggregates on whites and blacks to discriminate between them on loans, charging black people higher rates because of higher group default rates. He suggests that rationality justifies public policy in permitting insurers to discriminate against all young male drivers in charging them increased insurance costs because, on average, young men are more reckless than young women, even though this discriminates against those young men who drive carefully. (See, D'Souza holds feminist views, after all.) Why is *this* the rational response? These are life and death concerns, and increased insurance costs to young men—because there is no way to prove to an insurer that one is not reckless—does little to discourage recklessness. (Actually, I suspect it would have little effect anyway, since reckless is by definition, well, reckless, irrational, and so not open to cost-benefit calculation.) To follow this logic, public policy should dictate that while young women may get licenses at sixteen, young men shouldn't until twenty-one. All we need to justify this is acknowledgment of the stereotype that young women mature more quickly than young men. Now that's *rational* discrimination, though I rather suspect the auto industry would object on purely economic motives. And just as it is unfair to nonreckless young men, so it would be to ordinary nondefaulting black people. Rational discrimination is still discrimination, no less unjust because rational.

More seriously, if—as D'Souza admits—companies are not "in a good position to predict individual behavior" (281) in the case of gender, age, and reckless driving, why does *racial* membership fix the causal determination? Age does correlate to some extent with experience and judgment, both of which are factors related to recklessness. Because race fails to determine any individual characteristics, it cannot predict any individual behavior. To think otherwise about race can only mean that D'Souza indeed buys into the biological determinism regarding race he claims to deny.

For D'Souza, it is rational for employers—because efficient and economical as a rule—to discriminate against blacks seeking employment in favor of white candidates. Such a recruiting rule supposedly saves employers on recruitment and hiring costs because of the higher risk of failure among black candidates.

Nevertheless, efficiency requirements and profit maximization do not imply blind discrimination—itself a ticket to economic disaster (employing a white person off the street is as crazy as employing anyone else off the street sight unseen)—but assessment of the capabilities of each candidate.[12] Hiring discrimination against blacks in favor of whites (as groups) must be equally inefficient; segregation protects white incompetence, in the present as in the past. The sort of historically effacing criticism D'Souza directs at affirmative action as economically inefficient furnishes further evidence of his segregationist leanings. Clearly he is comfortable with social arrangements that effectively set blacks apart. More than this, he actively promotes these arrangements even as he self-consciously hides the terms of such promotion.

Furthermore, according to D'Souza's criteria, women earn on average one grade better than men in college. So, on "merit," and to cut the costs of recruitment for the vacant position in our department, I should rationally discriminate against men and consider only women for the position. Come to think of it, why should I bother even grading my student's papers if I can just assume that women will earn a grade higher than men? If I'm concerned about being evenhanded, I'll give As only to the best women, B+s to the best men and second-tier women, and so on. Sorry Dinesh, the best you can hope for is a B+; it's just rational discrimination, you understand.

In speaking of racism and criminal justice, D'Souza is close to his most outrageous. He chides the *New York Times*, in reporting "such gruesome crimes as rape," for "omit(ting) *the crucial detail of race*" (263, my emphasis). What is it about race and rape, or perhaps race and crime generally, that makes D'Souza undo his expressed embrace of color blindness? And why should news reports of rape declare the racial identity of the perpetrator, even of the *alleged* assailant? Does D'Souza want to foment racial antagonism? First, he claims, without substantiation, that "victims are unlikely to lie about the race of their offenders" (283). Susan Smith, Charles Stuart, and Jim Anderson may not belie that claim—they're perpetrators, not victims, I can hear D'Souza retort. Nevertheless, there are studies that demonstrate the disposition to misrepresent. Confronted with photographs of a white and black man arguing, the white subjects of the study later reported the black man as wielding a razor blade when it was the white man.

Second, D'Souza claims that no one believes that the criminal justice system is more racist now than fifty years ago. If so, there should be fewer blacks in prison rather than more, which patently is not the case. The largest difference between blacks and whites regarding criminal justice is in the arrest rates. D'Souza puts this down to "rational discrimination" once again. Police officers know that young black men are more likely than whites to commit crimes, so they pursue them more vigorously (283–84). There is another explanation, however. Arrest is the most discretionary phase in the criminal justice system, the most open to abuse, and therefore potentially the most discriminatory.[13] Considering Laurence Powell, Stacy Koons, and Mark Fuhrman, why would anyone think otherwise? D'Souza does. He concludes that "most scholars would give assent" to the claim that "although at one time discrimination was quite likely, at the present time the general conclusion is that race remains an important factor only in selected contexts." After Fuhrman?!

Was D'Souza to be serious about his commitment to (statistically based) "rational" discrimination in regard to criminality, he "should" discriminate no more than 40 percent of black men between the ages of eighteen and twenty-nine. Before and after these ages, the relation of black men to the criminal justice system drops off dramatically. So, to play D'Souza's probability game, he might want to avoid 1 of every 2.5 black men in that age group with whom he has contact (actually fewer, give his own class location). Committed to color blindness when it suits him, he'd likely be the first to cross the otherwise deserted street when a black man approaches him, though "the stranger" comes dressed in an Armani suit and carries his doctor's bag. Perhaps D'Souza would have those in trouble with the law wear a yellow-starred armband. Now *that* would make his rational discrimination easier![14] D'Souza's "rational discrimination" regarding race and crime articulates the transformation of the prison industry into the postmodern equivalent of the plantation system, warehousing young black men as they increasingly supply desperately cheap labor to a variety of industries as well as bodies for chain gangs.

I get the distinct sense from reading his book not that D'Souza hates black people but that he is in deep, paranoid fear of a black planet, for somehow he thinks it would be both incompetent and criminally dangerous. Hobbes takes on an explicitly racial hue. In discussing, and dismissing the force of, discrimination in all three areas—employment, lending, and crime—D'Souza completely ignores any analysis of underlying structural factors that enable the discriminatory differences he is seeking to dismiss. His discussion accordingly is partial, at best and at worst. By contrast, he might just consider the relation between joblessness and the disposition to crime. It turns out that the average rate of joblessness is 40 percent for young black men also, especially in inner cities. William Julius Wilson (1996) has found strong connection between crime and unemployment. If our social choice is yellow stars or dignified work, prisons or schools for our children, which would *you* choose?

Rational discrimination is not racist, D'Souza insists, "because rational discrimination is based on group conduct, not biology." Where judgments are based not on prejudices and stereotypes but "on the reality of group differences which are real," a person apparently may discriminate rationally without being racist (286). This argument makes no sense, even by D'Souza's reasoning. The critical outrage against what he is calling rational discrimination is not that the judgment may accurately apply to some black individuals, but that it is being used as the grounds for nefarious judgments and equally pernicious exclusions against all black people who are not so characterizable. That commitment is not only racist, it's about as close to a paradigm of racist judgment and application as can be found.

The only way the thesis that "rational discrimination is not racist" can be made to seem plausible is by assuming that all (or most) members of the group in question—here blacks—are less competent or qualified than whites, or that they are highly likely to be guilty of crimes or "pathological behavior." And on any reasonable conception of racism—not D'Souza's, as it turns out—these are racist presumptions. Such (mis)attributions run at the very base of D'Souza's world view, no matter his denials and qualifications. "It is difficult to compel people to admire groups many of whose members do not act admirably" (287); and "racial preferences ... treat incompetent individuals as competent" (297); and again, "why is it reasonable to expect that black students majoring in education with a C average at a community college should command incomes comparable with white students majoring in business with a B average at the University of Wisconsin or Cornell" (301). D'Souza's is the voice of the new segregationism: committed to the cultural autonomy of "embattled" whites and dominant racial norms that are statistically mobilized, shamelessly overgeneralized, and perniciously stereotypical, with the view to rationalizing the apartness, institutionally and spatially, of the ethnoracially and economically distinct.

THE ENDS OF D'SOUZA'S RACISM

So "the end of racism" in D'Souza's view is the end of white racism, not black. Black racism, he insists, is a rationalization for black failure. The end of racism thus is to be produced by black people digging in and acquiring the skills to compete effectively and successfully with whites. Here D'Souza leaves the lingering doubt of imputed genetically determined inferiority—he writes of a "black gene pool" not having changed substantially (478).

What we have then is this: Black people are cut loose socially, set apart, and left alone. White America is freed from responsibility save for not discriminating, other than rationally, in their own self-interests. So what else is new? If against all these odds a couple of black people succeed, fine. In his generosity D'Souza doesn't seem to mind an occasional black neighbor if they can afford it as a result of an honest day's labor. While white gangsters, corporate or organized, won't be excluded from Mr. D'Souza's neighborhood, no gangstas—especially if they're rap stars—need apply. Too many black neighbors, I sense, will drive down the value of his home. Nevertheless, D'Souza makes it abundantly clear that the likelihood of black success is culturally, if not genetically, unlikely. It's amazing what fear and trembling produce.

D'Souza's fear and trembling—and the general fear and trembling concerning blacks in America—are caused, he claims, by widespread black social pathology threatening the social fabric of American society. The attributed pathologies he lists and discusses are a curious mix: behavior that is asocial or antisocial (like being unmarried with children); responses to perceived wrongs suffered (as in "black middle-class rage"); heightened social expectations (expected government help, as in welfare and quota queens); ironic cultural expression and self-representation (for example, the "bad nigger"); what D'Souza calls "rap sheets"—violent rap lyrics, criminal braggadocio, and the like. D'Souza insists, in totalizing fashion, that blacks in America, despite their diversity, share a common culture that is "oppositional" (484) and that "is not racial but ethnic" (482). "Middle-class behavior by African Americans is seen as inauthentic, while low-class behavior is seen as genuinely black.... on many moral issues the tone in the black community is set from below" (485). Black culture is deemed ethnic rather than racial because historically rather than biologically produced, and gutt(e)ral rather than middlebrow. Thus, by turning all blacks into the racial lumpen proletariat he is able, self-servingly, to effect racism's exclusionary ends while evading the charge of racism. Talk about bad faith!

D'Souza insists, repeatedly, that "black culture" is characterized by a "vicious, self-defeating and repellant underside" (486), that "underclass blacks [are characterized by] their gold chains, limping walk, obscene language, and arsenal of weapons" (504). Moreover, "thirty-two-year-old black grandmothers *abound*" (516, my emphasis).[15] The slippage around blackness in D'Souza's mode of articulation is readily apparent. He chides the (black) *underclass* for pathological behavior, then not a moment later generalizes to blacks ("many blacks") as such, thus reducing "the black underclass" to pathology, blacks to the underclass, and the underclass to blacks. Moreover, the emotion-laden connotation of "pathology" links D'Souza's analysis, self-consciously I have to think, to those very old stereotypes of black people as moved by emotion and passion rather than by reason.

The concept of culture at work here is especially peculiar: deep enough to be absolutely determining of what is considered pathological behavior but shallow and superficial enough that it is unaffected or underdetermined by the political, economic, social, legal, and psychological conditions on which it is founded and in which it is embedded. Oddly, he seems to suggest, in addition, that pathological culture is acceptable if one is white and can afford it: "Rich whites, for example, may adopt cocaine habits but they can take advantage of expensive treatment programs that are unavailable to the crack addict. Similarly, when middle-class white teenagers get pregnant they frequently draw on the support of parents and grandparents; these resources do exist among poor blacks, but they are scarce" (485-86). In the land of Lockean libertarianism, one not only gets what one can pay for; those unable to pay, overwhelmingly black, get locked away. Three simple strikes (if one is not white) and you're out of sight, out of mind. For life.

D'Souza nowhere establishes without first presuming that the "problems endured by African Americans today are substantially the result of cultural pathologies on the part of blacks" (481). This is a claim that takes the notion of "cultural pathology" as unproblematic (as though it declares itself baldly without normative presumption), just as it totalizes all or nearly all blacks to "perpetrate" such pathological expression. Indeed, D'Souza lies down with odd bedfellows: Daniel Moynihan, the mainstream media, Louis Farrakhan. The sociological thorn of social control assumes new significance when all these folk climb onto a common podium rapping to a common tune.

Assuming for the moment what we should resist passionately, namely, that blacks exhibit the sorts of "cultural pathologies" D'Souza identifies, two related questions are raised: Why is it that these "pathologies" emerged only in the past thirty years? What underlying social, political, and economic conditions facing blacks changed in ways that might have spurred such cultural developments? D'Souza says nothing in response to the first question other than to link contemporary "cultural pathology" to "pathological cultural developments" among slaves. I have already noted this nonsense in discussing D'Souza's ignorance about slave conditions. But even were it plausible, it fails to explain, on his own terms, how it is that "black cultural pathology" manifested only from the mid-1960s on. All he says in response to the second question, amounts to half a sentence (in a book 700 pages long): what emerged "since the 1960s ... [was] a new environment of social permissiveness and government subsidy" (485).

D'Souza fails to consider an alternate reading of the social terrain: that the troubled and troubling behavior of some among the most disaffected, hopeless, nihilistic, and impoverished of young black people, especially men, that we have watched emerge in the last twenty-five years or so developed out of a radically intensified impoverishment at the very moment of heightened expectation. This in turn is a complex product of dramatic shifts in the socioeconomic structure and attendant prospects for young black people over this period. As William Julius Wilson points out, employed black men in their late twenties experience similar rates of crime as employed white men of this age. Not surprisingly, it is the jobless who tend to commit crimes, and (white anxiety notwithstanding) young black inner-city men are much more likely to be out of work than their white peers. So, when D'Souza reduces the range of possible determinants of contemporary black social difficulties to genes, culture, or racial discrimination (or some combination) (529), he reaches for the superficial account. There are structural considerations over which young black men have had no control. The history of racism has made blacks, in particular, more prone to the difficulties structurally produced, thus exacerbating the problems they face. One could say that the intersection of race, class, and gender gives precise location to the debilities at issue.

This is the analysis offered by the likes of Elijah Anderson and William Julius Wilson, whose work D'Souza invokes but misrepresents. "To understand illegitimacy in the black underclass, one must turn to the work of urban anthropologist Elijah Anderson who ... describes the inner city in the same immersed and detailed way that some Western scholars portray tribes in distant lands" (516). In the hands of D'Souza, Elijah Anderson becomes the bridge over which we are driven to return to the discourse of primitivism. The urban underclass, itself a term discursively thick and value laden, becomes the new primitive. Dinesh D'Souza assumes the figure of the missionary bearing the enlightened torch. Again!

In response to D'Souza one might ask what social responsibilities there are among individuals and those with institutional power to alter the social, political, and economic conditions underlying the reproduction of self- and other-destructive behavior. D'Souza's arguments are predicated on totalizing and vicious stereotypes, and his only policy response is to end all government assistance and civil rights protections while insisting that individual black people have a special responsibility to stand up to the peculiar problems they or group members face. This response reifies his commitments not just to already established forms of segregation but to the ongoing project of segregating those who don't assume and exhibit the culture of middle-class whiteness.

Now "[t]he only people who are seriously confronting black cultural deficiencies and offering constructive proposals for dealing with them," states D'Souza, "are members of the group we call the reformers" (521). In contrast to what he calls "the liberals," these are the black conservatives like Clarence Thomas, Shelby Steele, Thomas Sowell, Alan Keyes, Robert Woodson, and Glen Loury, some of whom have explicitly distanced themselves sharply from D'Souza's book. Indeed, the latter two resigned their affiliations with the American Enterprise Institute in protest. What then is it that D'Souza sees "the reformers" responding to, and what reforms are being promoted?

For D'Souza, "irrational racism"—bigoted prejudice—is for the most part historical racism, now long past. "Rational discrimination," by contrast, he claims is a legitimate response to perceived danger and loss. The market—profits and costs—is supposed to determine the ongoing viability of the rational discrimination. What little irrational racism exists, D'Souza concludes, can only be removed by harming liberal society—that is, by restricting freedom—a harm more than the harm of racism it alleviates. On the contrary, liberal democratic society restricts all kinds of behavior that might impinge on people's freedoms without anyone complaining about invasions of liberty. For instance, some states require couples wanting a divorce to seek counselling at their own expense.

Obviously, if contemporary racism is so curtailed by D'Souza in form and scope, permissible social responses will be restricted similarly. D'Souza briefly discusses four projected remedies for contemporary racism, rejecting the first three. The first proposal is to expand the logic of proportional representation for all racial groups (539). This, D'Souza thinks, "erodes the principle of merit which constitutes the only unifying principle for a multiracial society" (540). D'Souza stretches the concept of "merit" so that if it made any sense before, it fails to do so now. Thus, merit is not "just desert" in terms of effort, credentials, or qualifications relevant to performance. He extends the criteria to include nepotistic relation to the employer: "Admittedly in some cases the job goes to the nephew of the boss. This, in the boss's mind, is his nephew's 'merit'—to be related to him" (544). So much for merit as the common glue of D'Souza's "multiracial" society. In the private sector anything goes, including the most extreme forms of racist exclusion. Goodbye to even color blindness as ideal; welcome back segregation.

Second, the suggestion is to abolish racial preferences for all groups save African Americans (541). D'Souza projects that such preference will prove debilitating to African Americans. Of course, he is less sensitive to this concern when it comes to his own use of odious characterization. Third, D'Souza considers general enforcement of color blindness in both private and public sectors (542). This, he argues, acknowledges some forms of discrimination as rational and so justifiable, though it still outlaws them and so licenses forms of interference at cost to human freedom.

Finally, D'Souza suggests a policy of dual standards. On the one hand, strict race neutrality in the public sphere—color blindness in government hiring and promotion, criminal justice and voting district apportionment; on the other, the right to discriminate throughout the private sphere, as in renting out an apartment or in job hiring. In other words, D'Souza is "calling for a repeal of the Civil Rights Act of 1964 ... [which] should be changed so that its nondiscrimination provisions apply only to the government" (544). He defends the right to private discrimination in employment cases on grounds that "the job is the employer's to give" (544). Like Richard Epstein, upon whom he relies for this argument, D'Souza fails to acknowledge that employers have jobs "to give" only because their own existence is made possible by the society in which they live. Take "society" away—schools, credentialing, public facilities like roads, and so forth—and the enterprise would cease to be possible. Besides, it must be asked what values one would endorse in structuring the society in which one chooses to live.

In response to the shriveled (mis)diagnosis D'Souza develops for racism, he offers the soundbite solutions prompted by black conservatives. So, racism is no longer the prevailing problem for African Americans. It is black pathologies that need to be identified and boldly confronted; self-help and entrepreneurship are called for rather than external and governmental help; and blacks need to commit themselves to the pursuit of excellence (as though somehow they don't). D'Souza characterizes these jointly as "the best antiracism now" (527), in contrast to "the most formidable ideological barrier facing blacks [which] is not racism but antiracism" (528). This, to paraphrase Marx, is Hegel on his head; come to think of it, a rather headless Hegel at that.

These "solutions" to racism should be underpinned, D'Souza insists, by "a return to the classical conception of natural rights, and the distinction made by the ancient Greeks between civilization and barbarism" (533). He continues: "Civilized people are held together by a common understanding of virtue and depravity, of greatness and depravation" (533), in contrast it might be said to *deprivation*. Unless he is assuming the universalizing of his own particular principles, which presumes a peculiar form of relativism commonly known as narcissism, I fail to see why this can't be relativistic. Virtue and depravity for the Greeks, and indeed among them, differed significantly from prevailing standards today, even as some very broad and abstract generalities may be established as parameters.

America's problem is partly one of race, and partly a problem for blacks. These are often, but not always, coterminous. D'Souza rejects proportional representation and multiculturalism as false remedies to America's racial paradox, prompted by liberalism's commitment to cultural relativism. The "solution" he offers to the race problem (as though there is just one) is strict government neutrality regarding race. The "solution" to "the black problem" (not, note, "the problems *for* blacks") is self-promoted cultural reconstruction. By "acting white" (556) African Americans will best enable "civilizational restoration" (556). And whites walk off into the sunset, "free at last" of any implication in racism and the production of its many nefarious effects.

By contrast, the complex account of the conditions facing the racially marginalized today that I earlier claimed D'Souza ignores, one that takes seriously the implications of a transforming political economy, suggests an altogether different sort of policy response. If in this society we are serious about addressing injustice in the lives of blacks specifically, and the racially marginalized most emphatically, then there are three interactive conditions that need immediate consideration: jobs, housing, and education. Was I to add a fourth consideration and so make complicated matters significantly more complex still, I would add having to address dominant media representations of blackness and whiteness whether bald or subtle, explicit or implicit, brazen or nuanced. Resource availability determines educational opportunity, and so jobs, and by extension quality of housing. Where one lives largely determines where one goes to school, the quality of education one receives, and so the quality of housing one can afford. Further, as the example of D'Souza's text makes abundantly clear, the color of ideological (mis)characterization tilts understanding one way or another, with dramatic material effect. If we are to equalize opportunity in America, we have to be serious about tackling this (un)holy trinity (quaternity). The new segregationism renews the depths of inequalities, reinstating the conditions not so past. A detour, as I said earlier, via the past to the future.

"DISSING" D'SOUZA

The End of Racism is a "must *not* read," and definitely a "don't buy" book, unless one is concerned with how the new segregationism is being articulated. D'Souza projects a view more widely held, and so more problematic, than the outrageous one he looks to be expressing. The real problem in the United States, as he represents it, is not any more racism but "antiracism" (for which one may read "political correctness"), not exclusion but cultural relativism, not the absence of equal opportunity and equality before the law but of treating cultures as equal. In this sense, the populist "appeal" of Dinesh D'Souza's text turns on its rationalizing a bigoted folk wisdom, extending a veneer of credibility—the intellectual stamp of authority—to what "everyman" (every white man and white wannabes, that is) supposedly knows. Where social life is complex, D'Souza and his supporters would have it simple, if not simplistic. Where the history of racism runs deep, D'Souza would have it flat. Where the nature of racism(s) is varied, D'Souza would have it singular. Where the determinants of racism(s) are multiple and multifarious, D'Souza would have them reduced to a singularity. Where contemporary racism persists, if transformed, D'Souza would have it past, dissolved by definition.

D'Souza's line of attack on the Civil Rights tradition in this country only makes sense in the context of the now popular effort to efface history by excising from historical memory the conditions that black people have suffered, with devastating contemporary effects for poorer black people especially. It is only by way of this aphasia that D'Souza and those he speaks to (and for) can mobilize the claim that civil rights policies—affirmative action, voting rights reapportionment to establish black represented districts, integrated schools, and so forth—discriminate against white people.[16] The claim forgets, in the sense of denial, that it is black people, those not white, who have suffered racial terror at the hands of whites: who have been discriminated against, excluded, denied equal access, violated persistently, devalued, dumped upon environmentally, ignored. This denial is why he spends so much ink trying to belittle—to diminish—the degradation black people continue to experience under the effects of racism (slavery wasn't so bad after all, segregation was designed to protect blacks from the likes of Ku Klux Klan radicals, a small fringe minority, and then the civil rights establishment placed blacks in positions to discriminate against whites). What D'Souza denies at every turn is the history of racial power—in politics, education, employment, wealth creation, and cultural production—which has guaranteed disproportionate representation for whites.[17]

So, in terms of policy, conservatives like D'Souza are committed to policies that produce the new segregation, and rhetoric expressive of the new segregationism, leaving the racially marginalized to their own cultural pathologies. Liberals by contrast reaffirm paternalizing welfare statism. There is another path here that both conservatives and liberals ignore, for it would require substantive commitment to dramatic political, economic, and cultural change, as well as transformations in sensibilities and sensitivities. If we are to be serious about effecting really equal opportunity, this entails equalizing socially available resources like health care coverage and educational resources from the earliest ages. It means establishing nondiscriminatory access and vigorously enforcing antidiscriminatory statutes, especially regarding employment and housing but also healthy living environments conducive to a dignified and respectful life. Further, it requires resisting all forms of racial discrimination, in design and effect, privately and publicly, as contexts render evident. And it necessitates challenging racist stereotypes, representations, myths, and narratives, whether culturally embedded and subtle or socially explicit. This imperative holds especially regarding devaluing and demeaning racist characterization in opinion forming media.

In closing these all too partial reflections, I must comment on the way the militia movement in America is renewing blacks as scapegoats of anxious social transformation and as common targets, the easy effects of reinventing America as a paleface nation, land of white power and home of anarcho-racial terrorism. D'Souza wonders aloud whether, once the traditionally liberal suspicion of the state becomes redefined as a conservative commitment, this suspicion doesn't automatically get dismissed as bigotry (256). Well, not quite automatically, because not without good reason. For members of the Michigan or Montana militia and their associates, the state they reject is the welfare state, the state identified as providing for blacks as it is controlled by the cabal of Jewish bankers and politicians who dominate through PACs. Deregulation of the public sphere has licensed the return of the not-so-repressed and, since the Reagan "counter-revolution," the no-longer-suppressed. The militia movement has demonstrable ties to neofascist groups in Germany, Austria, and Russia, and it is known to circulate neofascist European literature in the United States. Just as the holocaust is denied by such groups in Europe (in one instance, gas chambers are characterized as an East German Disneyland), so on internet home pages devoted to Civil War history slavery is denied, its importance to the conduct of the Civil War dismissed, and black Americans are presumed to acquiesce in their own enslavement. Sound familiar? Historical memory once more gives way to hyperbolic fantasy.

Thus I conclude where I began, with my title. Dinesh dedicates his book to "My darling wife Dixie, who makes my life complete." Not wishing to disrespect a relation dear to his heart, I must observe that in his vituperative and totalizing views of black folk generally, and African Americans particularly, and in his more than superficial support for renewing segregating effects in America, Dinesh D'Souza (along with those for whom he speaks) is wedded to Dixie in more ways than one.

NOTES

CHAPTER 2
HATE, OR POWER?

1. On conflating racism and hatred see, for example, Paul Hockenos (1993). A number of programs on the resurrection of neo-Nazi movements in Central Europe and in the United States by Ted Koppel on *Nightline* invoked the generalized rubric of hate, as did one by Phil Donahue and Vladimir Posner. "Hate" was the title used by Bill Moyers for his PBS special on racism and prejudice. See also Leonard Zeskind, "And Now, the Hate Show," *The New York Times,* Tuesday, November 16, 1993.

2. It may be that expressions of racism were understood as prejudice by those critical of them as early as the mid-nineteenth century. Nevertheless, definitions of racism were offered for the first time only in the late 1930s, and the prevailing contemporary understanding of racism as prejudice is firmly anchored in 1950s social science, especially social psychology.

3. The disanalogies between racist and sexist expression run as deep as the analogies. Indeed, while identifying commonalities between racist and sexist assumptions, expressions, and movements, identifying the commonalities without strict qualification is evasively reductive. For simplicity's sake, I restrict myself here to comments about racism.

4. Not uncommonly, the prejudgment that turns out to be false will be forced later. It is not unusual for a white professor, grading blind to students' identities on the semester's first test to give the top grade to the only black person in the class, only to downgrade that student in later tests. I owe the example to Jan Boxill, "Affirmative Action as Reverse Discrimination," unpublished note on file with author.

5. For a fuller argument concerning antiracist pragmatics, see chapter 9 of Goldberg (1993a).

CHAPTER 3
TAKING STOCK: COUNTING BY RACE

1. George P. Smith (1989) reasserts the importance of eugenic considerations for applying the new reproductive technologies. Though he makes no mention of race, Smith recommends on grounds of social welfare that the state eugenically control the reproduction of populations marked by genetic disposition to disabling disease and disability. While his suggestions raise grave concerns about political morality, the history of both the definition and practice of eugenics should serve as warning of their deeply racialized implications. Underlying much of the celebration of these new biotechnologies seems to lie an image not so much of an *Ubermensch* as of a genetically ordered, disease-free *Idealmensch*, a biologically engineered race of perfectly healthy human beings. Genetic "defects" are to be bred out eugenically by restrictions on reproduction. The extension of the racializing project in and through sociobiology has been well exposed. It seems more deeply embedded in the newer phase of biosocial *hyp(e)*othesizing. E. O. Wilson (1993) has been examining those aspects of our urban environment toward which we display "biophobic" and "biophilial" dispositions. The biogenic disposition "we" supposedly display toward racialized ghettoes is self-evident.

2. Secondariness in the case of the census is best illustrated by the following: in the lead up to the 1980 U.S. Census, oversight hearings were scheduled, somewhat cynically, months *after* Congress had signed off on the categories presented to them by the director of the U.S. Census Bureau.

3. I am grateful to Nahum Chandler for this reference. On the distinction between functional and ideological social science, see Goldberg (1993a, 152–55).

4. Arjun Appadurai (1993, 799–800) suggests that census classification in a wide variety of modern societies, marching to their own technological requirements, has been influential in producing or reproducing fractured, fearful, and fixed social identities, which otherwise would be fluid and negotiable.

5. Stephen Steinberg (1989) points out that by 1790, slaves still included some Indians and whites, but their numbers were overwhelmingly black. Indeed, it is hard to think how the three-fifths clause could have been entertained, let alone sustained, if not premised upon black dehumanization.

6. A permanent U.S. Census Bureau was established in 1902 within the Department of the Interior, but was moved to the Department of Commerce and Labor a year later. It remained with the Department of Commerce when Labor split off in 1913. The marketing departments of major corporations are now among the primary consumers of census data, meaning that the government is effectively making a welfare (some might say a workfare) payment to Wall Street. By contrast, Sharon Lee (1993, 92, n. 1) sees the early census taking, up to the Civil War and emancipation, as servicing slavery. Lee insists that the primary census distinction was between free men and slaves. It is true that the census maps human labor resources, what more recently have been conceived as "social capital." Nevertheless, this both overstates the influence of slavery on the bureaucratic technology of population counting and fails to recognize the determining autonomy of racial discrimination. On census history, see U.S. Department of Commerce (November 1989).

7. Because federal coherence and control were limited in the early years of the republic, and the independence of the thirteen states in conducting their own affairs was paramount, the first census counts were disorganized and uneven in their application and results. For 1800, 1810, and 1820, I rely largely on the categories formulated by Massachusetts, the state that seems to have been most coherent in its administration.

8. In 1844, then House of Representatives member John Quincy Adams once confronted Calhoun regarding the latter's census-contrived distortions. Adams wrote in his diary: "[Calhoun] writhed like a trodden rattlesnake on the exposure of his false report ... and finally said that where there were so many errors they balanced one another" (Aptheker 1974, 15–16).

9. Bernard Cohn (1987, 234, 236), for example, notes that prevailing European perceptions of conditions in cities in India were prompted by their architectural layout, which suggested to them, huge crowds. These perceptions in turn licensed overestimations of urban populations in the early nineteenth-century British Census counts in India. Discretion exacerbated the effects of these (mis)perceptions: Enumerators in India were left to define the boundaries of family, for example, as well as to estimate whom among respondents could be counted as adult.

10. I have borrowed these numbers from Petersen (1987, 223). Paul Starr (1987, 44) notes that 10–15 percent of white Americans—however this is determined—offer no ethnic identity and another 35–40 percent offer two or more ethnic traditions as defining their heritage. In addition, as Petersen (1987,

189) points out, in a random survey across consecutive census counts, fully one-third of matched persons cited different ethnic origins from one survey to the next.

11. The bureau's publication (1990, 3, n. 2) attributes this difficulty in crosscensus comparisons not only to "changes in the census questionnaire and the way persons report race and ethnic origin," but also to "improvements in census procedures." Thus, we are faced by a strange paradox: as census procedures improve, the transhistorical comparisons—the very mandate of the census undertaking—become increasingly unreliable.

12. Manu Aluli Meyer, representing the group Ho'omau, as quoted in *The New York Times*, July 8, 1994, A18. The assistant division chief for special population statistics at the census bureau—a title in which Foucault would have delighted—referred to this complex hybrid of issues concerning census identification by way of the telling racial metaphor: "a can of worms."

13. The report on the racial rate of doctorates was issued by the American Council on Education, *The New York Times*, January 18, 1994, A6. Given that the proportion of whites earning doctorates across the same period remains constant at 88 percent, it would be interesting to determine whether any of the increase in rates for "Hispanics" or the decrease for blacks is a function of blacks reidentifying themselves as "Hispanic."

14. On Teja Arboleda, see *The New York Times*, July 8, 1994, A18.

15. Consider that there is no literature on "Hispanic" populations in the United States explicitly and self-consciously identified in terms of the category until 1978. Most of the literature on "Hispanics" dates from the mid-1980s. See Gerardo Marin and Barbara VanOss Marin (1991); Edna Acosta-Belen and Barbara Sjostrom (1988); and Rodney E. Hero (1992, esp. 2–5).

16. There is some evidence for these claims. Using exactly what I have questioned here, namely, racialized categories, 78 percent of black voters support the Democratic Party compared to 54 percent of "Hispanic" voters, and only 34 percent of white voters.

17. It was estimated, on the basis of crosscensus and birth-death rate comparisons, that 25,000 blacks "passed into the general community" *each year* from 1900–1910. If these figures are even half accurate, they are remarkable (Petersen 1987, 212).

18. On Dale Sandhu's case against Lockheed Missiles and Space Co., see *American Lawyer Media, L.P., The Recorder*, July 7, 1994, p. 4, which ironically reported the case under the byline, "Court Allows *Caucasian's* Bias Suit" (my emphasis). For the ways in which census information factors into determination of jury discrimination in the United States, see Hiroshi Fukurai, Edgar Butler, and Richard Krooth (1993). It should be noted that the authors commit the error of unproblematically reading the category "Hispanic" back into the pre-1970s

historical record. Thus, for example, they interpret *Hernandez v. Texas* (347 U.S. 475 1954) as the first recognition by the Supreme Court of the need for protection by Hispanics from jury discrimination. The Court, in fact, recognized the claims of Mexican Americans.

CHAPTER 4
MADE IN THE USA: RACIAL MIXING 'N MATCHING

1. Public Enemy, "Fear of a Black Planet," written by K. Shocklee, E. Sadler, and C. Ridenhour (Def Jam Records, 1990). All lyrics that follow in this chapter are from this song.

2. For example, Maria Root speaks of "the emergence of a racially mixed population ... transforming the 'face' of the United States." Root's "increasing presence of multiracial people" gives in to the premise of past purity (1992, 3).

3. On "ethnorace," see Goldberg (1993a, 74–78).

4. See Linda Chavez (1991) for a proponent of post-Mexicano Hispanicity. See Suzanne Oboler (1996) for a long critical look at the category "Hispanic."

5. The fabrication at work here is revealed in the ironic courtroom response of Steve Biko under prosecutorial interrogation. The exchange proceeded in the following terms. Prosecutor: Why does the Black Consciousness Movement characterize itself as "black?" You're not black, but brown. To which Biko quickly retorted: Why "white?" You're not white but pink. The story was recounted by journalist Donald Woods in eulogy of Biko upon his murder.

6. See, for example, Roger Omond (1985, 21–25). As an example of multiple reclassifications, Omond cites the case of a Mr. Wilkinson, who found himself reclassified five times from "mixed" to "European (white)" to "Coloured" to "white" to "Coloured," the last time at his own request so he could live legally with his wife, an Indian woman who at the same time applied successfully to be reclassified as "Coloured."

7. See Parker (1996).

8. On the "nihilistic threat" faced by blacks, see Cornel West (1993a) and Richard Wright (1965). On Wright's depiction of African-American nihilism, see Paul Gilroy (1993, 172); and on West's argument regarding black nihilism, see my chapter on West, and Adolph Reed (1993, 18–20).

9. See "A Cultural Gap May Swallow a Child," *New York Times*, October 8, 1993, A8. The Indian Welfare Act of 1978 grants American Indian tribes special preference in adopting children born to Indian parents. The case reported concerned a child fathered by an Oglala Sioux man and placed at birth by his white mother with white adoptive parents. The Oglala Sioux nation were suing the adoptive parents to re-place the now four-year-old boy with Indian relatives on Pine Ridge Reservation. His biological father had since married a woman

other than the boy's biological mother, and according to the report has shown no interest in the child.

10. Similar arguments appear on crossracial dating, particularly in contemporary campus settings. See Ben Gose (1996, A45–46). At the same time, as Pat Williams (1995, 221) points out, even where race and class intersect so that white adoptive parents are more likely to be better off than black adoptive parents, this likelihood sustains the demand for redistributing family resources, not for racially directed adoptions.

11. In current arrangements, mixed-race adoption takes on more troubling implications yet, for it affords those adoptive parents who can afford it the possibilities of a designer kid. The current yuppie flavor, reflecting stereotypes of the model minority and ethnic intelligence, is Korean. For approximately what it takes to buy a small Hyundai, and without import duties or local bureaucracy, those with impeccably white credentials can adopt a Korean kid (terms arranged no doubt for the right customer). What, one might ask *Time* magazine, happens to the child-as-property when tastes change? See also Patricia Williams (1995, 214–28).

12. Naomi Zack (1994) responds to the question about the desirability of mixed-race identity in something like this first way.

13. See Ernest Gellner (1983, chapters 2 and 3); and Eric Hobsbawm (1993, 62–65). On race, culture, and hybridity, see Robert Park (1950).

14. *Made in America*, the film starring Whoopi Goldberg and Ted Danson, broaches the subject of mixed-race relations for the 1990s, as *Guess Who's Coming to Dinner* did for the 1960s. While considerably more optimistic in conclusion than, say, *Jungle Fever*, *Made in America* ends up implicitly reinserting the ban on mixed-race progeny (American can breathe free again, Ted Danson is not the biological father of Whoopi Goldberg's daughter) even as it calls for the exuberance of the intercultural experience and the commodified appropriation of the wonders of the Other's cultural expression. I viewed the film in Mesa, Arizona, home to the second largest Mormon population in America, outnumbered in this suburb of Phoenix only by southwestern Catholics. The audience chuckled nervously at the thought of mixed-race offspring, but virtually danced in the aisles during the celebratory finale.

15. See Michele Collison (1993, A13–14). "A Twist on Affirmative Action: Listing of Italian Americans as Protected Group Triggers Debate at CUNY," *Chronicle of Higher Education* (November 24, 1993): A13–14.

16. Peter Caws points out that one's first culture, the one into which one is born, is not a culture that one owns but that one belongs to (1994, 371–87).

17. See Toni Morrison (1992); Paul Gilroy (1993, 217–23); Michael Wallace (1996).

18. A theory of (deracinated) cultural membership is worked out by Asa Kasher (1993, 56–79).

19. On the imperative to improvise, see Richard Wright (1954, 346–47); and Paul Gilroy (1993, 192–93).

CHAPTER 5
IN/VISIBILITY AND SUPER/VISION:
FANON AND RACIAL FORMATION

1. John Brigham (1996) examines this logic in the context of legal definition and administration of "Other(ed) countries," racially defined, within the United States—Harlem, American Indian reservations, the contested *ejido* or community lands of Northern New Mexico.

2. I am tempted to weaken the force of this by reformulating the dilemma as a product at least of racially conceived and not only racist societies. Elaboration of this distinction is beyond my scope here. See Goldberg 1993a, especially chapters 4 and 5.

3. Helen Watson (1994) discusses the complex dimensions of the veil for Islamic women.

4. Ahab's itself represents a stereotyped location of exploitative Semitic inner-city commercialism where parasitic capitalism and the illegal drug trade meet. Lee contrasts Ahab's with Victor's night-time, second-job location, a family restaurant run by a Jamaican immigrant who pointedly resists drug transactions on the premises. Significantly, Lee extends the contrast to Rodney's project barbershop, a front for his drug empire. The local hood and don-like father figure to his streetwise clockers, Rodney runs his trade on the exploited backs of teen labor.

5. I am grateful to my good friend and colleague, James Riding In, for furnishing me with U.S. Senate documentation of the "Bow and Arrow Ceremony" transcript, dating to November 1930.

6. This has been well documented in relation to Los Angeles by Mike Davis (1990), Victor Valle and Rudy Torres (1994), and others. While a more general phenomenon, it is perhaps especially pressing and visible in the case of Los Angeles.

7. Michel Foucault (1988, 145–62) notes that in seventeenth-century France and Germany the term "police" meant the administration of the state, and not simply the surviellance of the citizenry, a more general understanding of modes of discipline.

8. For elaboration of this point, see my chapter "Crime and Preference in the Multicultural City."

CHAPTER 6

WHITHER WEST? THE MAKING OF A PUBLIC INTELLECTUAL

1. In surfing the internet, I discovered West's "Toward a Socialist Theory of Racism," a paper published only in cyberspace. So his more radical work is being released to the relative anonymity of cyberspace, where electronic distance between text, author, and reader mutes the message. The euphoria over the public dimensions of internet space has hidden from scrutiny the levels of ordering—of time, of engagement, of perception and conception, of knowledge—commercial, hence privatized, framing places upon consumption. At the same time, it deregulates the circulation of racist representation and rationalization, in old form and new.

2. I do not mean to leave the impression that a public intellectual is drawn inevitably, though often inadvertently, by the power of representation into the language of power and representation of power's interests. The measure of critical power and the power of the critical intellectual is furnished precisely by the capacity to undo power's command of language, to redirect significance and to signify redirection, to undo the web of power's meaning as one means to undo power's web, to shatter institutional disciplines as one fractures disciplinary institutions.

3. Parenthetical page numbers within the text refer to Cornel West (1993a).

4. The book consists of eight short chapters and an introduction. Only the penultimate chapter on black sexuality had not appeared before as a discrete article. Four of the remaining seven chapters critique the current impasse of black political and intellectual leadership. The especially thin chapter on affirmative action (all of five pages) discusses the sorts of policies West thinks black leadership should be pursuing.

5. Obviously, the existence of a black middle class, or various fractions of such a class, long precedes this period. See E. Frazier (1965).

6. West makes a number of disparaging remarks about the clothing styles of black politicians and intellectuals that, he says, symbolize their critical distance from the real concerns and experiences of the bulk of black people. While he probably had Ron Brown in mind, it is clear from the counterexample he offers, namely, Adam Clayton Powell, that expensive tastes need not compromise representation of blacks' political interests. And while West wishes to render black academics more self-conscious about their dress so that they might be taken more seriously when addressing black church and community groups, this hardly commands that they dress like DuBois—or look like West, for that matter. In contrast to West's aesthetic privileging of DuBois's dress code, Paul Gilroy (1993, 17) provocatively notes that DuBois invested considerable personal capital in modeling his clothes and mustache on those of Kaiser

NOTES

Wilhelm II. A critique of the aesthetics of contemporary fashion needs to be more evenhanded than West's seemingly self-serving moralizing allows.

7. He includes in this litany, as I do not, the marginalization of humanistic studies, though this strikes me as less true than the others. The influence of humanistic studies has altered in kind, rather than diminished, and this may have to do with their transformed content, styles, and methods. But West's inclusion of humanistic stories implicitly, and uncritically, lauds its past effects. This romanticizes some questionable assumptions and practices in the history of the humanities.

· 8. For a sustained critical reading of the Thomas affair, see Toni Morrison (1992), in which West's chapter first appeared.

9. West commits two related errors in this account, however, one empirical, the other causal. First, he overstates the levels of black youth employed in Southern agriculture in the 1950s. He claims that 50 percent of all black youth were employed in agriculture, overwhelmingly in the South. Census reports for 1950 put this figure at more like one third. Second, he directly links the disappearance of these agricultural jobs to urban unemployment of black youth shortly thereafter (1993a, 54). The causal chain suggested here is misdirected: The unemployment level for black youth in northern cities by the mid-1960s was a function not so much of black youth migrating in large numbers from rural areas as it was of massive loss of blue collar manufacturing jobs from the mid-1950s on. The transformation in the U.S. economy that West notes (54) was already well under way much earlier than he acknowledges.

10. All he says here is that the prophetic framework involves moral assessment of the various perspectives held by black people, particularly of the responses to white supremacism, though the criteria for moral assessment are never specified other than to add that views will be chosen based on the appeal to black dignity, self-love, decency, and the rejection of any claims to cultural hierarchy (1993a, 30). West discusses at only slightly greater length the related conditions for "psychic conversion" in the closing chapter on Malcolm X.

11. I owe a great deal to insightful discussions about *Race Matters* with Howard McGary (who convinced me that it is a more complex book than a quick cursory read would have it), Tommy Lott, Paul Gilroy, Bill Lawson, Henry Giroux, and especially with my colleague, Pat Lauderdale.

CHAPTER 9
CRIME AND PREFERENCE IN THE MULTICULTURAL CITY

1. When asked whether the state should support programs promoting equal opportunity for those denied it, Californian voters by contrast are strongly supportive.

2. Actually, discussion of the apparent excesses of affirmative action programs, anecdotes that frame virtually every ordinary conversation that alienated white men seem to have about preference programs, covers up any discussion of the white men who claim to have been driven to take advantage of the programs. *Soul Man* aside, consider the case of the Malones, Irish American twin brothers, and the Boston Fire Department. Having scored poorly on their first test for the department, they were not hired. They then identified themselves as "Black" on the basis of having discovered a black grandmother, tested again with similar scores, were hired, and served undetected for ten years. It was only upon their application for promotion that an astute administrator noticed their falsified identification and fired them. They sued, *Malone v. Haley*. The case raises the complex of issues intersecting racial identity, racial self-identification, racism, compensatory and distributive justice, merit, and competence. See Christopher Ford (1994, 1231–85), Lewis Gordon (1994).

3. Given the difficulties I have mentioned regarding census-taking, the Census Bureau data must be taken as approximate.

4. Jonathan Kozol (1991) confirms in graphic and data-complemented detail what a conversation with any inner-city school teacher will tell you.

5. Prison building in the California state budget is displacing higher education. In 1980, spending on penal colonies made up just 2 percent of state spending, and higher education 12.6 percent. In this year's budget, prison's have climbed to 9.9 percent of the budget while higher education has slipped back to 9.5 percent. On current projections, by the year 2002, correctional spending (if ever there was a misnomer, this is it), at 18 percent, will have squeezed spending on higher education to 1 percent of the state budget. If the Pelican Bay prison is any indication, the point is to reduce bodies to solitary confinement and obliterate minds. See Fox Butterfield, "Prison-Building Binge in California Casts Shadow on Higher Education," *New York Times*, April 12, 1995, A11.

CHAPTER 10
WEDDED TO DIXIE:
DINESH D'SOUZA AND THE NEW SEGREGATIONISM

1. On the urbanizing determinations of Plessy-era segregationism, see John Cell (1982) and J. Kushner (1980). On contemporary segregation, see Douglas Massey and Nancy Denton (1993); Richard Ford (1995, 28–48); and Thomas Dumm (1993, 178–95).

2. At risk of sinking into minutiae, J. Angelo Corlett is not a "Sociologist" (265) but a philosopher.

3. Of the nearly 1,000 pages making up Darwin's two principal books, *The Origin of Species* (1859) and *The Descent of Man* (1871), just one chapter (thirty-four pages), "On the Races of Man," concerns race in any extended sense. The opening sentence reads: "It is not my intention here to describe the general *so-called* races of men," (Darwin, *The Descent of Man*, chapter 7, my emphasis).

4. Oddly enough, given his views about race and culture, D'Souza writes as though his "own" group were "white," "European" culture.

5. The ring of racism attendant on this claim is exemplified by the recent resistance to school desegregation by some white South Africans in the Afrikaner stronghold of Potgietersrust. In scenes reminiscent of Little Rock in the mid-1950s, white parents blocked the school entrance to black parents and children, rationalizing their resistance to desegregation in terms of the imperative to sustain white Afrikaner culture. See *New York Times*, February 22 and 23, 1996.

6. While the actual number of black-owned slaves is a bit higher than D'Souza states, free blacks often bought slaves, especially relatives, with the view to making them free. This fact places D'Souza's figure of black slave owners severely in question. Actually, because manumission was forbidden by law, slave registration under black relatives was tantamount to liberation. See Herbert Aptheker (1974, 8).

7. D'Souza is not above ad hominems, invoking any snide means necessary to attack relativism. In discussing Boas's influence, D'Souza mentions that Margaret Mead and Ruth Benedict "shared a lesbian relationship" (144), a comment irrelevant to an assessment of their work. I can only conclude that D'Souza refers to this relatively well-known relationship only to insinuate that their work on sexuality was nothing more than a rationalization for their own sexual practices. Likewise he speaks, with the ring of McCarthy, of Boas's "left-leaning" politics and "admiration for Soviet communism" (144 and 601, n. 139).

8. "Black activist groups have a financial interest in using racism to justify preferences and set-asides, and many white liberals have an ideological stake, derived from relativism, in blaming racism for group inequality" (396; compare with 346).

9. Nor is D'Souza beyond projecting stereotypical fabrications of views he wishes to pin on his adversaries to support his point (see, for example, 235).

10. Complementing D'Souza's repeated and pointed (ab)use of stereotypes is his litany of decontextualized quotes to exemplify views he wishes to dismiss. So, every twenty pages or so, he invokes in mantric fashion a series of quotes, items pulled from or out of their contexts and seemingly garnered from a keyword search conducted no doubt by his trusted assistants. However accurately these litanies may represent some particular facts or events, they reduce to caricature the positions and conditions D'Souza is seeking to attack or

criticize. They serve as argument by anecdote, dismissing general claims based on particular (and not particularly representative) counterclaims.

11. In his 150 pages of footnotes, D'Souza takes every opportunity to exhibit his erudition. It strikes me as salient, therefore, that he fails to acknowledge, let alone discuss, the only extended analysis in the literature of the claim that racism may not be inherently irrational. In "Racisms and Rationalities," chapter 6 of my previous book (1993, 117–47), now widely cited, I argue that there are forms of racial discrimination that may be rational. D'Souza's discussion mirrors many of my arguments. I argue that racisms nevertheless are necessarily morally unjustifiable. Thus, I draw a dramatically different conclusion from admitting racism's rationality than D'Souza does, a critical line he fails to consider, let alone pursue.

12. This is a version of J. J. C. Smart's (1956) critique of rule utilitarianism. It applies equally to D'Souza's line of argument about rational discrimination of banks in denying loans to all blacks because of the higher default rate among blacks as a group.

13. Some African Americans have filed a lawsuit against the Beverly Hills Police Department, which is almost exclusively white, for routinely using racial profiles to make unwarranted "specific, random stops of African-American males and then engaging in the harassment of the same group." See "Race Issue Rattles Celebrity Haven," *New York Times*, April 23, 1996, A10.

14. Michael Levin (1992, 5–29) actually suggests something approaching this for the New York subway.

15. D'Souza, so keen to cite references as testament to his erudition, is eerily silent on the page references to Elijah Anderson's (1990) work, which he claims here to be representing.

16. For a representative sample, see Clint Bolick, "Discriminating Liberals," *New York Times*, May 6, 1996, A15.

17. If any popular doubt remains about the depths of continuing racist sentiment and segregating rationalization, Ted Koppel's *Nightline* series on "America in Black and White," May 20–24, 1996, surely must have dispelled it. Rachel Ward, a black single mother who moved into Bridesburg, a white working-class neighborhood of Philadelphia, was run out within a week not only by the clamor of racial slurs and threats but as much by the "polite racism" of those "ordinary people" quietly committed to keeping their neighborhood white.

Bibliography

Acosta-Belen, Edna, and Barbara R. Sjostrom, eds. 1988. *The Hispanic Experience in the United States: Contemporary Issues and Perspectives.* New York: Praeger.

Anderson, Benedict. 1983. *Imagined Communities.* London: Verso Books.

Anderson, Elijah. 1990. *Streetwise: Race, Class and Change in an Urban Community.* Chicago: Chicago University Press.

Appadurai, Arjun. 1993. "The Heart of Whiteness. " *Callaloo* 16, no. 4:799-800.

Aptheker, Herbert. 1974. "Heavenly Days in Dixie: Or, The Time of Their Lives." *Political Affairs* 1-31.

Balibar, Etienne. 1991. *"Es Gibt Keinen Staat in Europa*: Racism and Politics in Europe Today." *New Left Review* 187 (May-June):5-19.

Bauman, Zygmunt. 1989. *Modernity and the Holocaust.* Oxford: Polity Press.

——. 1991. *Modernity and Ambivalence.* Ithaca, N.Y.: Cornell University Press.

Becker, Carol. 1995. "The Artist as Public Intellectual." *Review of Education/Pedagogy/Cultural Studies* 17, no. 4:385-96.

Bell, Derrick. 1992. *Faces at the Bottom of the Well: The Permanence of Racism.* New York: Basic Books.

Berube, Michael. 1995. "Public Academy." *The New Yorker* (January 9): 73-80.

Biale, David, Michael Galchinsky, and Susannah Heschel, eds. 1996. *Insider/Outsider: American Jews and Multiculturalism*. Berkeley: University of California Press.

Black Public Sphere Collective, eds. 1995. *The Black Public Sphere*. Chicago: University of Chicago Press.

Boynton, Robert. 1995. "The New Intellectuals." *The Atlantic Monthly* (March): 53–70.

Brenkman, John. 1995. "Race Publics." *Transition* 66, no. 2:4–37.

Brigham, John. 1996. "The Other Countries of American Law." *Social Identities* 2, no. 2 (Summer):237–54.

Brown, William Wells. 1880. *My Southern Home*. Boston: A.G. Brown.

Caws, Peter. 1994. "Identity: Cultural, Transcultural, and Multicultural." In *Multiculturalism*, ed. David Theo Goldberg, 371–87. Cambridge: Basil Blackwell.

Cell, John. 1982. *The Highest Stage of White Supremacy: The Origins of Segregation in South Africa and the American South*. Cambridge: Cambridge University Press.

Chavez, Linda. 1991. *Out of the Barrio: Toward a New Politics of Hispanic Assimilation*. New York: Basic Books.

Cohn, Bernard S. 1987. *An Anthropologist among the Historians and Other Essays*. Oxford: Oxford University Press.

Conk, Margo A. 1987. "The 1980 Census in Historical Perspective." In *The Politics of Numbers,* ed. William Alonso and Paul Starr, 187–234. New York: Russell Sage Foundation.

Darwin, Charles. 1859. *Origin of the Species*. New York: The Modern Library.

———. 1871. *The Descent of Man*. New York: The Modern Library.

Davis, Cary, Carl Haub, and JoAnne L. Willette. 1988. "U.S. Hispanics: Changing the Face of America." In *The Hispanic Experience in the United States*, ed. Edna Acosta-Belen and Barbara R. Sjostrom, 3–56. New York: Praeger.

Davis, F. James. 1991. *Who is Black? One Nation's Definition*. University Park, Pa.: Pennsylvania State University Press.

Davis, Mike. 1990. *City of Quartz*. New York: Verso.

DeMott, Benjamin. 1996. *The Trouble with Friendship: Why Americans Can't Think Straight about Race*. New York: Grove Press.

D'Souza, Dinesh. 1995. *The End of Racism*. New York: The Free Press.

Dumm, Thomas. 1993. "The New Enclosures: Racism in the Normalized Community." In *Reading Rodney King/Reading Urban Uprising*, ed. Robert Gooding-Williams, 178–95. New York: Routledge.

Early, Gerald. 1996. "Who is the Jew: A Question of African-American Identity." *Common Quest* 1, no. 1 (Spring):41–45.

Ellison, Ralph. 1948/1975. *Invisible Man*. New York: Vintage Books.

———. 1972. *Shadow and Act*. New York: Vintage.

Fanon, Frantz. 1968. *Black Skin White Masks*. Trans. Charles Lam Markmann. London: Paladin.

———. 1970. *A Dying Colonialism*. Trans. Haakon Chevalier. London: Pelican.

Ford, Christopher A. 1994. "Administering Identity: The Determination of 'Race' in Race-Conscious Law." *California Law Review* 82:1231–85.

Ford, Richard. 1994. "Imagined Cities." *Transition* 68:28–48.

Foucault, Michel. 1988. "The Political Technology of Individuals." In *Technologies of the Self*, ed. Luther Martin, Huck Gutman, and Patrick Hutton, 145–62. Amherst: University of Massachusetts Press.

Frazier, E. Franklin. 1965. *Black Bourgeoisie*. New York: The Free Press.

Frederickson, George. 1995. "Demonizing the American Dilemma." *New York Review of Books* 19 (October):10–15.

Fukurai, Hiroshi, Edgar Butler, and Richard Krooth. 1993. *Race and the Jury: Racial Disenfranchisement and the Search for Justice*. New York: Plenum.

Garvey, Marcus. 1926. "What We Believe." In *Philosophy and Opinions of Marcus Garvey*, vol. II, 81. New York: Addison.

Gates, Jr., Henry Louis. 1991. "Critical Fanonism," *Critical Inquiry* 17, 3:457–70.

Gates, Jr., Henry Louis, and Cornel West. 1996. *The Future of the Race*. New York: Alfred Knopf.

Gellner, Ernest. 1983. *Nations and Nationalism*. Oxford: Basil Blackwell.

Gilman, Sander. 1990. "'I'm Down on Whores': Race and Gender in Victorian London." In *Anatomy of Racism*, ed. David Theo Goldberg, 146–70. Minneapolis: University of Minnesota Press.

Gilroy, Paul. 1993. *The Black Atlantic: Modernity and Double Consciousness*. Cambridge: Harvard University Press.

Giroux, Henry. 1997. "In Living Color: Public Intellectuals and the Politics of Race." *Social Identities* 3, no. 1 (April).

Gluzman, Michael. 1996. "Modernism and Exile: A View from the Margins." In *Insider/Outsider: American Jews and Multiculturalism*, eds. David Biale et al., Berkeley: University of California Press.

Goldberg, David Theo. 1993a. *Racist Culture: Philosophy and the Politics of Meaning*. Oxford: Basil Blackwell.

———. 1993b. "The Semantics of Race," *Ethnic and Racial Studies* 15, no. 4 (October):543–69.

Goldberg, David Theo, ed. 1994. *Multiculturalism: A Reader*. Cambridge, MA: Basil Blackwell.

Goldberg, David Theo, and Michael Krausz, eds. 1993. *Jewish Identity*. Philadelphia: Temple University Press.

Gordon, Avery, and Christopher Newfield, eds. 1996. *Mapping Multiculturalism*. Minneapolis: University of Minnesota Press.

Gordon, Lewis. 1995. *Bad Faith and AntiBlack Racism*. New York: Humanities Press.

———. 1996. "Existential Dynamics of Theorizing Black Invisibility." In *Existence in Black*, ed. Lewis Gordon, 69–79. New York: Routledge.

Gose, Ben. 1996. "Public Debate Over Private Choice: Interracial Dating at Colleges Angers Many Black Female Students." *Chronicle of Higher Education* (May 10):A45–46.

Gossett, Thomas. 1965. *Race: The History of an Idea in America*. New York: Schocken Books.

Habermas, Jurgen. 1988. *Philosophical Discourse on Modernity*. Cambridge: Massachusetts Institute of Technology Press.

———. 1989. *The Structural Transformation of the Public Sphere*. Cambridge: Massachusetts Institute of Technology Press.

Hacker, Andrew. 1991. *Two Nations: Black and White, Separate, Hostile, and Unequal*. New York: Scribner's.

Hall, Stuart, Chas Critcher, Tony Jefferson, John Clarke, and Brian Roberts. 1978. *Policing the Crisis: Mugging, the State, and Law and Order*. London: Holmes and Meier.

Harvey, David. 1989. *The Condition of Postmodernity*. Oxford: Basil Blackwell.

Hero, Rodney E. 1992. *Latinos and the U.S. Political System: Two-Tiered Pluralism*. Philadelphia: Temple University Press.

Herzl, Theodor. 1904/1988. *A Jewish State*. New York: Dover.

Hobbes, Thomas. 1651/1975. *Leviathan*. London: Pelican.

Hobsbawm, Eric. 1993. "The New Threat to History." *New York Review of Books*, 40, no. 21 (December):62–65.

Hockenos, Paul. 1993. *Free to Hate: The Rise of the Right in Post-Communist Eastern Europe*. New York: Routledge.

hooks, bell. 1994. *Outlaw Culture: Resisting Representations*. New York: Routledge.

James, Joy. 1996. *Democratizing the Talented Tenth: Race Leaders, Women, American Intellectuals*. New York: Routledge.

Jordan, Winthrop. 1968. *White over Black: American Attitudes towards the Negro, 1550–1812*. Baltimore: Penguin.

Kasher, Asa. 1993. "Jewish Collective Identity." In *Jewish Identity*, ed. David Theo Goldberg and Michael Krausz, 56–79. Philadelphia: Temple University Press.

Kilson, Martin. 1993. "Anatomy of Black Conservatives." *Transition* 59:4–19.

Kozol, Jonathan. 1991. *Savage Inequalities: Children in America's Schools*. New York: Crown.

Kushner, J. 1980. *Apartheid in America: An Historical and Legal Analysis of Contemporary Racial Segregation in the United States*. Arlington, Va.: Carrolton Press.

Lee, Sharon M. 1993. "Racial Classifications in the US Census: 1890–1990." *Ethnic and Racial Studies* 16, no. 1 (January):75–94.

Lester, Julius. 1995. "The Outsiders." *Transition* 68, no. 4:66–89.

Levin, Michael. 1992. "Responses to Race Differences in Crime." *Journal of Social Philosophy* 23 (Spring):5–29.

McDougall, Hugh A. 1982. *Racial Myth in English History: Trojans, Teutons, and Anglo-Saxons*. Montreal: Harvest House.

Mann, Coramae Richey. 1993. *Unequal Justice: A Question of Color*. Bloomington: Indiana University Press.

Marin, Gerardo, and Barbara VanOss Marin. 1991. *Research with Hispanic Populations*. Newbury Park, Calif.: Sage.

Massey, Douglas, and Nancy Denton. 1933. *American Apartheid: Segregation and the Making of the Underclass*. Cambridge: Harvard University Press.

Morrison, Toni. 1992. *Playing in the Dark*. Cambridge: Harvard University Press.

Morrison, Toni, ed. 1992. *Race-ing Justice, Engendering Power*. New York: Pantheon.

Murray, Charles and Richard Herrnstein. 1994. *The Bell Curve: Intelligence and Class Structure in American Life*. New York: The Free Press.

Netanyahu, Benzion. 1995. *The Origins of the Inquisition in Fifteenth Century Spain*. New York: Random House.

Oboler, Suzanne. 1996. *Ethnic Labels, Latino Lives: Identity and the Politics of (Re)Presentation in the United States*. Minneapolis: University of Minnesota Press.

O'Malley, Patrick. 1995. "Gentle Genocide: State Policies and the Government of Desert Aboriginal Peoples in Central Australia." *Social Justice* 21, no. 4:46–65.

Omond, Roger. 1985. *The Apartheid Handbook: A Guide to South Africa's Everyday Racial Policies*. Harmondsworth: Penguin.

Park, Robert. 1950. "Mentality and Racial Hybrids." In *Race and Culture*, ed. Robert Park, 377–92. Glencoe, Ill.: The Free Press.

Parker, Kenneth. 1996. "Gendering a Language, Liberating a People: Women Writing in Afrikaans and the 'New' South Africa." *Social Identities* 2, no. 2 (Fall):199–220.

Petersen, William. 1980. "Politics and the Measurement of Ethnicity." In *The Politics of Numbers*, ed. William Alonso and Paul Starr, 187–234. New York: Russell Sage.

Pieterse, Jan Nederveen. 1996. "Racism and Social Development: Affirmative Action in the United States and India Compared." *Economic and Political Weekly*.

Reed, Jr., Adolph. 1993. "Class Notes." *The Progressive* 57, no. 12 (December):18–20.

Renoso, Cruz. 1992. "Ethnic Diversity: Its Historical and Constitutional Roots." *Villanova Law Review* 37, part 2:821–837.

Root, Maria P. 1992. "Within, Between, and Beyond Race." In *Racially Mixed People*, ed. Maria P. Root, 3–11. Newbury Park, Calif.: Sage.

Rosenbaum, Alan, ed. 1996. *Is the Holocaust Unique? Perspectives in Comparative Genocide*. Boulder: Westview Press.

Rosenberg, Alfred. 1970. *Race and Race History*. ed. R. Pois. New York: Harper and Row.

Said, Edward. 1978. *Orientalism*. New York: Vintage Books.

———. 1993. *Representations of the Intellectual: The 1993 Reith Lectures*. New York: Pantheon.

Schneider, Anne. 1981. "Differences between Survey and Police Information about Crime." In *The National Crime Survey: Working Papers, Vol. 1.*, ed. R. G. Lehnen and W. G. Skogan, 135–50. Washington D.C.: U.S. Government Printing Office.

Smart, J. J. C. 1956. "Extreme and Restricted Utilitarianism." *Philosophical Quarterly* 6:344–54.

Smith, George P. 1989. *The New Biology: Law, Ethics and Biotechnology*. New York: Plenum Press.

Starr, Paul. 1987. "The Sociology of Official Statistics." In *The Politics of Numbers*, ed. William Alonso and Paul Starr, 7–58. New York: Russell Sage.

Steele, Claude and Joshua Aronson. 1995. "Stereotype Threat and the Intelligence Test Performance of African Americans." *Journal of Personality and Social Psychology* 69 (November 5):797–811.

Steinberg, Stephen. 1989. *The Ethnic Myth*. Boston: Beacon Press.

Stocking, George. 1987. *Victorian Anthropology*. New York: The Free Press.

Taylor, Jared. 1992. *Paved with Good Intentions: The Failure of Race Relations in Contemporary America*. New York: Carrol and Graf.

Thomas, Laurence M. 1993. *Vessels of Evil: American Slavery and the Holocaust*. Philadelphia: Temple University Press.

———. 1996. "The Matrices of Malevolent Ideologies: Blacks and Jews." *Social Identities* 2, 1(February):107–34.

U.S. Bureau of the Census. 1990. *Census Profile #2*.

U.S. Department of Commerce. 1989. *200 Years of U.S. Census Taking: Population and Housing Questions, 1790–1990*, (November).

Valle, Victor and Rodolfo Torres. 1994. "Latinos in 'Postindustrial' Disorder: Politics in a Changing City." *Socialist Review* 23, no. 4:1–28.

Wallace, Michael. 1996. *Mickey Mouse History: The Politics of Public Memory.* Philadelphia: Temple University Press.

Watson, Helen. 1994. "Personal Responses to Global Process." In *Islam, Globalization and Postmodernity*, ed. Akhbar Ahmed and Hastings Donnan, 141–159. London: Routledge.

West, Cornel. 1993a. *Race Matters.* Boston: Beacon Press.

——. 1993b. "The Dilemma of the Black Intellectual." In *Keeping Faith: Essays on Religion, Philosophy and Politics*, 67–85. New York: Routledge.

Wieseltier, Leon. 1995. "All and Nothing at All." *The New Republic* (March 6):31–36.

Wilbanks, William. 1987. *The Myth of a Racist Criminal Justice System.* Monterey Calif.: Brooks/Cole.

Williams, Jeffrey. 1995. "Edward Said's Romance of the Amateur Intellectual," *Review of Education/Pedagogy/Cultural Studies* 17, no. 4: 397–410.

Williams, Patricia. 1995. *The Rooster's Egg: The Persistence of Prejudice.* Cambridge: Harvard University Press.

Wilson, E. O., ed. 1993. *The Biophilia Hypothesis.* Washington, D.C.: Island Press/Shearwater Books.

Wilson, William Julius. 1989. *The Truly Disadvantaged.* Chicago: University of Chicago Press.

——. 1996. *When Work Disappears: The World of the New Urban Poor.* New York: Alfred Knopf.

Wright, Richard. 1954. *Black Power: A Record of Reactions in a Land of Pathos.* New York: Harper and Brothers.

——. 1965. *The Outsider.* New York: Harper and Row.

Yanow, Dvora. 1993. "Administrative Implications of American Ethnogenesis." Paper presented to the Public Administration Section, American Political Science Association Annual Meeting, Washington, D.C., September, 1–5. Paper on file with author.

Young, Iris. 1990. *Justice and the Politics of Difference.* Princeton: Princeton University Press.

Young, Robert. 1994. *Colonial Desire.* London: Routledge.

Zack, Naomi. 1994. *Race and Mixed Race.* Philadelphia: Temple University Press.

INDEX

(by name)

INDEX

(by concept)

164, 171, 182, 186, 189–91, 193,
194, 198, 201, 215, 222, 223,
225, 226, 232
American Enterprise Institute, 179,
203, 219
American Indian (Native American),
36–37, 39, 42–48, 53, 57, 60, 71,
103, 138, 186, 231, 233
anonymity, 6, 83, 84, 88, 234
anthropology, 18, 28–29, 183–84,
218
Anti-Defamation League, 13, 203
antiessentialism, 80–81, 126
anti-Semitism, 54, 122, 131–32, 145,
188, 190
apartheid, 2, 18, 22, 41, 67–70, 95,
98, 102, 107, 153
Arabic, 98
archaeology, 88
Armenian, 183, 190
Asian and Pacific Islander (API), 37,
46–47, 57
assimilation, 35, 48, 102–03, 133,
138–39, 140, 143, 176, 186
Australia, 102–03, 190
authenticity, 72, 94, 119, 141, 215

"bad nigger", 192, 196, 215
Bantu, 67, 68
Battle of Algiers, 92
Bell Curve, The (Murray &
Hernnstein), 49, 170, 173, 176–77
Bering Straits Theory, 39, 65
Bill of Rights, 55
biology, 28, 182, 185, 205, 213, 228
black, 1–3, 6–7, 9, 11, 12, 13, 14, 19,
20, 21, 22, 25, 29, 34–41, 44, 48,
49, 51–52, 53, 56–57, 61–78,
79–83, 87–89, 91, 92, 97, 98–101,
104, 106, 108, 111–26, 129–47,
150–54, 159, 160, 161–74,
175–226, 228, 229, 230, 231, 232,
234, 235, 236, 237, 238

blackness, 3, 38, 41, 52, 63, 66,
71, 73, 76, 79–83, 87–89, 97,
112, 119, 146, 183, 216, 222
black-consciousness, 43, 63, 142
black cultural pathology, 71, 75,
113, 117, 125, 136, 181, 187,
191, 192–95, 196, 206, 216–17,
219
Black Entertainment Television, 203
Black or White (Michael Jackson), 60
Boer, 67
Bow and Arrow Ceremony, 103, 233
Brazil, 61
Britain (British), 41, 67, 176, 190,
193, 229
*Brown v. Board of Education, Topeka,
Kansas,* 174, 204
brown, 43–44, 52, 65, 72, 231

California(n), 39, 50, 54, 64, 104,
106, 149, 153, 154, 166, 207,
235, 236
capital, 3, 4–5, 33, 34, 64, 100, 111,
115, 117, 131, 132, 133, 134,
145, 155, 157, 196, 201, 229,
233, 234
Catholic, 183, 188, 232
Caucasian, 54, 230
Census, Bureau of, 29, 33–49, 50, 56,
62, 65, 163, 178, 228, 229, 235,
236
Chicanos, 186
Chinese, 36–37, 39–40, 42, 43, 46,
49, 186
Christian, 13–14, 134, 140, 197, 203
Christian Coalition, 13, 203
city, 4, 12, 15, 16, 17, 21, 25, 30, 46,
47, 50, 55, 72, 80, 83, 91–92, 97,
99, 104–06, 110, 119, 132, 141,
151, 153, 159, 160, 171, 172,
177, 206, 218, 227, 231, 233,
234, 236
Civil Rights Act (1964), 51, 55, 221

INDEX (by concept)

112, 151–55, 160, 167, 171, 181, 185, 190, 191, 200, 213, 223, 237, 238

liberalism, 12, 44, 69, 70, 109, 120, 123, 126, 181, 196–98, 222

libertarianism, 169, 194–95, 197, 217

Los Angeles, 4–5, 103–07, 134, 146, 152–53, 233

lynching, 19, 191, 199–200

Made in America, 232

Malone v. Haley, 236

Marranos, 188

March on Selma, 92

masochism (masochist), 82–84

medicine (medical), 38, 81, 85, 104, 130

memory, 75, 87, 133, 135, 137, 144, 160, 224, 226

merit, 135, 211, 220, 236

mestizo, 65

Mexican, 37, 42–43, 45–46, 48, 52, 64–66, 138, 231

migration, 39, 64–65, 104, 137, 140, 143

military industrial complex, 4, 106, 154, 171, 173

militia(s), 145, 225

miscegenation, 41, 60, 62, 67, 69, 102, 141

Mitchell v. Wisconsin, 17

mixed race (racially mixed), 11, 42, 44, 59–78, 231

modernity, 27, 74, 83, 86, 106, 116, 187

Moral Majority, 203

Mormon, 232

Moslem, 43

mulatto, 36, 39–41, 68, 76, 87, 178

multiculturalism, 4, 11, 46, 57, 59–60, 77, 110, 139, 154, 171–74, 182, 198, 222, 233

multiplier effect, 114, 116

My Southern Home (William Wells Brown), 174

NAACP, 202, 203

NAFTA, 52

nation, 2, 4, 13, 17, 22, 33–34, 41, 43–46, 53, 87, 95, 98, 102, 120, 131, 134, 138–47, 157, 158, 166, 171, 200, 203, 225, 231

national identity, 34, 102, 138

Nation of Islam, 22, 131, 145

National Association of Black Social Workers, 70–71

National Origins Act, 41

nationalism(s), 87, 138–45, 147

natural rights, 195, 221

Negro (negro), 9, 36–37, 39–44, 46, 68, 80, 87–90, 99–101, 127, 140–41

neoconservatism, 117–20, 175

New Deal, 7, 42, 51

New Mexico, 45, 50, 233

New York, 5, 50, 126, 134, 203, 209, 211, 227, 230, 231, 236, 237, 238

Nigerian, 44, 46

nihilism, 71, 112–16, 125, 218, 231

nonracialism, 12, 26, 47, 51, 69, 77

octoroon, 36, 39–40

Olin Foundation, 179, 203

one-drop rule, 62, 66, 71, 72, 159, 178, 202

Other, 21, 24–25, 29, 34, 37, 39, 40–43, 46–47, 50, 51, 53, 59, 76, 81, 83–84, 88, 100, 104, 106, 108, 123, 136, 142, 160, 176, 187, 232, 233

Pan Hawaiian, 37, 43

passing, 52, 72, 91, 107, 118, 137, 174

People v. Hall, 39

Philadelphia, 5, 50, 209, 238

sadism (sadist), 82–84
Samoan, 37, 44, 46
School Daze (Spike Lee), 72
segregation, 10, 11–12, 16, 41, 62,
    70, 141, 143, 153, 158, 162, 170,
    174, 175–226, 236, 237, 238
    new, 175–226
    old, 176
segregationism, 11, 12, 141, 176,
    181, 187, 196, 198, 199, 205,
    211, 214, 223–24, 236
    the new, 176, 181, 182, 187, 196,
    198, 214, 223–24
sexism, 20, 120
sexist, 19, 21–22, 23, 119, 121, 171,
    227
Shoah, 141
Sikh, 183
slavery, 38, 90, 105, 134–37, 143,
    178, 180, 181, 189–96, 224, 226,
    229
    black, 35, 190, 194, 237
social science, 18, 33, 48, 100, 162,
    208, 227, 228
    functional, 33, 228
    ideological, 33, 228
sociobiology, 28, 228
Soul Man, 47, 236
South Africa, 2–3, 4, 22, 41, 61,
    67–70, 76, 95, 97–98, 107, 137,
    237
Southern Baptist Convention, 13
State of California v. O. J. Simpson,
    149, 154
state, the, 11, 28, 30, 33, 51, 53, 85,
    96, 102–03, 106, 123, 225, 228,
    229, 233, 235, 236
stereotype(s/ing), 2, 3, 7, 15, 16, 20,
    50, 99–100, 132, 144, 145–46,
    155, 162–63, 168, 176, 179, 192,
    193, 196, 206–07, 210, 213–14,
    216, 219, 225, 232, 233, 237
structure(al), 4, 8, 14, 22, 24, 30, 31,
    52, 55, 56, 86, 89, 97, 100–101,

102–05, 113, 114, 115, 117, 120,
    123, 129, 159, 172, 183, 185,
    196, 213, 218, 221
subject, 10, 16, 21, 27, 30, 50, 55,
    66, 75, 81–85, 95, 99, 111, 119,
    142, 150, 172, 195, 212
Supreme Court, 10, 17, 18, 39, 119,
    231

technology, 30–32, 43, 45, 51–52,
    61, 66, 81, 96, 97, 106, 168, 229
Terminator 2, 60
Time Magazine, 151
Treatise on Government (Locke), 195
tribalism, 40, 42–43, 183
tribes, 40, 183, 218, 231
Truly Disadvantaged, The (William
    Julius Wilson), 49
Turk(s/ish/ey), 22, 183, 190
Turner Broadcast Station, 203

Ukrainian, 44, 46
underclass, 5, 18, 130, 202, 216, 218
UNIA (Universal Negro Improve-
    ment Association), 140–41
United States (U.S.), 2–11, 17, 22, 28,
    29, 30, 33–58, 59, 61–62, 65,
    70–71, 73, 76–77, 91, 98, 99, 103,
    112, 120, 130–31, 137, 139–40,
    144, 150, 158, 161, 163, 176,
    178, 181, 186, 187, 192–93, 199,
    203, 209, 223, 226, 227, 228,
    229, 230, 231, 233, 235
University of the Western Cape, 69

veil (veiling), 30, 86–87, 90–93, 95,
    101, 107, 152, 233
Venezuelan, 44
Vietnamese, 37, 44, 46, 207
visibility (invisibility), 10, 11,
    79–108, 110, 124, 133, 136, 142
Voice of Algeria, 94–95
voting rights, 51, 224

INDEX (by concept)